PENGUIN BOOKS

KILLING PABLO

Mark Bowden is the author of *Black Hawk Down, Bringing the Heat,* and *Doctor Dealer.* He has been a reporter at *The Philadelphia Inquirer* for twenty-one years and has won many national awards for his writing. His articles have appeared in *Talk, Men's Journal, Sports Illustrated, Rolling Stone, Playboy, Policy Review,* and many other magazines. The movie based on his bestseller *Black Hawk Down,* was released in December 2001.

The companion *Killing Pablo* television documentary is available for order from Knight Ridder Video at www.killingpablo.com or by calling (215)854-4444.

KILLING
PABLO

THE HUNT FOR THE
WORLD'S GREATEST OUTLAW

MARK
BOWDEN

PENGUIN BOOKS

PENGUIN BOOKS

Published by the Penguin Group

Penguin Group (USA) Inc., 375 Hudson Street, New York, New York 10014, U.S.A.

Penguin Books Ltd, 80 Strand, London WC2R 0RL, England

Penguin Books Australia Ltd, 250 Camberwell Road, Camberwell, Victoria 3124, Australia

Penguin Books Canada Ltd, 10 Alcorn Avenue, Toronto, Ontario, Canada M4V 3B2

Penguin Books India (P) Ltd, 11 Community Centre, Panchsheel Park, New Delhi – 110 017, India

Penguin Books (N.Z.) Ltd, Cnr Rosedale and Airborne Roads, Albany, Auckland, New Zealand

Penguin Books (South Africa) (Pty) Ltd, 24 Sturdee Avenue,
Rosebank, Johannesburg 2196, South Africa

Penguin Books Ltd, Registered Offices: 80 Strand, London WC2R 0RL, England

First published in the United States of America by Atlantic Monthly Press 2001
Published in Penguin Books 2002

5 7 9 10 8 6 4

Copyright © Mark Bowden, 2001
All rights reserved

PHOTO CREDITS—Insert page 1: Pablo as he appeared in 1983 (Reuters NewMedia Inc./CORBIS). Insert page 2: Map of Colombia (*The Philadelphia Inquirer*); Map of Medellín (*The Philadelphia Inquirer*). Insert page 3: Pablo and his wife Maria Victoria in 1983 (Reuters NewMedia Inc./CORBIS); Pablo embraces his wife, Maria Victoria, and his daughter Manuela (RCN). Insert page 4: President Bush with Colombian president Virgilio Barco (AP/World Wide Photos); Morris D. Busby (*The Philadelphia Inquirer*); Luis Galán (AP/World Wide Photos); Colombian president César Gaviria (*The Philadelphia Inquirer*). Insert page 5: A dinner party in the mid-1980s (Mark Bowden); Fernando Galeano (AP/World Wide Photos); A view from the comfortable living room of Pablo's suite at *La Catedral* prison (Mark Bowden); DEA agents Steve Murphy and Javier Peña (Mark Bowden). Insert page 6: Agent Joe Toft (Tim Dunn, freelance photographer); José Rodriguez-Gacha (*El Espectador*); Colonel Hugo Martinez (*The Philadelphia Inquirer*); Eduardo Mendoza (AP/World Wide Photos). Insert page 7: An exhibit at the *Policía Nacional de Colombia*'s museum (*The Philadelphia Inquirer*); The third page of a handwritten letter (Mark Bowden); The Colombian government and U.S. Embassy printed thousands of posters and handbills (RCN); A victim of *Los Pepes* (RCN). Insert page 8: Members of Colonel Martinez's Search Bloc (Mark Bowden); Pablo's grave in Medellín (*The Philadelphia Inquirer*).

THE LIBRARY OF CONGRESS HAS CATALOGED THE HARDCOVER EDITION AS FOLLOWS:
Bowden, Mark, 1951–

Killing Pablo : the hunt for the world's greatest outlaw / [Mark Bowden].

p. cm.

ISBN 0-87113-783-6 (hc.)

ISBN 0 14 20.0095 7 (pbk.)

1. Escobar, Pablo. 2. Narcotics dealers—Colombia—Biography. 3. Fugitives from justice—Colombia—Biography. 4. United States—Foreign relations—Colombia. 5. Colombia—Foreign relations—United States. 6. Police—Colombia. I. Title.

HV5805.E82 B69 2001

364.1′77′09861—dc21   00-048539

Printed in the United States of America
Set in Janson MT
Designed by Laura Hammond Hough

For Rosey and Zook

CONTENTS

PROLOGUE

December 2, 1993

On the day that Pablo Escobar was killed, his mother, Hermilda, came to the place on foot. She had been ill earlier that day and was visiting a medical clinic when she heard the news. She fainted.

When she revived she came straight to Los Olivos, the neighborhood in south-central Medellín where the reporters on television and radio were saying it had happened. Crowds blocked the streets, so she had to stop the car and walk. Hermilda was stooped and walked stiffly, taking short steps, a tough old woman with gray hair and a bony, concave face and wide glasses that sat slightly askew on her long, straight nose, the same nose as her son's. She wore a dress with a pale floral print, and even taking short steps she walked too fast for her daughter, who was fat. The younger woman struggled to keep pace.

Los Olivos consisted of blocks of irregular two- and three-story row houses with tiny yards and gardens in front, many with squat palm trees that barely reached the roofline. The crowds were held back by police at barricades. Some residents had climbed out on roofs for a better look. There were those who said it was definitely Don Pablo who had been killed and others who said no, the police had shot a man but it was not him, that he had escaped again. Many preferred to believe he had gotten away. Medellín was Pablo's home. It was here he had made his billions and where his money had built big office buildings and apartment complexes, discos and restaurants, and it was here he had created housing for the poor, for people who had squatted in shacks of cardboard and plastic and tin and picked at refuse in the city's garbage heaps with kerchiefs tied across their faces against the stench, looking for anything that could be cleaned up and sold. It was here he had built soccer fields with lights so workers could play at night, and where he had come out to ribbon cuttings and sometimes played in the games himself, already a legend, a chubby man with a mustache and a wide second chin who, everyone agreed, was still pretty fast on his feet. It was here that many believed the police would never catch him, could not catch him, even with their death squads and all their gringo dollars and spy planes and who knew what all else. It was here Pablo had hidden for sixteen months while they searched. He had moved from hideout to hideout among people who, if they recognized him, would never give him up, because it was a place where there were pictures of him in gilded frames on the walls, where prayers were said for him to have a long life and many children, and where (he also knew) those who did not pray for him feared him.

The old lady moved forward purposefully until she and her daughter were stopped by stern men in green uniforms.

"We are family. This is the mother of Pablo Escobar," the daughter explained.

The officers were unmoved.

"Don't you all have mothers?" Hermilda asked.

When word was passed up the ranks that Pablo Escobar's mother and sister had come, they were allowed to pass. With an escort they moved through the flanks of parked cars to where the lights of the ambulances and police vehicles flashed. Television cameras caught them as they approached, and a murmur went through the crowd.

Hermilda crossed the street to a small plot of grass where the body of a young man was sprawled. The man had a hole in the center of his forehead, and his eyes, grown dull and milky, stared blankly at the sky.

"You fools!" Hermilda shouted, and she began to laugh loudly at the police. "You fools! This is not my son! This is not Pablo Escobar! You have killed the wrong man!"

But the soldiers directed the two women to stand aside, and from the roof over the garage they lowered a body strapped to a stretcher, a fat man in bare feet with blue jeans rolled up at the cuff and a blue pullover shirt, whose round, bearded face was swollen and bloody. He had a full black beard and a bizarre square little mustache with the ends shaved off, like Hitler's.

It was hard to tell at first that it was him. Hermilda gasped and stood over the body silently. Mixed with the pain and anger she felt a sense of relief, and also of dread. She felt relief because now at least the nightmare was over for her son. Dread because she believed his death would unleash still more violence. She wished nothing more now than for it to be finished, especially for her family. Let all the pain and bloodshed die with Pablo.

As she left the place, she pulled her mouth tight to betray no emotion and stopped only long enough to tell a reporter with a microphone, "At least now he is at rest."

THE RISE
OF
EL DOCTOR

1948–1989

1

There was no more exciting place in South America to be in April 1948 than Bogotá, Colombia. Change was in the air, a static charge awaiting direction. No one knew exactly what it would be, only that it was at hand. It was a moment in the life of a nation, perhaps even a continent, when all of history seemed a prelude.

Bogotá was then a city of more than a million that spilled down the side of green mountains into a wide savanna. It was bordered by steep peaks to the north and east, and opened up flat and empty to the south and west. Arriving by air, one would see nothing below for hours but mountains, row upon row of emerald peaks, the highest of them capped white. Light hit the flanks of the undulating ranges at different angles, creating shifting shades of chartreuse, sage, and ivy, all of them cut with red-brown tributaries that gradually merged and widened as they coursed downhill to river valleys so deep in shadow they were almost blue. Then abruptly from these virgin ranges emerged a fully modern metropolis, a great blight of concrete covering most of a wide plain. Most of Bogotá was just two or three stories high, with a preponderance of red brick. From the center north, it had wide landscaped avenues, with museums, classic cathedrals, and graceful old mansions to rival the most elegant urban neighborhoods in the world, but to the south and west were the beginnings of shantytowns where refugees from the ongoing violence in the jungles and mountains sought refuge, employment, and hope and instead found only deadening poverty.

In the north part of the city, far from this squalor, a great meeting was about to convene, the Ninth Inter-American Conference. Foreign ministers from all countries of the hemisphere were there to sign the charter for the Organization of American States, a new coalition sponsored by the United States that was designed to give more voice and prominence to the nations of Central and South America. The city had been spruced up for the event, with street cleanings and trash removal, fresh coats of paint on public buildings, new signage on roadways, and, along the avenues, colorful flags and plantings. Even the shoe-shine men on the street corners wore new uniforms.

The officials who attended meetings and parties in this surprisingly urbane capital hoped that the new organization would bring order and respectability to the struggling republics of the region. But the event had also attracted critics, leftist agitators, among them a young Cuban student leader named Fidel Castro. To them the fledgling OAS was a sop, a sellout, an alliance with the gringo imperialists of the north. To idealists who had gathered from all over the region, the postwar world was still up for grabs, a contest between capitalism and communism, or at least socialism, and young rebels like the twenty-one-year-old Castro anticipated a decade of revolution. They would topple the region's calcified fuedal aristocracies and establish peace, social justice, and an authentic Pan-American political bloc. They were hip, angry, and smart, and they believed with the certainty of youth that they owned the future. They came to Bogotá to denounce the new organization and had planned a hemispheric conference of their own to coordinate citywide protests. They looked for guidance from one man in particular, an enormously popular forty-nine-year-old Colombian politician named Jorge Eliécer Gaitán.

"I am not a man, I am a people!" was Gaitán's slogan, which he would pronounce dramatically at the end of speeches to bring his ecstatic admirers to their feet. He was of mixed blood, a man with the education and manner of the country's white elite but the squat frame, dark skin, broad face, and coarse black hair of Colombia's lower Indian castes. Gaitán's appearance marked him as an outsider, a man of the masses. He could never fully belong to the small, select group of the wealthy and fair-skinned who owned most of the nation's land and natural resources, and who for generations had dominated its government. These families ran the mines, owned the oil, and grew the fruits, coffee, and vegetables that made up the bulk of Colombia's export economy. With the help of technology and capital offered by powerful U.S. corporate investors, they had grown rich selling the nation's great natural bounty to America and Europe, and they had used those riches to import to Bogotá a sophistication that rivaled the great capitals of the world. Gaitán's skin color marked him as apart from them just as it connected him with the excluded, the others, the masses of Colombian people who were considered inferior, who were locked out of the riches of this export economy and its privileged islands of urban prosperity. But that connection had given Gaitán power. No matter how educated and powerful he became, he was irrevocably tied to those others, whose only option was work in the mines or the fields at subsistence wages, who had no chance for education and opportunity for a better life. They constituted a vast electoral majority.

Times were bad. In the cities it meant inflation and high unemployment, while in the mountain and jungle villages that made up most of Colombia it meant no work, hunger, and starvation. Protests by angry *campesinos*, encouraged and led by Marxist agitators, had grown increasingly violent. The country's Conservative Party leadership and its sponsors, wealthy landowners and miners, had responded with draconian methods. There were massacres and summary executions. Many foresaw this cycle of protest and repression leading to another bloody civil war—the Marxists saw it as the inevitable revolt. But most Colombians were neither Marxists nor oligarchs; they just wanted peace. They wanted change, not war. To them, this was Gaitán's promise. It had made him wildly popular.

In a speech two months earlier before a crowd of one hundred thousand at the Plaza de Bolívar in Bogotá, Gaitán had pleaded with the government to restore order, and had urged the great crowd before him to express their outrage and self-control by responding to his oration not with cheers and applause but with silence. He had addressed his remarks directly to President Mariano Ospina.

"We ask that the persecution by the authorities stop," he'd said. "Thus asks this immense multitude. We ask a small but great thing: that our political struggles be governed by the constitution. . . . Señor President, stop the violence. We want human life to be defended, that is the least a people can ask. . . . Our flag is in mourning, this silent multitude, this mute cry from our hearts, asks only that you treat us . . . as you would have us treat you."

Against a backdrop of such explosive forces, the silence of this throng had echoed much more loudly than cheers. Many in the crowd had simply waved white handkerchiefs. At great rallies like these, Gaitán seemed poised to lead Colombia to a lawful, just, peaceful future. He tapped the deepest yearnings of his countrymen.

A skillful lawyer and a socialist, he was, in the words of a CIA report prepared years later, "a staunch antagonist of oligarchical rule and a spellbinding orator." He was also a shrewd politician who had turned his populist appeal into real political power. When the OAS conference convened in Bogotá in 1948, Gaitán was not only the people's favorite, he was the head of the Liberal Party, one of the country's two major political organizations. His election as president in 1950 was regarded as a virtual certainty. Yet the Conservative Party government, headed by President Ospina, had left Gaitán off the bipartisan delegation appointed to represent Colombia at the great conference.

Tensions were high in the city. Colombian historian German Arciniegas would later write of "a chill wind of terror blowing in from the provinces." The day before the conference convened, a mob attacked a car carrying the Ecuadorian delegation, and rumors of terrorist violence seemed confirmed the same day when police caught a worker attempting to plant a bomb in the capital. In the midst of all the hubbub, Gaitán quietly went about his law practice. He knew his moment was still a few years off, and he was prepared to wait. The president's snub had only enhanced his stature among his supporters, as well as among the more radical young leftists gathering to protest, who otherwise might have dismissed Gaitán as a bourgeois liberal with a vision too timid for their ambition. Castro had made an appointment to meet with him.

Gaitán busied himself with defending an army officer accused of murder, and on April 8, the day the conference convened, he won an acquittal. Late the next morning, some journalists and friends stopped by his office to offer congratulations. They chatted happily, arguing about where to go for lunch and who would pay. Shortly before one o'clock, Gaitán walked down to the street with the small group. He had two hours before the scheduled meeting with Castro.

Leaving the building, the group walked past a fat, dirty, unshaven man who let them pass and then ran to overtake them. The man, Juan Roa, stopped and without a word leveled a handgun. Gaitán briskly turned and started back toward the safety of his office building. Roa began shooting. Gaitán fell with wounds to his head, lungs, and liver, and died within the hour as doctors tried desperately to save him.

Gaitán's murder is where the modern history of Colombia starts. There would be many theories about Roa—that he had been recruited by the CIA or by Gaitán's conservative enemies, or even by Communist extremists who feared that their revolution would be postponed by Gaitán's ascension. In Colombia, murder rarely has a shortage of plausible motives. An independent investigation by officers of Scotland Yard determined that Roa, a frustrated mystic with grandiose delusions, had nursed a grudge against Gaitán and had acted alone; but since he was beaten to death on the spot, his motives died with him. Whatever Roa's purpose, the rounds he fired unleashed chaos. All hope for a peaceful future in Colombia ended. All those brooding forces of change exploded into *El Bogotazo,* a spasm of rioting so intense it left large parts of the capital city ablaze before spreading to other cities. Many policemen, devotees of the slain leader, joined the angry mobs in the streets, as did student revolutionaries like Castro. The leftists donned red armbands and tried to direct the crowds, sensing with excitement that their moment had arrived, but quickly realized that the situation was beyond control. The mobs grew larger and larger, and protest evolved into random destruction, drunkenness, and looting. Ospina called in the army, which in some places fired into the crowds.

Everyone's vision of the future died with Gaitán. The official effort to showcase a new era of stability and cooperation was badly tarnished; the visiting foreign delegations signed the charter and fled the country. The leftists' hopes of igniting South America's new communist era went up in flames. Castro took shelter in the Cuban embassy as the army began hunting down and arresting leftist agitators, who were blamed for the uprising, but even a CIA history of the event would conclude that the leftists were as much victims as everyone else. For Castro, an agency historian wrote, the episode was profoundly disillusioning: "[It] may have influenced his adoption in Cuba in the 1950s of a guerrilla strategy rather than one of revolution through urban disorders."

El Bogotazo was eventually quieted in Bogotá and the other large cities, but it lived on throughout untamed Colombia for years, metamorphosing into a nightmarish period of bloodletting so empty of meaning it is called simply *La Violencia.* An estimated two hundred thousand people were killed. Most of the dead were campesinos, incited to violence by appeals to religious fervor, land rights, and a bewildering assortment of local issues. While Castro carried off his revolution in Cuba and the rest of the world squared off in the Cold War, Colombia remained locked in this cabalistic dance with death. Private and public armies terrorized the rural areas. The government fought paramilitiaries and guerrillas, industrialists fought unionists, conservative Catholics fought heretical liberals, and *bandidos* took advantage of the free-for-all to plunder. Gaitán's death had unleashed demons that had less to do with the emerging modern world than with Colombia's deeply troubled past.

Colombia is a land that breeds outlaws. It has always been ungov-
ernable, a nation of wild unsullied beauty, steeped in mystery. From the
white peaks of the three cordilleras that form its western spine to the triple-
canopy equatorial jungle at sea level, it affords many good places to hide.
There are corners of Colombia still virtually untouched by man. Some are
among the only places left on this thoroughly trampled planet where bota-
nists and biologists can discover and attach their names to new species of
plants, insects, birds, reptiles, and even small mammals.

The ancient cultures that flourished here were isolated and stubborn.
With soil so rich and a climate so varied and mild, everything grew, so
there was little need for trade or commerce. The land ensnared one like a
sweet, tenacious vine. Those who came stayed. It took the Spanish almost
two hundred years to subdue just one people, the Tairona, who lived in a
lush pocket of the Sierra Nevada de Santa Marta foothills. European in-
vaders eventually defeated them the only way they could, by killing them
all. In the sixteenth and seventeenth centuries the Spanish tried without
success to rule from neighboring Peru, and in the nineteenth century Simón
Bolívar tried to join Colombia with Panama, Venezuela, and Ecuador to
form a great South American state, Gran Colombia. But even the great lib-
erator could not hold the pieces together.

Ever since Bolívar's death in 1830, Colombia has been proudly democratic, but it has never quite got the hang of peaceful political evolution.
Its government is weak, by design and tradition. In vast regions to the south
and west, and even in the mountain villages outside the major cities, live
communities only lightly touched by nation, government, or law. The sole
civilizing influence ever to reach the whole country was the Catholic
Church, and that was accomplished only because clever Jesuits grafted their
Roman mysteries to ancient rituals and beliefs. Their hope was to grow a
hybrid faith, nursing Christianity from pagan roots to a locally flavored
version of the One True Faith, but in stubborn Colombia, it was Catholicism that took a detour. It grew into something else, a faith rich with an-
cestral connection, fatalism, superstition, magic, mystery . . . and violence.

Violence stalks Colombia like a biblical plague. The nation's two
major political factions, the Liberals and Conservatives, fought eight civil
wars in the nineteenth century alone over the roles of church and state.
Both groups were overwhelmingly Catholic, but the Liberals wanted to
keep the priests off the public stage. The worst of these conflicts, which

began in 1899 and was called the War of a Thousand Days, left more than one hundred thousand dead and utterly ruined whatever national government and economy existed.

Caught between these two violent forces, the Colombian peasantry learned to fear and distrust both. They found heroes in the outlaws who roamed the Colombian wilderness as violent free agents, defying everyone. During the War of a Thousand Days the most famous was José del Carmen Tejeiro, who played upon popular hatred of the warring powers. Tejeiro would not just steal from wealthy landowning enemies; he would punish and humiliate them, forcing them to sign declarations such as "I was whipped fifty times by José del Carmen Tejeiro as retribution for persecuting him." His fame earned him supporters beyond Colombia's borders. Venezuelan dictator Juan Vicente Gómez, sowing a little neighborhood instability, presented Tejeiro with a gold-studded carbine.

A half century later, *La Violencia* bred a new colorful menagerie of outlaws, men who went by names like Tarzan, Desquite (Revenge), Tirofijo (Sureshot), Sangrenegra (Blackblood), and Chispas (Sparks). They roamed the countryside, robbing, pillaging, raping, and killing, but because they were allied with none of the major factions, their crimes were seen by many common people as blows struck against power.

La Violencia eased only when General Gustavo Rojas Pinilla seized power in 1953 and established a military dictatorship. He lasted four years before being ousted by more democratic military officers. A national plan was put in place for Liberals and Conservatives to share the government, alternating the presidency every four years. It was a system guaranteed to prevent any real reforms or government-initiated social progress, because any steps taken during one administration could be undone in the next. The famous *bandidos* went on raiding and stealing in the hills, and occasionally made halfhearted attempts to band together. In the end they were not idealists or revolutionaries, just outlaws. Still, a generation of Colombians grew up on their exploits. The *bandidos* were heroes despite themselves to many of the powerless, terrorized, and oppressed poor. The nation both thrilled and mourned as the army of the oligarchs in Bogotá hunted them down, one by one. By the 1960s Colombia had settled into an enforced stasis, with Marxist guerrillas in the hills and jungles (modern successors to the *bandido* tradition) and a central government increasingly dominated by a small group of rich, elite Bogotá families, powerless to effect change and, anyway, disinclined. The violence, already deeply rooted in the culture, continued, deepened, *twisted.*

Terror became art, a form of psychological warfare with a quasi-religious aesthetic. In Colombia it wasn't enough to hurt or even kill your enemy; there was ritual to be observed. Rape had to be performed in public, before fathers, mothers, husbands, sisters, brothers, sons, and daughters. And before you killed a man, you first made him beg, scream, and gag . . . or first you killed those he most loved before his eyes. To amplify revulsion and fear, victims were horribly mutilated and left on display. Male victims had their genitals stuffed in their mouths; women had their breasts cut off and their wombs stretched over their heads. Children were killed not by accident but slowly, with pleasure. Severed heads were left on pikes along public roadways. Colombian killers perfected signature cuts, distinctive ways of mutilating victims. One gang left its mark by slicing the neck of a victim and then pulling his tongue down his throat and out through the slice, leaving a grotesque "necktie." These horrors seldom directly touched the educated urbanites of Colombia's ruling classes, but the waves of fear widened and reached everywhere. No child raised in Colombia at midcentury was immune to it. Blood flowed like the muddy red waters that rushed down from the mountains. The joke Colombians told was that God had made their land so beautiful, so rich in every natural way, that it was unfair to the rest of the world; He had evened the score by populating it with the most evil race of men.

It was here, in the second year of *La Violencia,* that the greatest outlaw in history, Pablo Emilio Escobar Gaviria, was born, on December 1, 1949. He grew up with the cruelty and terror alive in the hills around his native Medellín, and absorbed the stories of Desquite, Sangrenegra, and Tirofijo, all of them full-blown legends by the time he was old enough to listen and understand, most of them still alive and on the run. Pablo would outstrip them all by far.

Anyone can be a criminal, but to be an outlaw demands a following. The outlaw stands for something, usually through no effort of his own. No matter how base the actual motives of criminals like those in the Colombian hills, or like the American ones immortalized by Hollywood—Al Capone, Bonnie and Clyde, Jesse James—large numbers of average people rooted for them and followed their bloody exploits with some measure of delight. Their acts, however selfish or senseless, were invested with social meaning. Their crimes and violence were blows struck against distant, oppressive power. Their stealth and cunning in avoiding soldiers and police were celebrated, these being the time-honored tactics of the powerless.

Pablo Escobar would build on these myths. While the other outlaws remained strictly local heroes, meaningful only as symbols, his power would become both international and real. At his peak, he would threaten to usurp the Colombian state. *Forbes* magazine would list him as the seventh-richest man in the world in 1989. His violent reach would make him the most feared terrorist in the world.

His success would owe much to his nation's unique culture and history, indeed to its very soil and climate, with its bountiful harvests of coca and marijuana. But an equal part of it was Pablo himself. Unlike any other outlaw before, he understood the potency of legend. He crafted his and nurtured it. He was a vicious thug, but he had a social conscience. He was a brutal crime boss but also a politician with a genuinely winning personal style that, at least for some, transcended the ugliness of his deeds. He was shrewd and arrogant and rich enough to milk that popularity. He had, in the words of former Colombian president César Gaviria, "a kind of native genius for public relations." At his death, Pablo was mourned by thousands. Crowds rioted when his casket was carried into the streets of his home city of Medellín. People pushed the bearers aside and pried open the lid to touch his cold, stiff face. His gravesite is tended lovingly to this day and remains one of the most popular tourist spots in the city. He stood for something.

For what, exactly, isn't easy to understand without knowing Colombia and his life and times. Pablo, too, was a creature of his time and place. He was a complex, contradictory, and ultimately very dangerous man, in large part because of his genius for manipulating public opinion. But this same crowd-pleasing quality was also his weakness, the thing that eventually brought him down. A man of lesser ambition might still be alive, rich, powerful, and living well and openly in Medellín. But Pablo wasn't content to be just rich and powerful. He wanted to be admired. He wanted to be respected. He wanted to be loved.

When he was a small boy, his mother, Hermilda, the real shaping influence in his life, made a vow before a statue in her home village of Frontino, in the rural northwest part of the Colombian *departamento,* or state, of Antioquia. The statue, an icon, was of the child Jesus of Atocha. Hermilda Gaviria was a schoolteacher, an ambitious, educated, and unusually capable woman for that time and place, who had married Abel de Jesús Escobar, a self-sufficient cattle farmer. Pablo was their second son, and she had already borne Abel a daughter. They would eventually have four more children. But Hermilda was cursed with powerlessness. For all her learning and drive, she knew that the fates of her ambition and her family were out of her hands. She knew this not just in some abstract, spiritual way, the way religious men and women accept the final authority of God. This was Colombia in the 1950s. The horror of *La Violencia* was everywhere. Unlike the relatively secure cities, in villages like Frontino and the one where Hermilda and Abel now lived, Rionegro, violent and terrible death was commonplace. The Escobars were not revolutionaries; they were staunchly middle class. To the extent that they had political leanings, they were allied with local Conservative landowners, which made them targets for the Liberal armies and insurrectionists who roamed the hills. Hermilda sought protection and solace from the child Jesus of Atocha with the urgency of a young wife and mother adrift in a sea of terror. In her prayers she vowed something concrete and grand. Someday, she said, she would build a chapel for Jesus of Atocha if God spared her family from the Liberals. Pablo would build that chapel.

Pablo did not grow up poor, as he and his hired publicists would sometimes later claim. Rionegro was not yet a suburb of Medellín, but a collection of relatively prosperous cattle farms in the outlying districts. Abel owned a house, twelve hectares, and six cows when Pablo was born, and he tended adjacent land that he had sold to a well-known local Conservative politician. The house had no electricity but did have running water. For rural Colombia, this would qualify as upper middle class, and conditions improved when they moved to Envigado, a village on the outskirts of Medellín, a thriving city that was rapidly creeping up the green slopes of the mountains around it. Hermilda was not just a schoolteacher but a founder of Envigado's elementary school. When they moved there, Abel gave up his farming to work as a neighborhood watchman. Hermilda was an important person in the community, someone well-known to parents and children alike. So even as schoolchildren, Pablo and his brothers and sisters were special. Pablo did well in his classes, as his mother no doubt expected, and he loved to play soccer. He was well dressed and, as his chubby frame attested, well fed. Escobar liked fast food, movies, and popular music—American, Mexican, and Brazilian.

While there was still violence in Colombia, even as he entered his teens, the raging terror of *La Violencia* gradually eased. Abel and Hermilda Escobar emerged from it all to create a comfortable life for themselves and their seven children. But just as the prosperity of the fifties in the United States bred a restless, rebellious generation of children, so Pablo and his contemporaries in Medellín had their own way of tuning in, turning on, and dropping out. A hippielike, nihilistic, countrywide youth movement called *Nadaismo* had its origins right in Envigado, where its founder, the intellectual Fernando Gonzáles, had written his manifesto "The Right to Disobey." Banned by the church, barely tolerated by authorities, the *Nadaistas*— the "nothingists"— lampooned their elders in song, dressed and behaved outrageously, and expressed their disdain for the established order in the established way of the sixties: they smoked dope.

Colombian dope was, of course, plentiful and highly potent, a fact that the world's marijuana-toking millions quickly discovered. It was soon the worldwide gold standard for pot. Pablo became a heavy doper early on and stayed that way throughout his life, sleeping until one or two in the afternoon, lighting up not long after waking up, and staying stoned for the rest of the day and night. He was plump and short, standing just under five feet, six inches, with a large, round face and thick, black, curly hair that he wore long, combing it left to right in a big mound that sloped across his forehead and covered his ears. He grew a wispy mustache. He looked out at the world through big, heavy-lidded hazel eyes and cultivated the bemused boredom of the chronic doper. Rebellion evidently took hold not long after he reached puberty. He dropped out of Lyceum Lucrecio Jaramillo several months before his seventeenth birthday, three years shy of graduation. His turn to crime appears to have been motivated as much by ennui as ambition.

With his cousin and constant companion Gustavo Gaviria, he had taken to hanging out nights at a bar in a tough neighborhood, the Jesús de Nazareno district. He told Hermilda that he wasn't cut out for school or a normal job. "I want to be big," he said. It was a testament to Hermilda's persistence, or possibly Pablo's broader plans, that he never fully abandoned the idea of education. He briefly returned to the lyceum two years later with Gustavo, but the two, older than their classmates and accustomed now to the freedom and rough-and-tumble of the Medellín streets, were considered bullies and were soon fighting with their teachers. Neither lasted the school year, although Pablo apparently tried several times, without success, to pass the tests needed to earn a diploma. He eventually just bought one. In later life he would fill shelves in his homes with stacks of unread classics and would talk sometimes of wanting to earn a higher degree. At one point, entering prison, he said he intended to study law. No doubt this lack of formal education continued to feed his insecurities and disappoint Hermilda, but no one who knew him doubted his natural cunning.

He became a gangster. There was a long tradition of shady business practices in Medellín. The stereotypical *paisa* was a hustler, someone skilled in turning a profit no matter what the enterprise. The region was famous for *contrabandistas*, local heads of organized-crime syndicates, practitioners of the centuries-old *paisa* tradition of smuggling—originally gold and emeralds, now marijuana, and soon cocaine. By the time Pablo dropped out of school, in 1966, drug smuggling was already serious business, well over the heads of seventeen-year-old hoodlums. Pablo got his start conning people out of money on the streets of Medellín. But he had plans. When he told his mother that he wanted to be big, he most likely had in mind two kinds of success. Just as the *contrabandistas* dominated the illicit street life of Medellín, its legitimate society was ruled politically and socially by a small number of rich textile and mining industrialists and landowners. These were the dons, the men of culture and education whose money bankrolled the churches and charities and country clubs, who were feared and respected by their employees and those who rented their land. Catholic, traditional, and elitist, these men held high public office and went off to Bogotá to represent Medellín in the national government. Pablo's ambition encompassed both worlds, licit and illicit, and this marks the central contradiction of his career.

The standing legend of Pablo Escobar has it that he and his gang got their start by stealing headstones from cemeteries, sandblasting them clean, and then reselling them. He did have an uncle who sold tombstones, and Pablo evidently worked for him briefly as a teenager. In later life he was always amused when the sandblasting stories were told, and he denied them—but then there was always much that Pablo denied. Hermilda has also called the story a lie, and, indeed, it doesn't seem likely. For one thing, sandblasting sounds too much like honest labor, and there is little to suggest that Pablo ever had an appetite for that. And he was deeply superstitious. He subscribed to that peculiarly pagan brand of Catholicism common in rural Antioquia, one that prays to idols—like Hermilda's child Jesus of Atocha—and communes with dead spirits. Stealing headstones would be an unlikely vocation for anyone who feared the spirit world. What sounds more likely are stories he later admitted to, of running petty street scams with his friends, selling contraband cigarettes and fake lottery tickets, and conning people out of their cash with a mixture of bluff and charm as they emerged from the local bank. Pablo would not have been the first street-smart kid to discover that it was easier and more exciting to take money from others than to earn it. He was exceptionally daring. Maybe it was the dope, but Pablo discovered in himself an ability to remain calm, deliberate, even cheerful when others grew frightened and unsteady. He used it to impress his friends, and to frighten them. On several occasions as a youth, Pablo later boasted, he had held up Medillín banks by himself with an automatic rifle, bantering cheerfully with the clerks as they emptied their cash drawers. That kind of recklessness and poise is what distinguished Pablo from his criminal peers and made him their leader. Before long his crimes would grow more sophisticated, and more dangerous.

The record shows that Pablo was an accomplished car thief before he was twenty. He and his gang took the crude business of pinching cars and turned it into a mini-industry, boldly taking vehicles (drivers would just be pulled from behind the steering wheel in broad daylight) and chopping them down to a collection of valuable parts within hours. There was plenty of money to be made in parts, and no direct evidence of the theft remained. Once he'd amassed sufficient capital, Pablo began simply bribing municipal officials to issue new papers for stolen vehicles, eliminating the need to disassemble the cars. He seems to have had few significant runins with the law during this period. The arrest records have vanished, but Pablo did spend several months in a Medellín jail before his twentieth birthday, no doubt making connections with a more violent class of criminals, who would later serve him well. Clearly the stint behind bars did nothing to dissuade him from a life of crime.

By all accounts, Pablo was enjoying himself. With their wide inventory of stolen engines and parts, he and Gustavo built race cars and competed in local and national car rallies. His business evolved. In time, car theft in Medellín was practiced with such impunity that Pablo realized he had created an even more lucrative market. He started selling protection. People paid him to prevent their vehicles from being pinched —so Pablo began making money on cars he *didn't* steal as well as from those he did. Generous with his friends, he would give them new cars stolen right from the factory. Pablo would draw up false bills of sale and instruct the recipients to take out fake newspaper ads offering the cars for sale, creating a paper trail to make it appear as though the cars had been obtained legitimately.

It was during this period, as a young crime boss on the make, that Pablo developed a reputation for casual, lethal violence. In what may have begun as simply a method of debt collection, he would recruit thugs to kidnap people who owed him money and then ransom them for whatever was owed. If the family couldn't come up with the money or refused to pay, the victim would be killed. Sometimes the victim was killed *after* the ransom was paid, just to make a point. It was murder, but a kind of murder that can be rationalized. A man had to protect his interests. Pablo lived in a world where accumulation of wealth required the capacity to defend it. Even for legitimate businessmen in Medellín there was little effective or honest law enforcement. If someone cheated you, you either accepted your losses or took steps yourself to settle the score. If you grew successful enough, you had to contend with corrupt police and government officials who wanted a piece of your profits. This was especially true in Pablo's new illicit business. As the amounts of money and contraband grew, so did the need to enforce discipline, punish enemies, collect debts, and bribe officials. Kidnapping or even killing someone who had cheated him not only kept the books balanced; it sent a message.

Pablo became expert at taking credit for crimes that could not be linked to him directly. From the start, he made sure that those he recruited to commit violent acts were never certain who had hired them. In time, Pablo grew accustomed to ordering people killed. It fed his growing megalomania and bred fear—which was akin to the respect he seemed to crave more and more.

Kidnapping for debt collection evolved soon enough into kidnapping for its own sake. The most famous case attributed to young Pablo was that of Envigado industrialist Diego Echavarria, in the summer of 1971. Echavarria was a proud Conservative factory owner, widely respected in higher social circles but disliked by many of the poor workers in Medellín, who were being laid off in droves from local textile mills. At the time, wealthy Antioquia landowners were expanding their country holdings by simply evicting whole villages of farmers from the Magdalena River Valley, leaving them no alternative but to move to the slums of the growing city. The unpopular factory owner's body was found in a hole not far from the place where Pablo was born. He had been kidnapped six weeks earlier and had been beaten and strangled, even though his family had paid a $50,000 ransom. The killing of Diego Echavarria worked on two levels. It turned a profit and it doubled as a blow for social justice. There is no way to prove that Pablo orchestrated this crime, and he was never officially charged with it, but it was so widely attributed to him that in the slums people began referring to Pablo admiringly as Doctor Echavarria, or simply *El Doctor*. The killing had all the hallmarks of the young crime boss's emerging style: cruel, deadly, smart, and with an eye toward public relations.

In one stroke, the Echavarria kidnapping elevated Pablo to the status of local legend. It also advertised his ruthlessness and ambition, which didn't hurt either. In coming years, he would become even more of a hero to many in Medellín's slums with well-publicized acts of charity. He had a social conscience, but his aspirations were strictly middle class. When he told his mother he wanted to be "big," he wasn't dreaming of revolution or remaking his country; he had in mind living in a mansion as spectacular as the mock medieval castle Echavarria had built for himself. He would live in a castle like that, not as someone who exploited the masses but as a people's don, a man of power and wealth who had not lost touch with the common man. His deepest anger was always reserved for those who interfered with that fantasy.

2

Pablo Escobar was already a clever and successful crook when a seismic shift in criminal opportunity presented itself in the mid-seventies: the pot generation discovered cocaine. The illicit pathways marijuana had carved from Colombia to North American cities and suburbs became expressways as coke became the fashionable drug of choice for adventurous young professionals. The cocaine business would make Pablo Escobar and his fellow Antioquia crime bosses—the Ochoa brothers, Carlos Lehder, José Rodríguez Gacha—and others richer than their wildest fantasies, among the richest men in the world. By the end of the decade they would control more than half of the cocaine shipped to the United States, netting a return flow measured in not millions but *billions* of dollars. Their enterprise became the largest industry in Colombia, and bankrolled the candidacies of mayors, councilmen, congressmen, and presidents. By the mid-eighties, Escobar would own nineteen different residences in Medellín alone, each with a heliport. He owned fleets of boats and planes, properties throughout the world, large swaths of Antioquian land, apartment complexes, housing developments, and banks. There was so much money rolling in that figuring out how to invest all of it was more than they could handle; many millions were simply buried. The flood of foreign cash triggered good times in Medellín. There was a boom in construction and new business start-ups, and unemployment plummeted. Eventually, the explosion of drug money knocked the entire country of Colombia off balance and upended the rule of law.

Pablo was perfectly positioned to take advantage of this wave. He had spent more than a decade building his local criminal syndicate and learning the ways of bribing officialdom. The cocaine boom initially attracted amateurs for whom cocaine was a glamorous flirtation with crime. But crime was already Pablo's element. He was violent and unprincipled, and a determined climber. He wasn't an entrepreneur, and he wasn't even an especially talented businessman. He was just ruthless. When he learned about a thriving cocaine-processing lab on his turf, he shouldered his way in. If someone developed a lucrative delivery route north, Pablo demanded a majority of the profits—for protection. No one dared refuse him.

A young Medellín pilot who went by the nickname "Rubin," and whose skills naturally led him into the cocaine business during those years, met Pablo for the first time in 1975. Rubin had grown up in a well-to-do family that had sent him to the United States to get an education. He had earned his pilot's license in Miami, and he spoke English fluently. When some of his friends, the Ochoa brothers, Juan David, Jorge, and Fabio, started shipping cocaine north, Rubin fell easily into the business with them. Before long he was buying and selling small planes in Miami, recruiting pilots to make the low-level flights. Rubin and the Ochoas were not professional tough guys, like Pablo and his gang, but playboys, relatively well educated young Colombians who considered themselves fashionable and smart. Very soon they were also rich.

Their very stylishness is what enabled them to ship and move cocaine, not any genius for business or connections with Antioquia's criminal class. They were comfortable in the upscale social circles in Miami where American buyers congregated. Rubin was perfect. He was handsome, fearless, even dashing. His boss at the time was a Medellín entrepreneur named Fabio Restrepo, one of the first *paisa* cocaine chiefs. In 1975 Restrepo was pulling together shipments of forty to sixty kilos of cocaine once or twice a year—and a kilo would sell for more than $40,000 in Miami. Whenever that much money is being made illegally, it attracts sharks.

Pablo originally contacted Jorge Ochoa to see about selling Restrepo some uncut product. Rubin accompanied Jorge to a small apartment in Medellín, where they were met at the door by a chubby young man with a thick mop of curly black hair who strutted alongside them comically, like a typical street tough. He wore a big pullover polo shirt, blue jeans that were rolled up at the cuff, and tennis shoes, and the apartment where they met him was a sty, strewn with trash and discarded clothing. To these two rich young dandies, Pablo was nothing but a local hoodlum. The fourteen kilos of cocaine he showed them in a dresser drawer was strictly small-time. They bought the cocaine from him and moved on, unimpressed—until Restrepo was murdered two months later. It was shocking. Somebody had simply killed him! And, just like that, there was a new man in charge of the cocaine business in Medellín. Rubin and the Ochoa brothers were surprised, after Restrepo's death, to find that they were now working for Pablo Escobar. There was, of course, no way to prove that Pablo had killed Restrepo, but he didn't seem to mind if people drew that conclusion. The playboy cocaine traffickers had underestimated the local hoodlum. The low-class, strictly small-time dealer had brutally and efficiently muscled his way in.

"There was not a single aspect of the business that was created, designed, or promoted by Pablo Escobar," Rubin says. "He was a gangster, pure and simple. Everybody, right from the start, was afraid of him. Even later, when they considered themselves friends, everybody was afraid of him."

In March 1976, Pablo married Maria Victoria Henao Vellejo, a shapely, pretty, dark-haired fifteen-year-old, so young that Pablo had had to obtain a special dispensation from the bishop (such things could be had for a fee). At age twenty-six, married, wealthy, and feared, if not respected, Pablo was on his way to achieving his dreams. But his rapid rise had already earned him dangerous enemies. One of them tipped off agents of the *DAS* (*Departamento Administrativo de Seguridad*), who arrested Pablo, his cousin Gustavo, and three other men, just two months after the wedding, as they returned to Medellín from a drug run to Ecuador.

Pablo had been arrested before. There was that stint he'd done at Itagui as a teenager, and he had been arrested again in 1974, caught in a stolen Renault. Both times he had been convicted and sentenced to serve several months in prison. But this was far more serious. The DAS agents found thirty-nine kilos of cocaine hidden in the spare tire of the group's truck, enough to place them in the big league of coke smuggling at that time, and to send them all to prison for a long time.

Pablo tried bribing the judge, who turned the money down flat. So the judge's background was researched, and it was learned that he had a brother who was a lawyer. The two brothers did not get along, and the lawyer agreed to represent Pablo in the case, knowing that the judge would likely recuse himself as soon as he found out, which is what happened. The new judge was more amenable to bribery, and Pablo, his cousin, and the others were freed. The manuever had been so bald that an appellate judge, just months later, reinstated the indictments and ordered Pablo and the others rearrested. But further appeals tied up the case, and in March of the following year, with Pablo still at large, the two *DAS* agents responsible for the arrest—Luis Vasco and Gilberto Hernandez—were killed.

Pablo was establishing a pattern of dealing with the authorities that would become his trademark. It soon became known simply as *plata o plomo*. One either accepted Pablo's *plata* (silver) or his *plomo* (lead).

None of the party boys in Medellín were complaining much about Pablo's methods, because they were all getting rich. Pablo absorbed the entrepreneurs, the lab rats, and the distributors like the Ochoas. He "insured" them. He oversaw their delivery routes, exacting a tax on every kilo shipped. It was pure muscle, an old-fashioned syndicate, but the result was to create for the first time a unified and streamlined cocaine industry. Once the coca leaves had been grown and refined by independent dealers, their shipments would be added to the loads controlled by Pablo's organization, a service for which they paid 10 percent of the wholesale U.S. price. If a big shipment was intercepted or lost, Pablo would repay his suppliers, but only for what the load had cost in Colombia. If only one or two shipments made it to Miami, New York, or Los Angeles, the sale would more than cover the cost of four or five lost or intercepted loads—and drug enforcement efforts were intercepting fewer than one load in ten. Losses were always far exceeded by profits.

And what profits. The appetite for white powder in America was seemingly inexhaustible. More money than anyone in Medellín had ever dreamed of seeing, money enough to remake not just lives but whole cities, whole nations! Between 1976 and 1980 bank deposits in Colombia's four major cities more than doubled. So many illegal American dollars were flooding the country that the country's elite began looking for ways to score its share without breaking the law. President Alfonso López Michelsen's administration permitted a practice that the central bank called "opening a side window," which allowed unlimited quantities of dollars to be converted to Colombian pesos. The government also encouraged the creation of speculative funds that offered exorbitantly high interest rates. These were ostensibly legitimate investments in highly speculative markets, but nearly everyone knew that their money was really being invested in shipments of cocaine. The government played along by turning a blind eye. Soon anyone with money to invest in Bogotá could readily cash in on the drug bonanza. The whole nation wanted to join Pablo's party.

With his millions, Pablo could now afford to buy protection for his cocaine shipments all through the pipeline, from growers to processors to distributors. He began traveling to Peru, Bolivia, and Panama, buying up control of the enterprise from top to bottom. He wasn't the only one. The Rodríguez Orejuela brothers, Jorge, Gilberto, and Miguel, were pulling together the threads of the Cali cocaine cartel at the same time. Competing in Antioquia—and sometimes collaborating—were José Rodríguez Gacha and the eccentric half German Carlos Lehder. Pablo's payoffs went from thousands to millions of pesos (hundreds of thousands of dollars), and there were few law-enforcement officials inclined to resist the juggernaut—especially when one considered the alternative. Pablo was even willing to play along a little, allowing a few shipments to be intercepted, enough to make law enforcement look like it was doing its job. He could afford it.

Nobody had a good handle on how much cocaine was flowing north. The estimates tended to be low by a factor of ten or more. American officials were estimating total shipments of five to six hundred kilos a year in 1975 when police in Cali stumbled over six hundred kilos in a single airplane. The seizure triggered a weekend war in Medellín, where various factions accused the others of either screwing up or selling out. Forty people were killed. But shipments of that size had become routine, and the vast majority of it got through. The tide of corruption and drug money simply swept away the relatively flimsy organs of law and authority. It happened so quickly that officials in Bogotá hardly noticed.

After skating away from his drug bust in 1976, Pablo knew he had little to fear from the law in Medellín. He was the unofficial king of the city. Rubin was in Miami during this period, so for a few years he didn't see Pablo or his friends the Ochoas. When he returned to Colombia in 1981, as he puts it, "The circus was in full swing." All of the cocaine kings had mansions, limousines, race cars, personal helicopters and planes, fine clothes, and fancy artwork (some, like Pablo, hired decorators to guide their taste in painting and sculpture, which tended toward the garish and surreal). They were surrounded by bodyguards, sycophants, and women, women, women. It was a higher life than anyone in Colombia had ever seen, and it was going to go higher still. The gangsters imported a nightlife to Medellín, opening lavish discos and fine restaurants.

Pablo in particular was known for his adolescent appetites. He and his buddies would play soccer matches under the lights on fields that he had paid to have leveled and sodded, paying announcers to call their amateur games as though they were big-time professional matches. Opponents and teammates were always careful to make Don Pablo look good. Soon he and the other cocaine kingpins would buy the best soccer clubs in the country. To entertain his closest friends, Pablo would hire a gaggle of beauty queens for evenings of erotic games. The women would strip and race naked toward an expensive sports car, which the winner would keep, or submit to bizarre humiliations—shaving their heads, swallowing insects, or engaging in naked tree-climbing contests. In the bedroom of one residence he kept, apparently for recreational purposes, a gynecological examination chair. In 1979 he constructed a lavish country estate on a seventy-four-hundred-acre ranch near Puerto Triunfo on the Magdalena River, about eighty miles east of Medellín. He called it "Hacienda Los Nápoles." The land alone cost him $63 million, and he had just started spending. He built an airport, a heliport, and a network of roads. He flew in hundreds of exotic animals—elephants, buffaloes, lions, rhinoceroses, gazelles, zebras, hippos, camels, and ostriches. He built six different swimming pools and created several lakes. The mansion was outfitted with every toy and extravagance money could buy. Pablo could sleep a hundred guests at a time, and entertain them with food, music, games, and parties. There were billiard tables and pinball machines, and a Wurlitzer jukebox that featured the records of Pablo's favorite performer, Brazilian singer Roberto Carlos. On display out front was a thirties-era sedan peppered with bullet holes, which Pablo said had belonged to Bonnie and Clyde. He would take his guests on jarring trail-bike excursions across his estate, or race them on Jet Skis across one of his custom lakes. Nápoles was an outrageous blend of the erotic, exotic, and extravagant. Pablo was its maestro. He enjoyed speed, sex, and showing off, and he craved an audience.

As his fortune grew and his fame spread, Pablo began tending his public image, conscientiously denying any official connection to his illicit enterprises and working hard to appear likable, although his reputation terrified even hardened Medellín criminals. He was stiffly formal in public, as if trying to measure up to a stature that ill suited him. His language became flowery and excessively polite. And he began courting the public, especially the poor.

Employing leftist rhetoric when it suited his needs, Pablo played upon popular resentments of the established powers in Bogotá and the historical hard feelings toward the United States. Marxist groups like the *FARC (Fuerzas Armadas Revolucionarias de Colombia,* or the Revolutionary Armed Forces of Colombia), *ELN (Ejército de Liberación Nacional,* or the National Army of Liberation), and a new urban movement calling itself M-19 enjoyed wide support from Colombia's educated youth. Rebellious Jesuits in Colombia were preaching liberation theology. After years of exploitation and political violence, including intimidation by the feared *autodefensas,* the private paramilitary squads employed by the wealthy to scare the peasantry into submission, the average poor citizen of Medellín despised the Colombian establishment. Bogotá, the seat of the national government, was in the hands of the wealthy elite, a privileged 3 percent who owned 97 percent of the country's land and wealth. Pablo, who was already wealthier than anyone in this 3 percent, portrayed himself as a champion of the people. His brother-in-law, Mario Henao, was a leftist intellectual who railed against the capitalist-imperialist influence of America. Mario provided Pablo with a patriotic rationale for his trafficking business and offered him a path to respectability. The flow of cocaine to North America and of dollars south could be considered a revolutionary tactic—at once sucking out Yankee dollars and corrupting the brains and bloodstreams of decadent *norteamericano* youth. By this reasoning, Pablo was not just enriching himself, he was striking a blow against the world establishment and using its own money to build a new, modern, hip, progressive Colombia. On an international scale, he was taking from the rich and giving to the poor.

He himself rarely used cocaine and was only a moderate drinker. His recreational drug of choice remained marijuana. Surrounded by bodyguards and worshipful associates, he had begun to see himself differently. It wasn't enough anymore to have succeeded on the streets of Medellín or to dominate the international drug trade; somewhere along the way Pablo had begun to see himself as a great man. His words and ideas assumed historical importance, and his ambition grew to fill the ever-larger space. He was like a gambler on a winning streak, rolling for higher and higher stakes. He began to see himself as an embodiment of the Colombian people, a vessel for their future, as though his goals were *their* goals, and his enemies, *their* enemies. He was fascinated with the career of Pancho Villa, the Mexican revolutionary who had challenged the United States directly in 1916 when he'd led raids into Texas and New Mexico. American troops, led by General John J. Pershing, had chased him back into Mexico, and then spent eleven months in Mexico in vain pursuit. The effort had turned Villa into a popular hero in Mexico (he was later assassinated by political enemies, in 1923). Pablo embraced a local legend that Villa had actually been Colombian. He began collecting memorabilia from that period of Mexican history and enjoyed dressing up and posing as Villa. Eventually, he would relive the Villa story, becoming the target of a U.S. military–assisted manhunt that would make Pershing's pursuit of Villa look like a trail ride.

Pablo became one of Medellín's most generous employers, paying salaries to workers in his cocaine labs that enabled them to buy houses and cars. Perhaps influenced by Mario Henao, he began spending millions on social improvements in the city, doing far more than the government ever had for the poor crammed into the city's expanding slums. He donated funds and leaned on his associates to raise millions for roads and electric lines, and he cleared soccer fields throughout the area. He built roller-skating rinks and handed out money at public appearances. He started a housing development for the poor called Barrio Pablo Escobar, which gave homes to people who lived in huts by the city's trash dumps. The Conservative Catholic Church in Medellín backed Pablo's social programs, and some priests would continue to support him throughout his life. He would show up for ribbon cuttings and dedications, displaying a reluctance to accept applause or thanks, but always allowing himself to be drawn out eventually to center stage. He would often take part in local soccer matches, demonstrating that despite his widening girth he could still move with surprising athleticism. By the end of the decade, the people's don was not just the richest and most powerful man in Antioquia; he was also its most popular citizen.

In an interview he gave to an auto-racing magazine in 1980, the thirty-year-old Pablo was feeling mostly generous about his fellow man. "I am a great friend and I do everything possible so that people appreciate me," he said. "What is worth most in life are friends, of that I am sure." Of course, friendship also had its hazards. "Unfortunately," Pablo added, somewhat ominously, "along life's paths one also meets people who are disloyal."

In private, he spoke softly and prided himself on his unruffled, casual good humor. When he was stoned he liked to tell stories, laughing about his own exploits and at the blundering of his enemies, but was otherwise content to watch and listen. He was a slob, lazy and self-indulgent in all his habits. He ate too much, guzzled Coca-Cola, devoured pizza and other fast foods, and spared no expense in recruiting young women—the younger the better—to satisfy his sexual appetite. Like others before him who amassed great wealth and power at a young age, Pablo grew increasingly self-righteous. He was already de facto above the law. In Medellín he had created a dual system of justice. The violence committed in the course of his business—the murder rate doubled in the city during this period—was studiously ignored by the police. It was considered part of the drug business, something separate from civil society. Pablo himself regarded murders committed by his men as matters of no consequence to society at large. It was strictly business, a grim necessity in a state without a strong legal system. In Colombia, one could waste a lifetime waiting for state-administered justice. One of the prerogatives of the wealthy and powerful in rural Colombia had always been enforcing their own justice—that's what lay behind the long and bloody tradition of *autodefensas,* or private armies. Once Pablo had made his first millions, he didn't look to the law for protection, and he resented its interference in his affairs. He considered it his right to use violence on his own account, and on occasion did so publicly. Once, when a worker was discovered stealing something from his estate, Pablo had the man bound hand and foot, and in front of horrified guests at Nápoles personally kicked the man into his swimming pool and then watched him drown.

"This is what happens to those who steal from Pablo Escobar!" he said. The warning no doubt resonated among his guests, many of whom were in a position to steal far more from *El Doctor* than the unfortunate servant had.

Most of Medellín accepted this system of private justice, because to oppose Pablo was unwise. Those who did became his enemies, and his enemies had a way of turning up dead. He had little stomach for idealism. For all his concern about Medellín's poor, Pablo's worldview was essentially cynical. One prospered by being smarter and more dangerous than the other guy. So when politicians or journalists in Bogotá started spreading the alarm about this emerging criminal power, defending the rule of law, he saw them as sanctimonious poseurs aligned with his rival cartels or with the United States. In Pablo's worldview, no one acted on principle. They pursued what was in their own best interests. Anyone who opposed him was simply "disloyal," not just to him personally but to Colombia.

Politics was the next logical step for a man of Pablo's ambition. In 1978 he was elected as a substitute city council member in Medellín. He helped underwrite the presidential campaign of Belisario Betancur that year, loaning the campaign planes and helicopters, and also contributed liberally to the campaign of Betancur's rival, Julio Turbay, who won the election. Two years later, Pablo backed the formation of a new national political movement, called the New Liberal Party, headed locally by former justice minister Alberto Santofimio and nationally by the enormously popular reformer Luis Galán. In 1982 he ran for Congress himself. He stood as a substitute, for Envigado representative Jairo Ortega. Under the Colombian system, voters elect a representative and a substitute, who is allowed full privileges of the office and sits in when the primary delegate is unable to attend congressional sessions. Ortega and Pablo were elected in the same balloting that elevated Betancur, on his second try, to the presidency.

So Pablo Escobar was a congressman. It was just a substitute position, but the victory seemed precisely the validation he had sought. He was now officially a respectable citizen, a representative of the people. The post conferred automatic judicial immunity, so Pablo could no longer be prosecuted for crimes under Colombian law. He was also entitled to a diplomatic visa, which he began using that year to take trips with his family to the United States. He posed in front of the White House with his young son, Juan Pablo, and began enjoying for the first time the mansions he had purchased for himself in Miami (one in Miami Beach and an $8 million spread north of the city in Plantation, Florida). Pablo had arrived. He told his friends that he intended someday soon to be president of Colombia.

By then, much of the ruling class in Bogotá had made its peace with drug trafficking. Some saw cocaine simply as a new industry, one that had created a new, wealthy, young social class—and one highly fashionable at that. The *narco* millionaires were comparable, to some, to the class of oil millionaires who had become powerful at the turn of the century. Pablo himself would argue, with some truth (perhaps with the voice of his leftist brother-in-law in his ear), that the wealth in some of Colombia's most established families had its seeds in crime—slaving, tobacco, and quinine smuggling, land seizures during the civil wars, gold and emerald smuggling . . . Colombia's history was rife with examples. Just as these wealthy classes had shaped Colombia's political and social agendas throughout history, the *narcos* had their own demands. They wanted the state to legitimize their enterprise, and given the money they were ready to spread around and the building boom going on in Medellín, some intellectuals saw the cocaine trade as potential economic salvation for Andean nations, akin to the discovery of vast oil fields in the Persian Gulf. Although this new *narco* class was made up of wealthy capitalists, the subversive nature of cocaine trafficking appealed to leftist nationalists, who applauded the great transfer of wealth from north to south.

The mistake Pablo made was to covet a public role in this process. He could have continued pulling strings in Colombian politics through a long, fat lifetime, but he insisted on stepping out from behind the curtain.

Pablo wanted the limelight. He wanted to be both the *contrabandista* and the don. He went to great and vicious lengths during the seventies to erase evidence of his more sordid criminal past (while still flaunting it in private), and undertook an aggressive campaign to be seen as a benevolent, law-abiding citizen. He hired publicists and paid off journalists. He founded his own newspaper, called *Medellín Cívica,* which produced occasional fawning profiles of its benefactor.

"Yes, I remember him," one Escobar admirer said in its pages. "His hands, almost priestlike, drawing parabolas of friendship and generosity in the air. Yes, I know him, his eyes weeping because there is not enough bread for all the nation's dinner tables. I have watched his tortured feelings when he sees street children—angels without toys, without a present, without a future."

Pablo sponsored art exhibitions to raise money for charity and founded "Medellín Without Slums," an organization that sought to continue his housing programs for the poor. He took walking tours of the city slums with two local priests, whose friendship implied the blessings of the church. The only hint of Pablo's personal agenda in this civic outreach was a forum he sponsored on the subject of extradition at a popular bar and disco in Medellín called Kevin's. Colombia had signed a treaty with the United States in 1979 that recognized the shipment of illegal drugs to be a crime against the United States. As such, it called for suspected drug traffickers to be extradited for trial to the United States, and, if convicted, imprisoned. The prospect struck fear into the hearts of men like Pablo Escobar, who long ago had learned they had little to fear from Colombia's justice system. Unsurprisingly, Pablo's forum on extradition denounced the practice as a violation of "national sovereignty." He made banning extradition a point of nationalist pride, and the centerpiece of his political agenda.

Pablo's election in 1982 marked the peak of his popularity and power. From any of his luxurious estates, it must have seemed to him that all of Colombia, if not all of South America, was within his grasp. In addition to his now frequent trips to the United States, he flew with his family to Spain and toured Europe. He had money and political position and was even beginning to exercise military power. The Colombian army's long-standing battle with Marxist guerrillas in the mountains and jungles had customarily been assisted by vigilantism—*autodefensas* underwritten by wealthy landowners and industrialists. Having assumed his place at the table of the nation's oligarchs, Pablo began to do the same. When the sister of his friends the Ochoas, Martha Nieves Ochoa, was kidnapped by M-19 in 1981 and held for an extravagant ransom, he and the Ochoas and their fellow *narco* bosses formed a private militia to combat the guerrillas. The militia was dubbed *Muerte a Secuestradores* (Death to Kidnappers), and it cloaked its bloody tactics (leaflets were dropped over a soccer stadium announcing the group's formation and promising to hang kidnappers from trees in public parks) in pious rhetoric against criminality, creating the rich and uniquely Colombian irony of a movement against criminal kidnappers funded and led by a longtime criminal kidnapper.

Pablo still employed populist rhetoric when it suited him, but he and the other *narco* kingpins had long since found themselves natural enemies of the Communists in the hills. The Middle Magdalena Valley, the lush green divide between the Central and Occidental Cordilleras in the Antioquia region, had been a stronghold of the *FARC,* Colombia's dominant guerrilla group. Wealthy landowners had for decades employed private armies to protect their property and families and to terrorize campesinos who exhibited any sympathy for the rebels. By the mid-eighties, Pablo and his associates were the wealthiest landowners in Colombian history. They could afford to do more than just defend themselves and scare rural villagers. Armed with sophisticated military equipment and trained by Israeli and British mercenaries, they began to go after the guerrillas more aggressively than even the Colombian army had. In the process, these *narco*-funded paramilitary groups formed close ties with the army, and together they had the *FARC,* the *ELN,* and M-19 on the run. Battling Communists further legitimized Pablo and the other *narcos* in the eyes of some Colombians. Some elected officials and journalists—many of them paid well for their efforts—began to argue for the legalization of cocaine trafficking. This was an extreme position, one that would have turned Colombia into an outlaw nation, but it had the effect of making Pablo's campaign against extradition seem moderate and even reasonable. Colombia's leadership was increasingly inclined to be agreeable. Both candidates for president in 1982 reportedly had their campaigns underwritten by drug traffickers.

With his election, Pablo became a popular public figure. To an increasingly admiring Bogotá press, he became the "*paisa* Robin Hood." In April 1983, the magazine *Semana* profiled him warmly, noting only that the sources of his wealth "never cease to be the object of speculation." Waving his diamond-and-gold Rolex, admitting to his ownership of a fleet of planes and helicopters and vast real estate holdings worldwide, in the article Pablo traced the origin of his estimated $5 billion fortune to a "bicycle rental business" he said he had started in Medellín when he was sixteen years old. "I dedicated some years to the lottery, then I got into the business of buying and selling cars, and, finally, I ended up in property." It was, of course, preposterous. He was infamous worldwide in law-enforcement circles as a cocaine trafficker, and in private he flaunted the origins of his fortune. But if the price of political success meant constructing a false, legitimate excuse for his wealth, Pablo was willing to wink and nod his way to power. By the end of that year, his prospects seemed ascendant and limitless.

Pablo was much more than a rich smuggler; he embodied the youthful spirit of the age. Throughout the civilized world, a new generation was coming of age, one that had strikingly different attitudes toward recreational drug use than its parents had. The illegality of these popular drugs was part of their appeal. Using them was an act of defiance, an assertion of hipness. Whether they thought about it or not, everyone who snorted cocaine was executing a small bow to their intrepid Colombian suppliers. Just as Pablo's billions were the sum total of every furtive transaction, his risk was the sum total of all his users' petty risks. At the end of the long chain of illicit commerce that delivered the numbing substance to their nasal membranes, Pablo ran the Big Risk and reaped the Big Reward. He and the other *narco* kingpins were, at least for this brief period, popular heroes, the embodiment of cool, as glamorous as they were dangerous in pop-culture portrayals such as the TV program *Miami Vice*. In real life, Pablo played his role with panache. He would proudly point out to visitors at Nápoles the small plane that had flown his first shipments of the drug, mounted over the entrance to his estate. He built small, remote-controlled submarines that could carry up to two thousand kilos of cocaine from the northern coast of Colombia to waters just off Puerto Rico, where divers would remove the shipment and transport it to Miami in speedboats. He would send fleets of planes north, each carrying one thousand kilos. There was no way customs and law enforcement would intercept more than a tiny fraction. Eventually he was buying used Boeing 727s, stripping out the passenger seats, and loading as much as ten thousand kilos per flight. There was nothing to stop him.

But here things began to turn. Pablo was, foremost, a creature of Colombia. No matter how successful he became or what his image was in the larger world, he was primarily concerned with his place at home. In Colombia, it was one thing to grow rich shipping contraband and to liberally spread that prosperity, but when Pablo sought respectability, polite Colombian society rebelled. When he applied for membership to an old-line country club in Medellín, Club Campestre, a social center for the city's traditional ruling class, he was rejected. When he tried to take his seat in El Congreso the following year, it provoked a political storm that dashed Pablo's dream of social status and political power. It triggered one of the bloodiest decades in Colombia's history.

3

Newly appointed justice minister Rodrigo Lara could not have known what a dangerous step he was taking when he went after political "hot money" in 1983. Lara was a handsome, ambitious former senator with long, straight hair and bangs that fell rakishly across his face. Charming, gregarious, and passionate, he was a rising star at age thirty-five in the dissident faction of the Liberal Party, the Liberal Renovation Front, which Pablo had helped bankroll in Medellín. They called themselves the "New Liberals" and were headed by the charismatic Luis Galán, whom many Colombians saw as heir to the progressive reform tradition of Gaitán.

Galán had been defeated in a three-way race for the presidency in 1982 by Belisario Betancur, who by law had to appoint members of the opposition to several cabinet posts. He had picked Lara for the justice post, and the young minister wasted little time going after the creeping *narco* influence, which had been a theme of Galán's campaign. It was an issue popular with the public and the press, but decidedly unpopular with the nation's political leadership; nearly everyone running for office in both the Liberal and Conservative Parties had taken money from the cocaine trade. Lara made the issue his own. His denunciations of hot money delighted the U.S. embassy and marked Lara as a man of principle, but his motives were not all selfless. The New Liberals saw the Medellín faction backed by Pablo—and on whose slate he had been elected—as a rival. So Lara's attack on hot money was a way of protecting his own political base. He did not receive much support from Betancur. The new president was notably silent on the subject. The attitude in Bogotá power circles was merely watchful. They would let Lara march down that path, and it would remain to be seen whether making an issue of hot money would prove politically wise.

In the summer of 1983, Pablo was infamous in law enforcement worldwide, but he was not yet that well known in Colombia outside of Medellín. He had taken great pains to whitewash his criminal record during his campaign as Ortega's alternate, and the fawning stories about him in Bogotá's press had done little to enlighten the populace. While his name and associations were known within the halls of power, his election as an alternate to El Congreso did not itself create a public stir. Lara knew who Pablo was, and knew there was no more blatant example of hot-money influence than his election. He did not begin by accusing Pablo of drug trafficking directly, but he made it clear that the Medellín ticket was tainted by such associations. It is unlikely that Lara fully comprehended how dangerous an enemy he was making, but by the end of that summer he would find out.

Ortega, the primary Envigado representative, spread the word that he intended to publicly answer Lara's accusations. And on the appointed date, August 16, 1983, Pablo Escobar came to the capitol for the first time. Seats in the observation area, usually empty, were full. There were packs of reporters and photographers. Among the crowd was Carlos Lehder, the flamboyant cocaine trafficker, with his own entourage of bodyguards and consorts. All the public seats to the chamber were filled, but because Lehder, like Pablo, published his own small newspaper, he was admitted to the balcony press gallery. The hallways outside the chamber were crowded, and there was a low buzz of excitement. No one knew for sure what to expect, only that the *narcos'* progress into Colombia's government and public life had been publicly challenged, and there was going to be some kind of showdown.

Pablo arrived with a platoon of bodyguards, a chubby man with long, uncombed hair wearing a cream-colored suit and a dress shirt open at the collar. He was at first barred by the doormen, who refused him entry to the chamber because he was not wearing a tie. So Pablo borrowed one with a bold floral print. There was an audible gasp when he swept into the hall with his bodyguards. All eyes were on him as he took his seat toward the back of the chamber. He seemed ill at ease at the center of so much attention, and when he was seated he began chewing nervously on his fingers.

The house president, César Gaviria, immediately stepped down from his place at the front rostrum and loudly called for the removal of all body-guards from the chamber. Gaviria was tense. He knew exactly who Pablo was, and feared the man was capable of anything. He had images of gun-fire erupting inside the chamber itself. But with a nod from Pablo, the gunmen left quietly.

On the desk of every delegate in the room had been placed a photo-copy of a check for one million pesos (about $13,000) from someone named Evaristo Porras, made out to Rodrigo Lara.

After the normal preliminaries, Ortega rose and asked to address the chamber. With his notorious alternate seated silently beside him, the con-gressman announced that he intended to talk about hot money, and that he welcomed the chance. He had no personal axe to grind, he said, but he wanted to respond to certain allegations made by the justice minister. Lara watched from a seat at the front of the room.

Ortega asked if Señor Justice Minister knew of this man named Porras. Across the room, Lara shook his head no.

Ortega went on to explain that Porras was a man from Leticia, a town on Colombia's southern border, who had done time in a Peruvian prison for trafficking drugs. The check—Ortega waved it in front of him—was a contribution to one of Lara's successful campaigns for the Senate. Ortega said that Lara had not only accepted the hot money, but had phoned Porras to thank him for the contribution. The congressman then produced a small machine and played what he said was a tape recording of that phone call. Few in the hall could make out a word of the recording.

"Let the Congress analyze the minister's conduct with this person who offered him a million pesos," said Ortega. "But far be it from me to try to detain the minister of justice's brilliant political career. I only want him to tell us what kind of morality he is going to require of the rest of us. Relax, Minister. Just let the country know that your morality can't be any different from that of Jairo Ortega and the rest of us."

Ortega's comments were met with wild cheering from Lehder and his entourage in the press gallery. When this breech of protocol drew loud reproaches from other reporters and editors, Lehder glared back at them. In his seat on the House floor below, Pablo just sat, picking his teeth with short, fat fingers, rocking in the high-backed swivel leather chair, listening and watching silently, sometimes with a small, pained smile.

When Ortega finished, Lara stood to reply. He did not recall Porras or his check, but he knew it was entirely possible that the man had once contributed to one of his campaigns. It was an outrageous accusation. Covered in mire, Ortega was pointing to a spot on the lapel of an honest man.

"My life is an open book," Lara said. He offered to resign his office the moment any suspicion "whatsoever" fell upon his honesty, adding that the same could not be said of "complacent ministers affected by the blackmail and the extortion being perpetrated against Colombia's political class.

"Morality is one thing, but there are levels: one thing are the checks that they use to throw mud . . . but it is another thing when somebody runs a campaign exclusively with these funds," said Lara, his voice now singing with sarcasm. He was clearly unafraid of contrasting his integrity with that of men like Ortega and Escobar. "[We have] a congressman who was born in a very poor area, himself very, very poor, and afterwards, through astute business deals in bicycles and other things, appears with a gigantic fortune, with nine planes, three hangars at the Medellín airport, and creates the movement 'Death to Kidnappers,' while on the other hand, mounts charitable organizations with which he tries to bribe a needy and unprotected people. And there are investigations going on in the United States, of which I cannot inform you here tonight in the House, on the criminal conduct of Mr. Ortega's alternate."

Pablo had no shortage of defenders. Ortega's argument was not without appeal in the chamber. He had appealed to a fellowship of sinners. If even Lara had accepted a tainted check, which of them would survive scrutiny? Another congressman from Medellín, also on the slate financed by the cartel, rose to portray the attack on Pablo as meritless and entirely political.

"It was only when Representative Escobar joined our movement that all kinds of suspicion were thrown on the sources of his wealth," the congressman said. "I, as a politician, lack the ability to investigate the origin of any assets. . . . Representative Escobar has no need to rely on others to defend his personal conduct, which, on the other hand and as far as I know, has not been subjected to any action by the law or the government."

Pablo made no comment as he left the hall that day, departing as he arrived, inside a phalanx of bodyguards. Outside the chamber, he was besieged by reporters. Ducking away from one who pursued him with a tape recorder, Pablo approached two congressmen conversing in the corridor. He stood awkwardly and silently beside them. One of the men, Poncho Renteria, startled and frightened, tried to break the ice by introducing Pablo.

"Professor," he said to his colleague, "you who have lived history— this is one of the superheavies of Envigado, Pablo Escobar."

Renteria's colleague looked Pablo up and down and, *Escobar* being a somewhat common name in Colombia, jokingly asked,"Which of the Escobars are you?"

Pablo managed a polite smile but said nothing. Two congressmen from Medellín then walked up, and Pablo left with them.

He was furious. The following day, Lara was notified by lawyers that he had twenty-four hours to present evidence supporting his accusations, otherwise legal action would be taken against him.

Lara knew that there was no doubt in all of Colombia—or the world, for that matter—about Pablo's criminality. This attack by Ortega confirmed that Lara had a bigger fight on his hands than anyone had imagined. And he was up to the challenge. Lara understood immediately that he was engaged in nothing less than a struggle for the soul of Colombia. Either the nation was for sale or it was not. He denounced the corruption and violence caused by drug trafficking and called for "a frontal fight, clear, open, without fear or retreat, running all the necessary risks." He called the Porras check a "smoke screen."

"My accusers could not forgive the clarity of my denunciation of Pablo Escobar, who through clever business deals has manufactured an enormous fortune," Lara said. Citing the vast sums of money earned by drug trafficking, Lara noted, "This is an economic power concentrated in a few hands and in criminal minds. What they cannot obtain by blackmail, they get by murder."

Lara had powerful friends. Days after the confrontation, the newspaper *El Espectador* unearthed stories from its files of Pablo's 1976 arrest for drug trafficking. There were mug shots of Pablo and his cousin Gustavo. Any pretense of Pablo's innocence was blown. So damaging was the story that Pablo's men raced around Medellín in a pathetic attempt to buy up every copy of the newspaper. Their efforts, of course, only heightened interest in the story. It prompted a renewed criminal investigation into the deaths of the policemen who had arrested him, and a new warrant was issued for Pablo's arrest. Weeks later, the judge who issued the warrant was murdered in his car. Then ABC-TV aired a documentary that accused Pablo of being Colombia's premier drug trafficker, worth more than $2 billion. He denied the accusation in an on-air interview. Claiming that he had made his fortune in "construction," he nevertheless argued for the great benefits the drug trade had brought to Colombia, reducing unemployment and providing capital for broad economic growth and investment. In the full context of these new revelations, Pablo's denials and posturing seemed ridiculous and self-serving. His fall from grace was hard and fast.

Over the next few months, Pablo was publicly denounced by Galán and kicked out of the New Liberal Party. The Congress began proceedings to lift his parliamentary immunity, and the U.S. embassy revoked his diplomatic visa. Cardinal Alfonso López Trujillo renounced church support for Pablo's social programs in Medellín. Lara signed an arrest and extradition order for Lehder, who went into hiding. It was the first time the government had moved to implement its 1979 extradition agreement.

"The more I learn, the more I know of the damage that the *narcos* are causing the country," said Lara. "I will never again refuse the extradition of one of these dogs."

Then the government, adding insult to injury, seized eighty-five of the exotic animals at Pablo's Nápoles estate, charging that they had been brought into the country illegally.

Pablo fought back. He announced that unless the government renounced the extradition treaty, he and Carlos Lehder would shut down fifteen hundred businesses and put tens of thousands of people out of work. He held a political rally in Medellín and denounced Lara as a hypocrite and a tool of the U.S. embassy. But the revelations of past arrests and new arrest warrants were too much to overcome. Pablo's political career was finished. He was never again able to shake his identification with drug trafficking. He angrily withdrew from politics in January 1984, issuing a petulant statement reflecting his belief that he was more attuned to the masses of Colombians than were his new political adversaries.

"The attitude of politicians is very far from the people's opinions and aspirations," he said.

Pablo complained bitterly to his friends about his sudden shift in fortune. He could not fathom Lara's behavior because he did not believe that anyone acted out of principle. The world was divided between those who lived in a dream, believing in right and wrong, good and evil, and those who lived with their eyes open, who saw there was only power and its prerogatives, reward and punishment, *plata o plomo.* Lara was clearly no fool. If he was immune to greed and fear, if he rejected hot money and was willing to risk his life, then to Pablo there could be only one explanation. The justice minister must be on the payroll of his enemies, either the Cali cartel or the United States or both. He was convinced of it. In his public statements he began referring to Lara as the U.S. representative in the Betancur administration. This was not a struggle between right and wrong; it was a power struggle, pure and simple. And that was a fight Pablo was convinced he could win.

Lara was murdered three months later. Riding in his chauffeur-driven Mercedes in northern Bogotá, he was hit by seven bullets from a machine pistol wielded by an ex-convict on a motorcycle. Lara had become increasingly fearful for his family's safety, and had arranged with the U.S. embassy for them to live temporarily under assumed names in Texas. But at the same time he had become increasingly heedless of his own. He had committed himself to this struggle and seemed to accept death as a possible outcome. The bullet-proof vest given him by U.S. ambassador Lewis Tambs was found on the seat beside him. It probably would not have helped.

4

Pablo was right about one thing. One of the strongest forces behind the move against him and Colombia's other cocaine billionaires was the United States. In response to a growing epidemic of cocaine use in America, President Ronald Reagan had created a cabinet-level task force in January 1982 to coordinate the nation's efforts against drug smuggling. He had appointed Vice President George Bush to lead it. It was not until Bush was elected president in 1988 that the U.S. war on drugs would formally shift its emphasis from trying to stop drugs from crossing the borders to going after *narco* kingpins, but Bush began moving in this direction early on. After

Lara's murder, the Colombian government recognized the cocaine cartels as a threat and were increasingly willing to accept American assistance. The drug lords would eventually become not just law enforcement targets but military ones—an important distinction that the hunt for Pablo Escobar would make clear. Even though few who thought seriously about the drug problem believed it could be stopped or even curbed by arresting a few cartel bosses, it proved a lot easier to get the U.S. Congress worked up about a cabal of billionaires infecting America's youth than about the amorphous smuggling problem. Marshaling public support for war, or even just war spending, requires enemies, and Colombian cocaine barons colorfully fit the description.

During this same period, mainstream attitudes toward cocaine use in the United States underwent a dramatic shift. In June 1986, University of Maryland basketball star Len Bias, the number-two pick in the National Basketball Association draft, collapsed and died at a campus party after snorting cocaine. The decade-long flirtation with the white powder by affluent young Americans had begun to sour anyway, but Bias's death sealed it. Seemingly overnight, cocaine the harmless party drug became cocaine the killer. Suddenly the stories of wild parties and excesses in Hollywood showed a darker side, in stories of overdose and addiction. Cocaine lost all its stylishness when it started showing up on city streets in its cheap, smokable form, crack. It was now a ravenous social epidemic, spurring petty crime waves and destroying lives. Traffickers like Pablo became not guides to the zeitgeist but criminals. They were no longer purveyors of the world's most desired substance; they were authors of a modern plague. People didn't stop using cocaine. But it was no longer fashionable or even okay to be open about it. Bewildered yuppie cocaine kingpins, who just a few years earlier had been the life of the party all over America and who saw themselves more as dashing facilitators than hardened criminals, were being hauled into court in chains, charged under stiff organized-crime statutes, and facing potential life terms in prison. The men behind the giant cocaine cartels in Colombia were no longer just gangsters; they had become enemies of the state.

At least some of the sudden open hostility Pablo encountered when he took his seat in the Colombian House of Representatives was a consequence of American pressure. While the *narcos* were not yet American targets, the U.S. government was growing concerned about links between them and Colombia's guerrillas. A secret CIA intelligence estimate issued in June 1983 reported, "These guerrilla groups initially avoided all connections with narcotics growers and traffickers, except to condemn the corrupting influence of drugs on Colombian society. Now, however, several have developed active links with the drug trade, others extort protection money from the traffickers, and some apparently use profits from drugs to buy arms." At the same time Pablo and the other *narcos* were collaborating with the Colombian army against the *FARC, ELN,* and M-19, arrangements of convenience were being struck in various regions. The guerrillas were finding it more profitable to join the *narcos* than to fight them. Instead of taxing the Medellín cartel, the insurgents had begun negotiating deals to protect coca fields and processing labs. "In fact, the *FARC* in some areas established quotas, taxes, wages and rules for workers, producers and owners of the coca fields," the CIA report said.

The new U.S. ambassador to Colombia, Lewis Tambs, was a conservative Republican who had coauthored the Sante Fe Report, the U.S. government blueprint for containing communism in Latin America. At his final briefing before leaving for the Bogotá post in April 1983, he had been instructed to concentrate on the drug problem as his first priority. On his arrival, the gregarious ambassador said he had only "two songs on my harp, Marxism and drugs," and given the new evidence linking the *narcos* and the guerrillas, the tunes were intertwined. The connection had strong implications in Washington, where the idea of using the U.S. military and spy agencies to combat drugs was still a novel and controversial idea. Fighting communism was neither. It had been the primary thrust of U.S. foreign policy since the end of World War II. If Marxism and drugs were becoming one tune in Colombia, then Pablo and his associates were courting a powerful and implacable enemy. In Lara, Tambs had found his first important ally. When the justice minister had launched his campaign against hot money, he was armed with information and support from the U.S. embassy.

With Lara's permission, the U.S. State Department had begun testing herbicides on coca fields, and in March 1984, government forces had struck two heavy blows against the Medellín cartel. Under Lara's leadership, *La Policía Nacional de Colombia* (*PNC*) raided a huge cocaine-processing facility on the Yarí River in the southern jungles. Called Tranquilandia, it was a complex of fourteen labs and camps housing forty workers. The *PNC* seized fourteen metric tons of cocaine, the largest such find in history. In the weeks before this raid, Betancur's aroused forces (with American assistance) had found and destroyed seven airstrips, seven aircraft, and twelve thousand chemical drums, and had seized cocaine estimated to be worth more than $1 billion. It had been the worst month ever for the Medellín cartel. Less than a month later, Lara was dead.

His killing created a powerful backlash against the Medellín cartel, one that would now erupt into open warfare. Cocaine would never again be seen as just another new industry in Colombia. The esteemed editor of *El Espectador*, Guillermo Cano, would write, "For some time now these sinister men have managed to create an empire of immorality, tricking and making fools of the complacent, doling out crumbs and bribes upon them while a cowardly and often entranced populace stood idly by, content with their illusions and entertained by stories of their jet-set lives."

Respectable Colombian society had picked a fight with the most powerful man in their country, and there would be hell to pay.

Killing the justice minister was an act of war against the state. Outrage in Colombia forced President Betancur to embrace both Lara's crusade and the American aid it required. He placed the entire country under a state of siege and authorized the national police to begin confiscating the *narco* kingpins' estates and other assets. He vowed at Lara's grave to enforce the extradition treaty with the United States.

American involvement in the Tranquilandia raid was widely publicized, and it prompted Pablo to write an angry letter to Ambassador Tambs, who had publicly accused him of owning the Tranquilandia labs. Calling the charge "tendentious, irresponsible and malicious," Pablo wrote that the ambassador was trying to set the stage for extradition "of some sons of Colombia. . . . Señor Ambassador, as a Colombian citizen and a member of Congress of the Republic [Pablo would not be formally stripped of his seat until December 1984], I want to express my most energetic and patriotic protest over the improper interference of North American boats and authorities in Colombian territory, in a way that entails the most flagrant violation of the sovereignty of our motherland."

Soon after Tambs received this letter, Pablo fled the country. For the rising star from Medellín, it had been a swift fall. Just a year earlier he had been a newly elected alternate to El Congreso, with private ambitions for the Presidential Palace. He and the cocaine industry seemed on the road toward respectability and power. With his parliamentary immunity, Pablo felt untouchable. His lavish parties at outlandish Nápoles attracted the most beautiful and powerful people in Colombia. He was a kingmaker who, it seemed, would sooner or later be king. And, just like that, he was cast out. Days after Lara's murder, Pablo boarded a helicopter in Medellín and made the short flight north to Panama City, where the other kingpins of the cartel—Carlos Lehder, José Rodríguez Gacha, the Ochoa brothers— had already gathered in exile.

For some time they had been eyeing Panama as a more hospitable place to do business. A representative of Manuel Noriega, then commander of the Panamanian army and soon to be the nation's dictator, had approached Pablo and the Ochoas in 1983 with an offer to provide a safe haven and protection for their industry for a $4 million fee. The cartel had made a $2 million down payment, but when all the ringleaders suddenly turned up in Panama City, there was no warm reception.

"The officer who made the deal was a black man, and the day Pablo and the others showed up with the rest of the money, I swear he turned white," recalled Rubin, who was with the group in Panama City.

It was more than Noriega had bargained for. Apparently he had envisioned a comfortable way station for the cartel, and a modest slice of illicit funds for himself. It was a busy time for the man the Panamanians called "Pineapple Face." He was plotting the moves that would soon make him Panama's dicator, playing games with Oliver North and the CIA, and delving deep into marijuana trafficking. Just dealing with his rivals in Panama was a full-time job. The last thing he needed was to turn Panama into the new world capital of the cocaine industry. That would invite more attention from his *norteamericano* friends than he wanted.

Whatever the intentions of Gacha, the Ochoas, Lehder, and the others, Pablo immediately began trying to negotiate a deal to return home. His fondest hope had always been to be a rich, respected don in Medellín. Now he was not just an outlaw but an exile. Looking for a way to erase the humiliations of the last eight months and restore himself, he was prepared to make a grand gesture, one that Colombia could not ignore.

In May, just weeks after fleeing, he and Jorge Ochoa met in the Hotel Marriott in Panama City with Alfonso López, the former Colombian president. It was a meeting of old friends. López was an elder statesman, bald and near-sighted, one of the distinguished elders of Colombia's Liberal Party and someone who had enjoyed campaign support from drug traffickers during his career. He was accompanied by Alberto Santofimio, the former justice minister who had founded the Medellín faction of the New Liberal party, which had welcomed Pablo as a candidate two years earlier. The two drug bosses told López that they represented "the dome," the top one hundred Colombian drug traffickers, and made an unprecedented offer. Pablo said he and the others would "dismantle everything" and return the billions deposited in Swiss bank accounts to Bogotá banks if the government would let them keep their fortunes and promise not to extradite them. The offer, which López conveyed to the Colombian president, was intriguing enough for Betancur to send his attorney general to Panama City.

The attorney general was presented with a six-page written proposal addressed to President Betancur. Clearly pleased at the prospect of returning home, Pablo had been in an especially convoluted and flowery mood when he wrote the proposal. The letter offered this preamble:

> In the search for a re-engagement with the country, with its government and with ourselves, as of a few months ago, we are requesting wise and opportune counsel from those, without being permissive or indulgent, who have better understood that our presence in the national life is worthy of study, review and modification. Mr. Alfonso López Michelsen, former President of the Republic, accepted to receive us in the first few days of May in the City of Panama and in a gesture of eminently patriotic goodwill, agreed to take our message of peace to the government. . . . It came to a good end when the Attorney General of the Nation, Mr. Carlos Jimenez Gómez, personally received us. Today we consider that the advice, eagerly sought, has taken real form. In effect, the Attorney General, Mr. Carlos Jimenez Gómez, who finds himself in Panama, has accepted to receive us personally to listen to our concerns.

Pablo went on to deny responsibility for Lara's death, which had been widely attributed to him, and to pledge the traffickers' support for Colombian democracy and law by helping to "eliminate once and forever any drug trafficking in our country." He and Ochoa claimed to represent traffickers who controlled 70 to 80 percent of the Colombian cocaine business, and who earned about $2 billion annually from it. Labs and airstrips would be turned over to the government, and fleets of boats and planes would be sold. They would cooperate with crop-substitution projects to wean Colombian farmers from the lucrative coca. In a "suggestions" section at the bottom of the document, the traffickers asked for a change in the extradition treaty and the right to appeal extradition orders to the Colombian Supreme Court. They also asked to be forgiven for past crimes. In a nutshell, Pablo was offering to go straight and rid Colombia of drug trafficking, provided he could live with his fortune in Medellín without fear of arrest or extradition.

It was a generous offer, even if it didn't include (as was erroneously reported later) a pledge to pay off Colombia's $10 billion national debt. It was probably an offer Pablo and the others could never have made good. Even if they were willing to give up their exorbitant *narco* profits, the many thousands of Colombians employed at all levels of the industry were unlikely to simply close up shop because Pablo had decided to retire with his billions. It was summarily rejected by both Colombian Conservatives and the U.S. embassy, who criticized López and Betancur for even opening a dialogue with criminals. The deal was politically untenable. Given the anger still felt in Colombia over Lara's murder, any deal Betancur struck with the *narcos* would be seen as capitulation. It was the first of many attempts Pablo would make to negotiate a return to the life he wanted for himself and his family. But he had gone too far. His denials about involvement in Lara's death were not believed, and they were later disproved when some of those closest to Pablo began cooperating with the police. Murdering the justice minister was a crime his country could never forgive.

Pablo didn't give up. He grew bitter. He always believed that he was somehow attuned to the masses of his countrymen, that they loved and supported him. He was, if anything, an ugly caricature of his country, unthinkably rich in natural resources but violent, stoned, defiant, and proud. Pablo saw his fate and the country's as the same, and as notorious as he became, he never stopped being a patriot. With so much money, he might easily have sought shelter in a dozen places around the world, but his vision of himself and his future was focused exclusively on Colombia. He did not want to live anywhere but in his home city of Medellín. Those who stood in his way were not just his enemies but tools of the oppressor, traitors to the state.

In the coming years especially, Pablo would become something of a pamphleteer. He liked to write, and he occasionally wrote well. Unlike his formal pronouncements, which tended to be comically overblown, his brief messages to associates or to his enemies were usually concise and polite and often displayed a subtle wit, except when anger made him sarcastic. Years later, when he was running from the national police, moving from hideout to hideout, the police found thirty pages of notes that they believed he had written and left behind in a hurried escape. In them, Pablo appeared to be trying to sketch out some kind of broadside, a rationale for his predicament. He blamed his persecution on the "gringos" who had "forced, by means of economic pressure, a government of slaves to engage in a fratricidal war against the so-called drug cartels."

He had grown up in an essentially lawless state, one he called "morally timid," and believed his philosophy of enforcing his own justice to be the only realistic alternative.

> If you are robbed, what do you do? Who do you turn to? The police? If someone crashes your car, do you expect the traffic police to solve your problem and to compensate you for your damages by forcing your aggressor . . . to pay damages? If you are not paid what you are owed do you believe that Colombian tribunals will force your creditor . . . to pay the debt? If members of the police and armed forces assault and abuse you, whom do you go to? I don't think one single person has mentally considered the above questionnaire anything other than a useless exercise of hope, which we all lost many years ago, faced with the criminal ineptitude of our police and judicial systems. Here, the guerrilla groups, crooks and coercive state systems (police and army) have been applying the death sentence on their enemies. . . . Total ineptitude. And then they go and insult the ones who dare to call things by their name.

These meandering thoughts ultimately failed to cohere into an argument. If Pablo was trying to craft some manifesto to relate his own struggle to that of Marxist heroes Che Guevara and Fidel Castro, he failed—not because he lacked intelligence but because he lacked convictions. His only cause, ultimately, was himself. At his most grandiose, he identified his own ambitions with those of his countrymen, but there was no rationale or ideology behind this parallel. Pablo asserted it simply because it sounded good. He wanted to be a man of the people, a hero to the masses, and what Pablo wanted, Pablo got. So even as more and more

Colombians turned on him, he remained in his own mind the people's one true representative. He would keep trying to work out a deal with the government of Colombia, despite his growing contempt for it, because he wanted most of all to live out that fantasy. It could not be done in Panama City or Managua or Havana or any of the capitals of Europe or Africa where he might have found safe haven. The true man of Colombia could not be cut off from his roots. The rest of Pablo Escobar's life struggle was to set himself back up, on his own terms, as Don Pablo, *El Doctor,* in Medellín, in his hometown of Envigado.

Pablo fled Panama when Noriega's army double-crossed him. Panamanian forces raided one of the cartel's lab complexes on the Colombian border in May. Shipments of chemicals needed for processing cocaine were seized by customs officials, and some of the Ochoas' men, including the pilot Rubin, were arrested and falsely implicated in a plot to murder Noriega. Pablo flew to Managua, on a path that very nearly delivered him into the hands of the U.S. Drug Enforcement Administration (DEA).

He surfaced in Nicaragua in dramatic fashion. A rotund American pilot and cocaine trafficker named Barry Seal had been busted by the DEA in Florida and, facing up to fifty-seven years in prison, had begged the DEA to take him on as an informant. He flew a C-123 transport plane to Managua on June 25, 1984, to pick up a 750-kilo shipment of cocaine. A camera hidden in the nose of the airplane captured images of the exiled Pablo and Rodríguez Gacha as they supervised the loading. The DEA intended to use Seal to set up a big sting, one that would lure Pablo, Rodríquez Gacha, and maybe even Lehder and the Ochoa brothers to Mexico, where they could all be arrested and brought to the United States to stand trial. It was clear that Pablo, at least, intended to continue working with Seal. He had given the informant a list of goodies to bring him back from the States. Life on the run had evidently cut into *El Doctor's* lifestyle. He wanted Seal to bring him video recorders, ten-speed bicycles, Johnnie Walker Black Label Scotch, Marlboro cigarettes, and one more thing . . . $1.5 million in cash.

Pictures of Pablo and Gacha loading drugs at a Nicaraguan airport caused quite a sensation in Washington. It proved a connection between the Marxist Sandinista regime and top Colombian cocaine traffickers. Oliver North, the National Security Council adviser coordinating the

Reagan administration's efforts (legal and illegal) against the Sandinistas, saw the photos as a tremendous public relations coup. He wanted to release them immediately but was asked not to by Ron Caffrey, chief of the DEA's cocaine desk in Washington. But it proved impossible to keep the pictures quiet. The administration was trying to convince Congress to continue funding for the Contras, the pro-democracy rebel forces battling the new Sandinista regime. The presence of Colombian *narco* kingpins shipping cocaine from Nicaraguan soil was very helpful to their case. The information leaked, first to the head of the U.S. Army Southern Command, General Paul Gorman, who told a chamber of commerce crowd in San Salvador that "the world will soon be given proof" that the Sandinista regime was abetting drug trafficking, and then to *The Washington Times*. The stories appeared only after Seal had delivered Pablo his goodies.

Seal would be murdered two years later, tracked down and killed by one of Pablo's *sicarios*, or paid gunmen, in Baton Rouge, Louisiana, after unwisely refusing to enter the U.S. Witness Protection Program. When Pablo and Jorge Ochoa were indicted in Miami for their part in the 750-kilo shipment, a car bomb was exploded outside the Bogotá residence of tough-talking Ambassador Tambs. Five months later the ambassador fled Colombia for good. Bogotá had become a hardship post.

The near miss with the DEA and the troubles in Panama may have convinced Pablo that no matter how hot things were for him in Colombia, he was safer there than anywhere else. There were signs that his prolonged absence was undermining his control in Medellín. When kidnappers seized his seventy-three-year-old father, Abel, in October, Pablo responded immediately with a vicious and concerted campaign. Gunmen turned Medellín inside out, killing scores of people, anyone even suspected of associating with the kidnappers. Sixteen days later, Abel was released unharmed and told his friends that no ransom had been paid. His kidnappers had been scared into letting him go.

After that, Pablo simply returned home. He and Maria Victoria threw a huge christening party for their daughter, Manuela, who had been born that summer at their Nápoles estate. No matter how hot things got—he would soon be the most wanted fugitive in Colombia and eventually the most wanted man in the world—Pablo Escobar had decided to fight his battles on his home turf. He would never leave Colombia again.

5

For the rest of his life, with one brief respite, Pablo was at war with the state. At the center of the struggle remained extradition, the one fate he feared more than any other—even death. He had proclaimed, "Better a tomb in Colombia than a prison cell in the United States."

Death was his strategy against extradition, that and money. His policy of *plata o plomo* became so notoriously effective that it would ultimately threaten to undermine Colombia's democracy. Already, by the end of 1984, he was untouchable in Medellín. He moved openly around the city, attending bullfights and nightclubs, throwing parties at his estates, all while officially a fugitive. Popular and powerful, he had clearly bought off the police and courts there. Anyone who considered standing up against him was marked for assassination. In July, the judge appointed to investigate the murder of Justice Minister Lara was murdered in Bogotá.

In the fall of 1985 Pablo offered once more to turn himself in if the government would promise not to extradite him to the United States. When it again refused, he settled in for a long fight.

Pablo formed an "organization"—in fact a flimsy pretense, in whose name he acted on behalf of himself and the other primary targets of extradition—called "the Extraditables," which vowed a fight to the death against the procedure. It gave him an outlet for his urge to take part in national affairs, and it gave him a chance to write. Pablo penned long communiqués by hand in a script that was half printing, half cursive, often enlarging and capitalizing certain words for emphasis. Pen in hand, he worked himself into heights of rhetorical indignation. With his American indictments and the pending Colombian arrest warrants, Pablo knew that he was just one misstep away from a life behind bars in the United States. His hatred of extradition was a matter of both personal survival and national pride.

Extradition was a kind of insult to Colombians and Pablo knew that his communiqués struck a popular chord. It implied not only that the nation was too weak to administer justice itself (which was true) but that the United States represented some higher moral authority. Pablo made an odd spokesman for this position; he was arguing, in essence, that Colombia alone had the right to arrest and punish him. He warned the nation's leaders that if they persisted in this agreement with the United States it would lead to a bloodbath. After one of their number, Jorge Luis Ochoa, was arrested in Spain, the Extraditables faxed a statement to newspapers, radio, and TV in Bogotá: "We have found out that the government is trying by whatever means possible to extradite citizen Jorge Luis Ochoa to the United States. For us, this is the vilest of outrages. . . . In case Jorge Luis Ochoa is extradited to the United States, we will declare absolute and total war against this country's political leaders. We will execute out of hand the principal chieftains."

Whether prompted by Pablo's threats or concern for Colombian sovereignty—or perhaps both—government authorities successfully contested U.S. efforts to extradite the drug trafficker. He was flown back to Cartagena, where he posted bail and promptly disappeared.

Pablo's primary target during these middle years of the 1980s was the country's judicial system, to which he offered *plata o plomo*. When a lawsuit was filed against the extradition treaty in 1985, Pablo bribed the office of Colombia's attorney general for a favorable recommendation and then went to work on the judges, one of whom received a letter, probably written by Pablo, that read:

> We, The Extraditables, are writing to you because . . . we know that you have said publicly and cynically that the extradition treaty is constitutional. . . . We are not going to ask or beg or seek compassion, because we do not need it. VILE WRETCH. We are going to DEMAND a favorable decision. . . . We will not accept stupid excuses of any kind: we will not accept that you go sick; we will not accept that you go on holiday; and we will not accept that you resign. The decision will be made by you within fifteen days of the arrival of the recommendation of the Attorney General's office.

The letter went on to make it clear that a decision against extradition would be handsomely rewarded, while defiance would result in the judge's family being killed and cut into pieces. "We swear before God and the life of our children that if you fail us or betray us, you will be a dead man!!!"

It was hardly an idle threat. Four other judges connected to the case, each of whom had received similar threats but who refused to comply, were murdered. More than thirty judges had already been killed since Lara's assassination. *Plata o plomo* had every official in Bogotá living in fear or under suspicion; they were either targets of the Medellín cartel or presumed to be its lackeys. In November 1985, days after the assassinations of the four judges weighing the extradition issue, the guerrilla group M-19 stormed the Palace of Justice in Bogotá, demanding, among other things, that the government renounce the 1979 extradition treaty. The terrorists held hostage the entire Colombian Supreme Court and its staff, prompting a government siege that left forty rebels and fifty Palace of Justice employees dead, including eleven of the twenty-four justices. The raid crippled the Colombian legal system and effectively killed President Betancur's efforts to negotiate a peace settlement with the *FARC* and M-19. Destroyed in process were some six thousand criminal case files, including records of the criminal proceedings against one Pablo Escobar. It was later reported that the guerrilla group had been paid about $1 million by Pablo and other traffickers to carry out the raid.

There were still a few brave souls in public life who defied *plata o plomo*, but by the end of 1986 not many of them were still alive. That same month the utterly cowed Colombian Supreme Court declared the extradition treaty invalid because of a technicality—it had been signed by a delegate of the president, not the president himself. *Semana* magazine applauded the decision, declaring that the treaty had "offended the dignity" of Colombia. Pablo set off fireworks in Medellín to celebrate the victory. His newspaper, *Medellín Cívica*, called it "The Triumph of the People."

It was a short-lived triumph. The United States had too much influence in Colombia to lose extradition that easily. Just days later the newly elected president, Virgilio Barco, promptly re-signed the treaty.

But victories like this were increasingly rare. Colombia had been corrupted and terrorized to its core. *El Espectador* editor Guillermo Cano wrote sadly, "It seems we have decided to live with crime and declare ourselves defeated. . . . The drug cartel has taken over Colombia." Weeks later the white-haired, sixty-one-year-old Cano would himself be killed while driving in Bogotá, his backseat piled with wrapped Christmas presents, shot down by one of Pablo's *sicarios* on a motorbike.

Pablo's ugly struggle continued. His lawyers (and *sicarios*) chipped away at the cases against him. Murders and bribes resulted in his name being left off the indictment of those responsible for Lara's murder, and the old charges against him for killing the *DAS* agents who'd arrested him in 1976 were dropped when the records mysteriously vanished. Recognizing that its judicial system was stymied, Colombia did away with jury trials (people were too frightened to serve in any trial remotely related to drug trafficking) and began attempting to protect judges by hiding their identities. But often even these "faceless" judges were gunned down. Pablo also tried in various ways to escape American justice. Betting that the United States had more interest in fighting Communists than *narcos*, his lawyers approached the U.S. attorney general in 1986 with an offer to trade information against Communist guerrillas, the *FARC*, *ELN*, and M-19, in return for amnesty from his drug crimes.

With the offer, Pablo made a gesture. He betrayed his longtime cartel associate Carlos Lehder. Colombian police were tipped off to a party Lehder had planned for February 4, 1987. The colorful, eccentric cartel leader was arrested and immediately extradited, flown from Bogotá to Tampa on a DEA plane. Photographers were allowed to snap pictures of him in the back of the plane, wearing combat boots, sweatpants, and a striped shirt, looking resigned and oddly bemused as he waited to depart. He would be sentenced to 135 years in prison in the United States and would not forget Pablo's betrayal.

Still, the United States was not interested in making a deal with Pablo Escobar. It was a sign of how seriously the Reagan administration was taking the drug problem. In April of 1986, the president had signed National Security Decision Directive 221, which for the first time declared drug trafficking a threat to national security. The directive opened the door to direct military involvement in the war on drugs, which was placing a growing emphasis on attacking the crops, labs, and traffickers in Central and South America. This was an unprecedented mixing of law enforcement and military missions, and Reagan directed that any American laws or regulations prohibiting such an alliance were to be reinterpreted or amended. The departments of Defense and Justice were directed to "develop and implement any necessary modifications to applicable statutes, regulations, procedures and guidelines to enable U.S. military forces to support counter-narcotics efforts." Beginning that summer, U.S. Army troops joined DEA agents and Bolivian police in raiding fifteen cocaine-processing labs in that country.

Inside Colombia, Pablo kept upping the ante. In December his *sicarios* killed the former chief of the nation's counternarcotics police and two legislators who had spoken out in favor of extradition. In January 1987 the former minister of justice, now the Colombian ambassador to Hungary, was stopped in a snowstorm in Budapest and shot five times in the face. He survived. Andrés Pastrana, the journalist son of a former president and Conservative candidate for mayor of Bogotá, was kidnapped, and a week later Attorney General Carlos Hoyos was killed in a hail of machine-gun fire in Medellín. A caller to a local radio station announced Hoyos's "execution" and called him "a traitor and a sellout." When a judge prepared to indict Pablo for Guillermo Cano's murder, he received a note from the Extraditables:

> We are friends of Pablo Escobar and we are ready to do anything for him. . . . We know perfectly well that not even the slightest evidence exists against Mr. Escobar. We have also heard rumors that after the trial you will be given a foreign diplomatic position. But we want to remind you that, in addition to perpetrating a judicial infamy, you are making a big mistake. . . . We are capable of executing you at any place on this planet . . . in the meantime, you will see the fall, one by one, of all the members of your family. We advise you to rethink, for later you will have no time for regrets. . . . For calling Mr. Escobar to trial you will remain without forebears or descendants in your genealogical tree.

By the end of 1987 there were killings in the news almost every day in Bogotá. The new U.S. ambassador, Charles Gillespie, began warning Washington that the escalating violence in Colombia was threatening to topple the state, and the National Security Council began preparing a "comprehensive national strategy" to shore up the government. Noting the state of siege, President Barco declared martial law.

Through it all, Pablo orchestrated the war in relative peace, living with defiant openness in homes in and around Envigado and at his giant *finca*, Nápoles, which his lawyers had managed to wrest back from the state. It was during this period, in September 1988, that Roberto Uribe met Pablo for the first time. A Medellín criminal lawyer, Uribe had been retained by one of Pablo's bodyguards who had been charged with the kidnapping of Pastrana (who was released unharmed and later would be elected president of Colombia). Uribe was a bookish, frail man with a broad, round forehead, a man with more reverence for the letter of the law than for its larger intent. He had found a mistake in the draft of the indictment against his client and had used it to have the charges dismissed. Pablo invited Uribe out to Nápoles for a meeting.

When he arrived at Nápoles at noon, Pablo was asleep. The lawyer had been there before as a tourist; on a bus tour from Medellín. Now he was a guest of the great man himself, and he was nervous. He was offered a chair by one of the swimming pools, where he sat, and sat, and sat. Pablo awakened two hours later, then spent three hours meeting with his lieutenants. Uribe sipped coffee and accepted some of the food that servants offered him. Finally, early in the evening, the drug boss wandered out to the pool, dressed in a T-shirt, shorts, and white Nike athletic shoes—exactly as in the pictures Uribe had seen. Pablo apologized for the delay and said that he hadn't known Uribe was waiting for him.

"I thought you were here to see my brother," he said sheepishly.

Uribe found him charming. Pablo's manner was relaxed—Uribe later realized he had probably been stoned—and he spoke to the lawyer like an old friend, someone he was taking into his confidence. He laughed with delight as Uribe explained the legal technicality that had freed his client, and said he wanted the lawyer to file similar motions for all of the men charged.

From that day forward, Uribe was one of Pablo's lawyers and confidants. He began seeing him regularly, and liked him. Working for Pablo Escobar vastly increased his status and income, so he was prepared simply to dismiss all the stories about the man's ruthlessness. How could someone so calm, someone who never raised his voice, who never swore, who was so unfailingly polite, be as violent a man as people said? When Uribe sat with him and talked, the terrible stories about Pablo became impossible for him to believe. What the lawyer saw was a generous man, someone who was a sucker for any hard-luck story. He was rarely in a bad mood. In time, Uribe noticed that just about everyone introduced to Pablo for the first time was afraid, as he had been, but that within minutes the fear had evaporated. Pablo had the gift of putting people at ease.

It was all the more remarkable considering that the unruffled drug boss was at the center of such a violently raging storm. He was now fighting escalating wars on two fronts, against the government and the Cali cartel. The southern-based cocaine-trafficking organization, headed by Gilberto and Miguel Rodríguez Orejuela, had grown richer and more powerful and was challenging the Medellín operation's control of routes and markets. Pablo believed the Cali cartel was responsible for a massive explosion outside his eight-story Medellín apartment building in January of that year. Eleven-year-old Juan Pablo and four-year-old Manuela were asleep in the penthouse when the bomb carved a thirteen-foot hole in the street, killing two watchmen, shattering windows throughout the neighborhood, exploding water mains, and cracking the building's facade from end to end. In the blast, Manuela suffered ear damage that left her partially deaf. The Escobars fled, and police exploring his luxury penthouse found expensive original paintings, among them priceless ones by van Gogh and expensive original works by Salvador Dalí. They also found Maria Victoria's collection of hundreds of shoes. In the basement of the building were eight antique Rolls-Royces and a bullet-proof stretch Mercedes limousine. Pablo struck back against the Rodríguez Orejuela brothers in a bombing campaign against their national chain of legitimate drugstores.

Police raids were also disruptive, and occasionally scary. Pablo was usually tipped off well in advance of any effort to arrest him, and he had homes scattered throughout the mountainous Medellín area, but now and then the police achieved enough surprise to catch him, literally, with his pants down. In March of that year, about one thousand national police officers raided one of his mansions in the mountains outside Medellín. They arrived in helicopters and in tanks and encircled the area. Pablo fled in his underwear, avoiding the police cordon on foot. Close calls like this led to retaliatory bombings and kidnappings. In May 1989, Pablo's men set off a car bomb in Bogotá alongside a vehicle carrying General Miguel Maza, the head of the *DAS*. Six people were killed and fifty more injured. The wheels of Maza's car melted on the asphalt in the heat of the blast, but the sturdy general, who was leading the hunt for Pablo, stepped out unhurt.

As these battles raged, Pablo's army of lawyers (which after September included Uribe) held a series of meetings with President Barco's government, attempting to revive the deal Pablo had offered in Panama City four years earlier. By now he had upped his demands and backed away from his offer to return money in foreign banks to Colombia. He wanted full pardons for himself and everyone else associated with the Medellín cartel and an end to extradition. In return, he promised they would get out of the trafficking business.

There were good reasons to want out. The Bush administration was shifting the focus of the drug war from intercepting boats and planes at the border to attacking cocaine's South American roots. The U.S. crackdown had already hurt them. Pablo's mansions and property in Florida had been seized. Ever since Lara's big raids back in 1984, U.S. airborne and satellite surveillance had been steering Colombian assault forces to scores of labs and coca fields, inflicting heavy losses on the industry. Angry when the talks with Barco went nowhere, Pablo kidnapped both the son and the sister of government negotiator German Montoya, Barco's chief of staff. His son was released, but his sister, Marina Montoya, was murdered. These acts of public vengeance and coercion turned all but Pablo's hard-core local supporters against him and the other *narcos*. He had gone from hero to pariah in the space of eight years, and the suits in Bogotá and Washington were more than fed up.

In Colombia it has always been hard to tell for sure who exactly is trying to kill you, but by 1988 Pablo was sure that somebody was. His enemies had both the motive and the means. There had been the bomb outside his apartment building in January, and then in June of the following year a team of British mercenaries, former Special Air Service commandos, came after him at his Nápoles estate. They aborted the attempt when one of their helicopters crashed into a mountain. Both attempts were widely attributed to the Cali cartel, but there was no telling. By 1989 the scaffolding of Pablo's once fearful organization was shaky. Nothing he was doing worked. He had bombed or bribed just about every official in Colombia, but it was clear no one in Bogotá was going to cut a deal that would jeopardize all-important ties with the United States government. So Pablo began trying to work some influence in Washington. He had tried to retain a lobbying firm managed by Henry Kissinger in an effort to influence the Reagan administration, and he retained a lawyer who worked in the same firm as Jeb Bush, son of the president-elect, hoping to eventually persuade the younger Bush to approach his father. Both efforts failed.

The future did not look bright. The Liberal Party candidate for president, Luis Galán, was wildly popular and certain to be elected in 1990. Galán was a charismatic forty-six-year-old reformer who had become a fearlessly outspoken enemy of the cartel. He had vowed to rid Colombia of drug traffickers, and he made no secret of his desire to ship them off to the United States for trial and imprisonment. His election threatened to undo all the progress Pablo had made by cowing and corrupting the Colombian judiciary. Galán was the nation's darling at that moment. Many

Colombians compared him to the national hero Gaitán. Killing Galán would stir up an unholy wrath.

Pablo's grudge with Galán ran deep. The popular politician had backed Lara's public attacks on Pablo in 1984 and had thrown him out of the New Liberal political movement. Galán was where all these troubles had begun. Pablo met with Gacha and some of their *sicarios* in the summer of 1989 at a farm owned by Gacha, and there the two men debated the pros and cons of killing the candidate. Both realized the storm that would follow might destroy them, but Pablo pointed out that Galán's election might do the same. They decided to order the hit.

On August 18, a *sicario* with a Uzi submachine gun shot down Galán as he made a campaign speech before supporters in Soacha, a town southwest of Bogotá. Three months later, in an effort to kill Galán's successor candidate, César Gaviria, his men planted a bomb on an Avianca airliner, blowing it out of the sky. One hundred and ten people were killed, including two Americans. It was an act of audacious cruelty with implications beyond any that Pablo had imagined.

These two atrocities would prove to be fatal mistakes. They made Pablo enemies who were far more powerful than any he had faced before. Downing a commercial airliner was an attack on global civilization. It meant Pablo now posed a direct threat to American citizens, which meant, as we shall see, that some in the Bush administration believed he could be legally targeted for assassination. Killing Galán had made Pablo public enemy number one in Colombia. The Avianca bombing made him public enemy number one in the world.

By the end of the summer of 1989, Pablo Escobar was forty years old. He was one of the richest men in the world, and perhaps its most infamous criminal. No longer just a law enforcement target, he was now a military target. To the men of America's secret counterterrorism community, the ruthless doper from Medellín had become a clear and present danger.

THE FIRST WAR

1989–1991

1

In time, no one in Colombia knew Pablo Escobar better than Colonel Hugo Martinez of *La Policía Nacional de Colombia* (*PNC*), even though the two men had never met. The tall, taciturn man who was nicknamed "Flaco" (Skinny) knew Pablo better than even the drug boss's closest family members and henchmen, because there were things he would say and do before his associates that he would not before his family, and there was a side of him that his family saw that he showed to no one else. The colonel saw it all. He knew Pablo intimately. He recognized his voice, knew his habits, when he slept, when and how he moved, what he liked to eat, what his favorite music was, how it was that criticism written or broadcast against him infuriated him but how he delighted in any political cartoon that portrayed him, no matter how crudely. The colonel knew what kind of shoes Pablo wore (white Nikes), what kind of sheets he liked on his bed, the preferred age of his sexual partners (girls of fourteen or fifteen, usually), his taste in art, his handwriting, the pet name he had for his wife ("Tata"), even what kind of toilet he preferred to use—since he had new facilities installed in all of his hideouts, and they were always the same. The colonel felt he understood Pablo, could see the world through his eyes, how he felt unjustly hounded and persecuted (mostly, nowadays, by the colonel). Martinez understood this last part so well he could sympathize with it, at times. There was truth even in the worldview of a monster, and the colonel believed he was chasing a monster. He never grew to hate Pablo, although he did fear him.

On August 18, 1989, the same day that Pablo's *sicarios* killed front-running presidential candidate Luis Galán, another group of his hit men killed *PNC* colonel Waldemar Franklin, chief of the Antioquian police. Franklin and Colonel Martinez had been friends. They had come up together through the ranks. When Franklin was assigned to Antioquia, Martinez and the other top officers in the *PNC* knew there would be trouble for the Medellín cartel. Franklin couldn't be bought or bullied. He had steered the raid that rousted Pablo in his underpants from the mansion outside Medellín that spring, one of his closest calls yet, and Franklin's men had recently raided a cartel laboratory and seized four metric tons of cocaine. This was bad enough, but Franklin sealed his fate when his men stopped Pablo's wife, Maria Victoria, and his children, Juan Pablo and Manuela, at a road block. The drug boss's family was taken to police headquarters in Medellín, where they were held for hours before Pablo's lawyers negotiated their release. Pablo would later complain to Roberto Uribe that Maria Victoria had been refused permission to give Manuela a bottle of milk. Pablo had always denied ordering the murder of Galán, but to Uribe he admitted that he had ordered Franklin killed over that bottle of milk.

Galán's killing had the anticipated effect. President Barco launched an all-out war against the cartel. He suspended habeas corpus, which meant people could be arrested and detained without being charged with a crime, and once again he authorized army and police to seize the cartel leaders' luxurious *fincas*. Shadow ownership of property was declared a crime, which made it harder for Pablo and the other *narcos* to disguise their holdings. But the biggest step Barco took was to invite further American help in this growing fight.

The *narcos* could see the United States government closing in on them. The kingpins had all been indicted by the U.S. Justice Department, most of them, like Pablo, more than once. They knew the DEA had been active in the country for years. Having long since compromised the Colombian police and military, they were holding their own at home, but President Bush had campaigned in 1988 saying he favored taking direct military action against traffickers in other countries. It was clear which "other country" he had in mind. Colombia was the source of nearly 80 percent of the cocaine making its way to the United States. In April 1986 President Reagan had signed a classified National Security Decision Directive that declared the flow of drugs across U.S. borders to be a "national security threat," which opened the door to U.S. military involvement. Bush had headed a cabinet-level task force against drugs as vice president. As president, he declared war on drugs. Just weeks after Galán's murder, Bush signed National Security Directive 18, calling for more than $250 million worth of military, law enforcement, and intelligence assistance to fight the Andean drug cartels over five years. A week later he authorized another $65 million in emergency military aid to Colombia alone, and he authorized sending a small number of U.S. Special Forces troops to Colombia to train its police and military in rapid-strike tactics. He followed that a month later with his Andean Initiative, which called for "a major reduction in the supply of cocaine." Bush told reporters, "The rules have changed. When requested, we will for the first time make available the appropriate resources of America's armed forces." Bush had always pledged that military action would depend on the approval of the host country, but even that caveat had begun to erode. In June 1989, the newly appointed U.S. drug czar, William J. Bennett, had all but advocated sending U.S. military hit squads to kill the infamous *narcos.* "We should do to the drug barons what our forces in the Persian Gulf did to Iran's navy," he had said. Stories from Washington, all of them read carefully at the breakfast tables of *narcos* in Colombia, revealed that senior U.S. officials were weighing such steps, and that the U.S. Justice Department was working on an opinion that would approve unilateral U.S. military action against *narcos* and terrorists in other countries, *with or without* the approval of host governments.

Indeed, in August of that year the army's counterterrorism unit, Delta Force, had prepared to raid a house in Panama where Pablo was reported to be staying. The plan called for Delta to seize him and then turn him over to DEA agents, who would arrive after the drug boss was in custody. The raid was called off when agents discovered that the reports were false; Pablo had not left Colombia. Nevertheless, the aborted mission showed how much the rules had changed under Bush. Over the next five years, the United States would basically underwrite a secret war in Colombia. U.S. spending for international antidrug efforts would grow from less than $300 million in 1989 to more than $700 million by 1991—and those dollars didn't even reflect the sums spent on the secret military and spy units deployed. The U.S. might have been considering acting unilaterally, if necessary, but Bush clearly preferred cooperation from Colombia. Barco had resisted opening that door until Galán's murder. That had changed everything.

In the four months after Galán's death, Barco's government shipped more than twenty suspected drug traffickers to the United States for trial. And with the new bonanza of American assistance, Barco created special police units, one of which was based in Medellín and was dedicated to hunting down José Rodríguez Gacha, the Ochoa brothers, and Pablo Escobar.

It was called the *Bloque de Búsqueda,* or Search Bloc. This was the command given to Colonel Martinez. It was a position he'd neither sought nor desired. Nobody wanted it. It was considered so dangerous that the PNC decided the command would be rotated monthly, like a hot potato.

There was, of course, a great flourish of official encouragement and praise when it was announced that Martinez was to be awarded the post first. With his wry sense of humor and practical bent, the colonel saw this for what it was and accepted the task grimly. He wasn't an obvious choice. There were better commanders, men with more field experience who had already distinguished themselves in combat against *narcos* or guerrillas. There were better investigators, men with impressive records tracking down fugitives. But these were all men who, because of their successful careers, had sufficient clout to duck an unwanted assignment. The colonel was quiet and bookish, with an aloof manner that seemed ill suited to leading men in the field. Tall and fair-skinned, he looked more European than Colombian. He was forty-eight, at a point in life where a man feels it is now or never for his life's goals. He was from Mosquera, a pretty little mountain village a few hours east of Bogotá, a place out of some timeless story of Colombian legend. Flowers cascaded down steep cultivated slopes to a central market and park, where on evenings, weekends, and holidays townspeople congregated and strolled. The colonel was the son of a local businessman who ran a cafeteria and worked in a store. He had joined the police force right out of high school. One of his older school buddies, José Serrano, had gone to the academy a year before, and seeing him return home in his cadet's uniform excited Martinez, prompting him to enlist. When he completed his courses at the academy in Bogotá, he was given a variety of postings, including station commander in the small town of Perreda, where he was promoted to chief of investigations. He went to law school at night during those years, and when he finished, the department sent him to Spain for a course in criminology. He married, and his wife bore him three sons and a daughter. In the years that followed, through most of the eighties, Martinez, then a major, held a variety of command positions at police headquarters in Bogotá. With the ongoing struggles against the FARC and other leftist guerrillas, there were plenty of combat postings, but Martinez was always more of an administrator and academic than a field officer. He had a long, lined face with a jutting straight nose and a thin-lipped mouth that could either make him look cruel or, when he smiled crookedly, reveal a crisp, quiet sense of humor. This new job would demand both cruelty and wit. It would also demand more courage than the colonel believed he possessed. In addition to Franklin's murder, the magistrate who issued the warrants for the most recent raids had been killed, as had a reporter from *El Espectador* who had written approvingly of the effort. There was a sense that Pablo could reach anyone, anywhere, any time. To make the threat explicit, Pablo responded to the creation of the colonel's Search Bloc by issuing a public pronouncement that it would not last fifteen days. In the world's most dangerous country, the job of going after Pablo was the most dangerous position of all.

Not to mention the near impossibility of the task. Pablo practically owned Medellín, his home city, including enough of its police force that one of the rules for this newly constituted Search Bloc was that it could not contain even one native Antioquian, or *paisa*, for fear he would secretly be on Pablo's payroll. Instead, the national police had assembled a collection of men from different units, including Colombia's FBI, the *DAS,* and its special branch of judicial police, the *DIJIN* (*Dirección Central de Policía Judicial e Investigación*). All were considered elite and incorruptible. Some were used to working in uniforms under straightforward military command, and others were essentially undercover cops who worked in plainclothes as civilians. None of them were familiar with one another or with the city, and they had no local sources or informants. They didn't dare ask the Medellín police force for help, because it was known to be largely on the cartel's payroll. The whole Search Bloc, even its plainclothesmen, stood out sharply because none spoke with the thick *paisa* accent. On their first foray out into the city, eighty men in ten vehicles, they got lost.

Within the first fifteen days, thirty of the colonel's two hundred men were killed. Despite elaborate precautions to protect the men and hide their identities, Pablo's army of *sicarios* picked them off one by one, often with the help of the Medellín police. They shot them down on the street, on their way home from work, even at home with their families when they were off duty. The funerals for these slain officers left the *PNC* reeling. At police headquarters in Bogotá the top command considered pulling the plug on the Search Bloc. The colonel and his top commanders asked that they be allowed to stay. While the killings grieved and frightened them, it also angered them and hardened their resolve. Instead of withdrawing, the *PNC* sent the colonel another two hundred men.

Martinez was proud that, as bad as things were in that first month, his men had managed to mount one impressive raid. Informed that Pablo was staying at a *finca* in the jungle that was about a two-hour helicopter flight from Medellín, the Search Bloc planned an assault. But the maps showed that on the way to the targeted *finca*, the choppers would have to fly over a Colombian army base. If they attempted to do so without getting permission from the base commander, it was likely the base defense forces would try to shoot them down. Martinez suspected that if he informed the commander of an army base in Antioquia of their mission, Pablo would be tipped off immediately. So he risked it. To avoid radar they flew over the base fast and low, so low that the colonel feared they would hit electric and telephone wires. But they made it. They hit the jungle *finca* from the air, coordinating the assault with ground troops who had moved in quietly the night before. Pablo escaped, but only narrowly. Under the circumstances, the colonel considered the raid a triumph.

Still, at the end of October 1989, according to the rotation plan, the colonel asked to be replaced. He was told he had done such a good job, the department wanted him to stay. His request the following month was similarly rejected.

Pablo's response to the Search Bloc's initial raid was swift and pointed. A car bomb was discovered in the basement of the apartment building in Bogotá where the colonel's family lived. His oldest son, Hugo Jr., was now a cadet at the national police academy, but his wife, daughter, and two younger sons had been home. The bomb had been found after someone telephoned a tip to the police, so it probably had been just a warning. But it was a chilling one. Pablo should not have been able to find them. Nearly all the residents of their building were high-ranking national police officers, the only ones who knew of the colonel's dangerous new job. Obviously someone among them had passed the word. The betrayal was aggravated when, instead of rallying around their besieged colleague, the other families in the apartment building held a meeting and voted to ask the colonel and his family to leave.

The day after the bomb was found, the colonel boarded a helicopter in Medellín and flew home to help his family pack. He told only his commander, General Octavio Vargas, where he was going that morning.

He was stuffing boxes bitterly in the apartment when a retired police officer, someone he had known since his days in the academy, arrived at his door. The colonel was surprised and alarmed. How had this man known to find him in Bogotá?

"I come to talk to you obligated," the retired officer said with a pained expression. Martinez asked what he meant.

"If I did not agree to come talk to you, they could easily kill me or my family," he said.

Then he offered the colonel $6 million, a bribe from Pablo Escobar to call off the hunt. Better yet, the officer explained, "Continue the work, but do not do yourself or Pablo Escobar any real damage." Pablo also wanted a list of any snitches inside his own organization.

Sometimes the fate of an entire nation can hinge on the integrity of one man. The bribe came at the lowest point in the colonel's career. He had been given a suicide mission, one with little chance of success. He attended funerals almost every day. The national police had constructed special funeral chapels in Medellín and in Bogotá just to handle the demand. The bomb in the basement of the apartment building had made it clear that Pablo could find the colonel's wife and children. This move was not going to protect them; it was designed to protect the apartment building's other residents. His own department was, in effect, abandoning him and his family to their fate.

And for what? Martinez could not even see the wisdom in going after Escobar. Cocaine was not Colombia's problem; it was the *norteamericanos'* problem. And even if they did away with *El Doctor*, as the United States insisted, it was not going to curb the cocaine industry.

Here was a generous ticket out. *Six million dollars.* Enough money to support himself and his family in luxury for the rest of their lives. But the colonel did not consider the bribe for any longer than it took him to have those thoughts. His gut rebelled against it. He cursed at his former friend, and then his anger turned to pity and disgust.

"Tell Pablo that you came but did not find me here, and then leave this matter as if it had never occurred," he said.

Martinez had known other police officers who took bribes, and he knew that money was just the hook on *El Doctor*'s line. Once he had accepted the bribe, Pablo would own him, just as he owned his friend who had approached him with the offer—*I come to talk to you obligated.* Martinez could see himself forced into a similar humiliating betrayal somewhere down the road. It would be like handing over his whole career, all the years of work and study, all the things he took professional pride in, to this thug. It would be like turning over his soul.

   After he dismissed his old friend, Martinez drove to police headquarters and informed Vargas of the bribe. They agreed it was a good sign.

   "It means we're getting to him," said Martinez.

   They were—in part because they had a new kind of help.

2

On the first night he spent in Bogotá, in September 1989, the American popped open a beer in his upstairs room at the Hilton and started counting explosions. He was too keyed up to sleep, so he pulled a chair up to his window and peered down, looking for flashes. The city was surprisingly modern. In recent years he had spent a lot of time in Central American cities, in San Salvador and Tegucigalpa, and these had been hardship posts, dingy, dangerous, and decidedly Third World. Bogotá reminded him more of some modern European capital, with its high-rises and distinctive architecture and wide, busy avenues humming with traffic that lit up the night in all directions. It reflected a muscular modernity with deep roots in an exotic and, to the American, a mostly unknown past. He was excited. Colombia was a new mystery to unravel, a new package to unwrap, the kind of challenge he relished. The Hilton was in the northern sector, where the dense cityscape was creeping ever higher up the hills. There were fine old cathedrals dating back to the sixteenth century and modern glass-skinned office buildings. To the south the city opened into a smoggy sprawl of shantytowns, housing the influx of refugees who'd started pouring into the city decades ago to escape violence and had since swollen the city's population to seven million. But the American couldn't see that the first night. What he saw was the elegant glow of Bogotá's skyline and the lights along the busy highways. He didn't see any flashes from the explosions, even though they sounded close. Some even rattled the windows.

   He knew that weeks before, a popular presidential candidate named Luis Galán had been murdered and that the Barco government had cracked down on the Medellín cartel. These bombs were part of the cartel's response. They kept going off for hours. The American, an army officer, had been fully briefed on the situation, so one or two explosions wouldn't have surprised him, but when his count passed twenty, and then thirty, and finally reached forty-four, he told himself, *Damn, this is going to be fun.*

The blasts that night were mostly pipe bombs, none of them very large, strategically placed at the entrances to banks, shopping centers, office buildings—places where Bogotános would be sure to see damage the next morning, but no place where there might be people working at night, even security guards. Bogotá, along with ten other Colombian cities, was under curfew from dawn to dusk. This night of the explosions—it was not the first or last that summer—was meant as a message to the government. *We can attack anywhere we want as often as we want.*

From the briefing he had been given before making this trip, it certainly sounded like the country was coming apart. It had included a chronology of outrages committed just in the previous five months:

- March 3: José Antequera, leader of the Unión Patriótica Party and candidate for president, assassinated.
- March 11: Hector Giraldo, lawyer and adviser to the newspaper *El Espectador*, whose editor Guillermo Cano had been murdered, was himself kidnapped and murdered.
- April 3: An active-duty Colombian police colonel is stopped at a roadblock and four hundred kilos of cocaine are found in the trunk of his car.
- April 21: Bucaramanga's popular radio newsman Luis Vera is murdered.
- May 4: The father of self-exiled investigative judge Martha Gonzales is murdered, and her mother is injured in the attack. Gonzales had fled Colombia after indicting Pablo Escobar and José Rodríguez Gacha for murder.
- May 30: A powerful car bomb explodes in Bogotá in an apparent effort to kill DAS Director General Miguel Maza, killing six onlookers but leaving the general unscathed.
- June 3: The son of President Barco's secretary-general is kidnapped.

- June 15: A well-known Medellín radio reporter, Jorge Vallejo, is killed.
- July 4: The governor of Antioquia, Antonio Roldan, is assassinated in Medellín when his car is destroyed by a remote-controlled bomb.
- July 28: A judge who had issued warrants for the arrests of Escobar and José Rodríguez Gacha is murdered.
- August 16: Carlos Valencia, magistrate of the superior tribunal, is assassinated. He had ratified lower-court indictments of Escobar and Gacha.
- August 17: More than four thousand appeals court judges begin a national strike protesting their vulnerability.

A day after the judges' strike began, Galán and Colonel Franklin had both been killed. There were reportedly British and Israeli mercenaries training *narco* killers in more sophisticated tactics. Given this bloody record, the American felt that the night of the pipe bombs actually showed some restraint. Evidently the traffickers were trying to avoid further alienating the public, which had taken Galán's assassination hard. The idea evidently was not to strike a blow but to send a message. The audacity made it clear why Colombia had asked the United States for help. The American was part of the military package.

He was part of a secret unit in Bogotá headed by an army major who, at least according to his current identity papers, was named Steve Jacoby. Members of the unit were new kinds of spies, surveillance experts selected and trained by the army to provide "operational" intelligence during planning for the ill-fated Iran hostage rescue mission ten years earlier. The idea was to plug what the army saw as a critical gap in the spying services provided by the CIA and the National Security Agency (NSA). These established spook bureaucracies, created and lavishly nourished by the Cold War, were primarily responsible for gathering intelligence for broad foreign-policy making. More and more, small-scale, specialized military operations were being launched in exotic places on short notice. What military leaders needed for these was timely, specific information, things like How many doors and windows does the target building have? What kind of weapons are carried by the bodyguards? Where did their target like to eat dinner? Where did he sleep last night, and the night before that? They needed someone to provide detailed local logistics, information about indigenous vehicles, safe houses, hiding places, and so on. This kind of information was not a specialty of the big spy outfits. Over the decade since its creation, the army's own small spy unit had changed its name often, in part to protect its secrecy. It had been called ISA, for Intelligence Support Activity, the Secret Army of Northern Virginia, Torn Victory, Cemetery Wind, Capacity Gear, and Robin Court. These days it was called Centra Spike.

Centra Spike was designed to offer an array of support intelligence, but its primary specialty was finding people. Eavesdropping on radio and telephone conversations from the air, its members were capable of pinpointing the origin of a radio or cell-phone call with amazing accuracy within seconds. Radio direction finding had long been one of the military arts, but only in recent years had it become accurate enough for tactical purposes. During World War II, surveillance teams could do little more than determine the general direction of a radio signal. Using three different ground-based receivers, monitors could at best triangulate a signal back to a region of a country. The German army tried this technique in France in mostly vain efforts to track resistance fighters sending messages to England. From each position on the triangle, they projected lines toward where the signal was strongest. Where the three lines intersected was the radio, or at least its broad vicinity. Twenty years later, during the Vietnam War, army direction finders had so improved both equipment and technique that they could place the origin of an intercepted signal to within a half mile. Twenty years after that, Centra Spike could pinpoint a radio or cell-phone signal to within a few hundred meters. What was more remarkable was the electronic package now used to accomplish that feat. Instead of triangulating from three receivers on the ground, they did it from one small aircraft. The airborne equipment substituted the three separate ground locations by taking readings from different points along the plane's flight path. As soon as a target signal was received, the pilot would begin flying an arc around it. Using computers to do precise, instantaneous calculations, they were able to begin triangulating off points in that arc within seconds. If the aircraft had time to complete a half circle around the signal, the location of its origin would be known to within two hundred meters. This could be done regardless of weather conditions or preventative measures taken by targets on the ground. Even a coded radio signal could not disguise its point of origin.

At first, this method required a very large aircraft, because the vari-ous antennae used to triangulate the signal had to be kept far apart. The ability to accomplish the task with a smaller plane meant you could be less conspicuous. So Centra Spike's precision and its low profile made it feasible for the first time to find people without attracting attention, even over a crowded city. This was the idea anyway. The unit's previous missions had primarily been against rebel units in mountains or jungles. Here in Colom-bia, against the Medellín cartel, they were going to stretch themselves.

Various American agencies had been working out of the embassy in Bogotá for years, relying on more conventional ways of gathering intelli-gence. The CIA had its own long-standing connections, but they had al-ways been oriented more toward the Marxist insurrections in the hills. The counternarcotics stuff had only recently been redefined as a CIA mission, and there were plenty of chiefs back at headquarters who were not sold on the idea. But the agents in Colombia were fully engaged. With deep pockets and a strong reputation for secrecy, the spy agency was already playing on murderous rivalries between the Cali and Medellín cartels. The DEA worked mostly with the Colombian police and had become skillful at exploiting divisions between it and the army or the separate secret police agency *DAS*, as well as internal hostility between the *DAS* and its own plainclothes investigatory agency, the *DIJIN*. The Bureau of Alcohol, Tobacco, and Firearms had an agent in Bogotá, and the FBI had made some headway infiltrating the cartels with informants captured in the United States, traffickers offered a chance to avoid long prison terms by return-ing to Colombia to play the very risky game of double-cross. All these efforts were extremely difficult. The cartels had such a brutal reputation that it was exceedingly hard to find anyone willing to spy or inform on them. Reward money was only marginally effective, because those motivated by money could make a lot more by selling drugs or taking bribes. Cultural differences made penetrating the cartels with American agents virtually im-possible; even Hispanic Americans found the Colombian dialect and cul-ture vastly different than Mexico's or Puerto Rico's. The agencies were not always smart about who they sent down, either. Steve Murphy, a big, ag-gressive DEA agent from West Virginia, was assigned to Bogotá with only a hasty, weeks-long introduction to Spanish. He spent most of his first year in Bogotá at a desk in the embassy, thumbing through a thick Spanish-English dictionary, trying to make himself useful by translating articles from the various Bogotá dailies. Centra Spike offered a seemingly magical shortcut to the dangerous, time-consuming, and difficult task of intelligence gathering. Its agents could literally pluck information out of the air.

For the first month, Centra Spike's team lived in hotel rooms, moving frequently. Those who worked at the embassy commuted back and forth to work in armored, unmarked cars with an armed escort. They avoided restaurants and bars and did their professional best to blend in colorlessly. Secrecy was not just Centra Spike's protection; it was an essential part of its strategy. So long as their target remained unaware of Centra Spike, the unit would hear and see a lot more. In time, the unit's goal was to electronically infiltrate the cartel and crawl inside the heads of the men who ran it. Only a handful of people at the U.S. embassy, the ambassador and the CIA station chief, and maybe one or two trusted aides, knew Steve Jacoby's mission in Bogotá. The host government wouldn't know. They were informed only that the United States, at Colombia's invitation, was going to begin some fairly sophisticated surveillance. To the world at large, Jacoby and the men who worked with him in Bogotá were just midlevel bureaucrats in the six-hundred-man workforce, at work on something to do with the computers, something administrative and mundane.

For the men of Centra Spike, flying to a new place just meant pulling out a different passport and a different set of credit cards and other carefully falsified documents, all of them as official as a newly minted hundred-dollar bill, complete with backup files, photos, history . . . for anyone who cared to check. Shifting identities had been hard at first, but by now for these men it was like putting on a new pair of shoes. They might pinch a little for the first few days, but then they loosened up and you didn't even notice them. Jacoby himself was a study in nondescript, the kind of face and body your eye would pass over without a second thought: with average height, a broad face, big soft hands, built thick but not fat, the kind of guy with more pressing and important things to do than work out, and a manner that seemed self-absorbed and quiet unless he had reason to turn his heavy-lidded eyes on you. Then you might see an active, cynical sense of humor. He would appear to be a clever man but not a serious one, skeptical of authority but in a safe, grumpy, amusing sort of way. Harmless. Curmudgeonly. A workaholic. You could tell that about him. He had the pasty complexion and rumpled shirt and suit coat of a man who had sat too many hours in an office chair behind a desk or computer. He seemed distant at first and gruff, but then warm and likable. He did not appear to be a complicated or particularly accomplished man. Within his top-secret world, he was considered the best.

Telecommunications was often the critical weakness of criminal, guerrilla, or terrorist organizations. Jacoby's unit succeeded by staying one or two steps ahead in a rapidly evolving field. When it was impossible to penetrate an organization with a spy, Centra Spike could get inside from a distance, placing "ears on target." It still meant that guys like Jacoby would have to move in and stay, often in very dangerous places. In San Salvador, members of the team would leave their hotels in the morning and drive to their airport base as fast as they could go, speeding ninety miles an hour through railroad underpasses where guerrillas liked to lob grenades. For techies like them, few jobs offered the same mix of intellectual stimulation and heart-pounding danger and excitement. If a detachment of Marxist guerrillas was hiding in the hills of Nicaragua, there wasn't time to do laboratory experiments and write papers and wait for peer reviews. Centra Spike had to come up with a way to find them and track them, for as long as necessary. The unit had ample funding to move fast, adapt, and improvise, and its members enjoyed the urgency and importance men feel when others' lives depend on their work. Add to that the sense of doing good, of making the world a better place, of serving the United States of America. The work was so compelling that it had undone more than one marriage in the unit, and made some of the men strangers to their children.

This Colombian mission was not a cold start-up. CIA station chief John Connolly had begun thinking about the logistics before the team arrived. First off, they had to get their aircraft into the country. Anyone looking for America's most sophisticated eavesdropping equipment would be watching for something high-flying and fancy, something with great bulbous features on the top or bottom, probably bristling with antennae. They wouldn't be searching for two perfectly ordinary-looking Beechcrafts, an older model 300 and a newer 350. Inside and out, the Beechcrafts looked like standard two-prop commercial planes, outfitted for about six passengers, the kind of plane employed by charter services or big companies with enough money to fly their executives from place to place without getting slick. In a country with mountain roads as iffy as Colombia's, such transports were typical.

But these were no ordinary Beechcrafts. Modified by Summit Aviation in Delaware, at the northernmost tip of the Chesapeake Bay, they were $50 million spy planes crammed with state-of-the-art electronic eavesdropping and direction-finding equipment. If someone looked *very* closely—for instance, with a tape measure—they would discover the Beechcrafts' wingspans to be about six inches longer than that of the normal models, because the plane's two main eavesdropping antennae were installed inside. Five more antennae could be lowered from the belly of the plane once it was in flight. Inside, until they took off, the planes looked like standard models. Centra Spike's operators would board carrying laptop computers, and set up for listening only after the plane had reached an altitude of twenty to twenty-five thousand feet. Then antennae would be lowered, panels folded down from the inner walls, and the computers plugged into the plane's mainframe and power center. The two operators wore headsets with earphones, one in each ear, so they could monitor four frequencies simultaneously. The computer screens before them displayed graphically the plane's position and the estimated position of the signals they locked on to. Since the plane flew so high and could listen through cloud cover, there was no tip-off below.

There was another nifty secret feature to Centra Spike's capability. So long as their target left the battery in his cell phone, Centra Spike could remotely turn it on whenever they wished. Without triggering the phone's lights or beeper, the phone could be activated so that it emitted a low-intensity signal, enough for the unit to get a fix on its general location. They would activate the phone briefly when their target was most likely sleeping, then move the plane into position to monitor any calls he might make when he awoke.

It was important that it not be obvious who owned these planes, so a dummy corporation called Falcon Aviation was created, which would have a contract to do something entirely innocuous. What the CIA set up was ingenious. Falcon Aviation would be officially conducting an aviation safety project, a survey of Colombia's VOR (VHF omnidirectional radio range) beacons. These are transmitters located at all airports to help pilots find their way to runways. VOR beacons are a standard feature of international air safety, and it would not appear unusual for the U.S. embassy, with the agreement of the local authorities, to be running routine checks on the equipment. It would give Centra Spike's pilots an excuse to fly just about wherever they wanted. There were only a few dozen VOR beacons in Colombia, so anyone who understood the details of aviation-industry infrastructure would know such work would take only weeks, but so few people paid attention to such things that the contract would serve as sufficient cover for the unit for years if necessary.

Centra Spike found blocks of hotel rooms for Jacoby, his pilots, and the highly skilled eavesdroppers (mostly native Spanish-speaking soldiers) who would man the planes and work the equipment, as well as for the support personnel who would work at the embassy sorting, collating, translating, and interpreting the daily haul of conversations, beeper transmissions, faxes, e-mails, and so on. Arrangements were made to transfer money, sometimes in large amounts, without attracting attention or suspicion. By early October 1989, at about the same time Colonel Martinez's Search Bloc began working in Medellín, Falcon Aviation was flying and listening. The pilots would file a flight plan at Palencaro Air Base north of Bogotá, but as soon as they were out of that tower's tracking range, they would fly off to begin the hunt.

3

In the fall of 1989, the U.S. embassy in Bogotá was not sure exactly how the Medellín cartel worked, or even who was in charge. Pablo was considered just one of the big names. The Colombian authorities believed he was the boss, but information from the local police and army was regarded with suspicion by the Americans. All of the cartel leaders were now infamous. *Fortune* magazine listed them annually with the richest men in the world, but José Rodríguez Gacha, "El Mexicano," the fat man who often sported a Panama hat with a snakehead on its band, was thought to be the richest and most vicious of them all. *Fortune* had put Gacha on its cover, estimating his worth at $5 billion. Before Centra Spike landed, their briefing indicated that Gacha was the real power atop the cartel.

U.S. intelligence agencies believed it was he, not Pablo, who had ordered the hit on Galán.

So the fat man was Centra Spike's first target, and it didn't take them long to find him. He had been hiding from the national police ever since they had seized his estate north of Bogotá immediately after Galán's murder. A well-placed police informant revealed that Gacha had regular phone conversations with a woman in Bogotá. That information was passed to the U.S. embassy through the DEA, and Centra Spike started listening for the calls. They found him immediately, in a *finca* on a hilltop southwest of Bogotá. It was the only dwelling on the hill and was conspicuously elegant for a such a remote spot. Jacoby passed on the location to the CIA station chief, and it was given to President Barco.

The response was immediate and surprising, and answered any uncertainty the Americans had about Barco's intentions. The coordinates were given to the Colombian air force, which launched a squadron of T-33 fighter-bombers on November 22 to destroy the *finca* and everyone in it. Embassy officials were taken aback. No one had anticipated that the Colombians would simply kill the people Centra Spike had helped them find.

As it happened, the bombing sortie never forced the issue, because the lead pilot, a Colombian colonel, noticed that just beyond the *finca*, over the lip of the hill, was a small village. If any of the bombs overshot by even a small margin, they were certain to hit the thirty or forty smaller homes below. To avoid a tragedy, the colonel called off the bomb run at the last minute, but not soon enough to stop all four fighters from streaking about fifty feet over the rooftop of a severely startled Gacha. The cocaine boss was on the phone (with Centra Spike listening in) when the jets boomed overhead. He shouted with surprise and anger and immediately fled. A number of his key lieutenants stayed, however, and were arrested the next day when a police unit assaulted the house from helicopters. The army seized $5.4 million in cash at the *finca*. A judge promptly found fault with the legal basis for the raid, and most of these men were released; some of them would later be identified by Centra Spike as key figures in the cartel.

The last-minute decision to abort the bombing brought heavy criticism on the pilots and on the air force, which was accused of selling out, of letting Gacha get away. There was some reason to suspect this because he had long-standing friends within the Colombian military who had collaborated with his paramilitary squads against the Communist guerrillas. The national police, who were the most serious go-getters in the war against the cartel, accused the air force of intentionally bungling the mission, tipping off Gacha and enabling him to escape. The U.S. embassy found itself adjudicating the dispute, reviewing imagery of the hill, approach speeds, and likely bomb trajectories. The air force even offered to fly Jacoby in the backseat of a T-33 over the site. He declined. The review concluded that the colonel had been prudent.

The hunt for Gacha and the other cartel leaders assumed an even higher level of importance to the United States when, just five days later, an Avianca airliner was blown out of the sky shortly after taking off from Bogotá for Cali. The bombing had been planned two weeks earlier at a meeting attended by Pablo, Gacha, and some of their top lieutenants and *sicarios*. They'd discussed two bombings, the most important of which was an attack on the *DAS* building in Bogotá. Plans for this were set in motion, and then Pablo suggested the Avianca bombing. He said wanted to kill César Gaviria, the candidate who had taken up Galán's standard and was now the front-runner in the campaign for president. Gaviria had been serving as Galán's campaign manager, and at the funeral Galán's son had asked him to finish off the run.

This session also produced a new communiqué from the Extraditables, written by Pablo: "We want peace. We have screamed out loud for it, but we cannot beg for it. . . . We do not accept, nor will we ever accept, the numerous arbitrary raids on our families, the ransacking, the repressive detentions, the judicial frame-ups, the anti-patriotic and illegal extraditions, the violations of all our rights. We are ready to confront the traitors."

Carlos Alzate, one of Pablo's veteran *sicarios*, recruited a young man in Bogotá to do a job for them. He was to carry a briefcase on the flight that they told him contained a recording device. Once aloft, he was instructed to secretly tape the conversation of the person seated next to him. In fact, the briefcase contained five kilograms of dynamite. The hapless bomber—Alzate called him the "*suisso*," or suicide—was instructed, once in flight, to flip a toggle switch on top of the suitcase to activate the recorder. All 110 passengers were killed. Gaviria was not on the plane. He had a ticket, but his staff had decided weeks earlier to avoid all commercial flights—for safety reasons, but also because Gaviria's presence on a commercial flight tended to panic the other passengers, who did not want to fly with someone who was so clearly a target for assassination.

Ever since the downing of Pan Am 103 over Lockerbie, Scotland, the year before, threats to air travel had been elevated to a primary concern by the United States and other world powers. International air travel was regarded as vital to the civilized world and also highly vulnerable to anyone unscrupulous enough to attack it. Deterring and punishing those who would take aim at commercial airplanes had become a priority in the counterterrorism community worldwide. Concern about the Medellín cartel heightened when some of Pablo's men were caught trying to buy 120 Stinger antiaircraft missiles in Florida. Weeks after the Avianca bombing, President Bush released a strenuously reasoned opinion by the U.S. Justice Department's Office of Legal Counsel concluding that it *would not* violate the Posse Comitatus Act for the army to be used against criminal suspects overseas. The Avianca bombing was significant for another reason. In the eyes of the Bush administration, it marked Pablo Escobar, José Rodríguez Gacha, and other cartel leaders as a direct threat to American citizens—two of those on the doomed flight had been American citizens. As such, the *narcos* were now men who, in the eyes of the Bush administration, could legally be killed.

For nearly two decades in the United States, the issue of targeting foreign citizens for death had been governed by Executive Order 12333, the pertinent parts of which read as follows:

2.11 *Prohibition on Assassination*

No person employed by or acting on behalf of the United States Government shall engage in, or conspire to engage in, assassination.

2.12 *Indirect Participation*

No agency of the Intelligence Community shall participate in or request any person to undertake activities forbidden by this Order.

The executive order dated back to 1974, when it was issued by President Gerald Ford to effectively preempt legislation gathering steam in Congress, which was investigating abuses by American intelligence agencies. It was a compromise designed to prevent left-wing lawmakers from carving such a prohibition into law and, as an executive order, presumably preserved the right of the president to make exceptions. Soon after Bush took office in 1989, the chief of the international law branch of the army's judge advocate general's office, W. Hays Parks, began work on a formal memorandum to further clarify Executive Order 12333. Dated November 2, and signed off on by legal counsels for the State Department, CIA, National Security Council, Department of Justice, and Department of Defense, it concluded:

> The purpose of Executive Order 12333 and its legal predecessors was to preclude unilateral actions by individual agents or agencies against selected foreign public officials, and to establish beyond any doubt that the United States does not condone assassination as an instrument of national policy. Its intent was not to limit lawful self defense options against legitimate threats to the national security of the United States or individual U.S. citizens. Acting consistent with the Charter of the United Nations, *a decision by the president to employ clandestine, low visibility or overt military force would not constitute assassination if the U.S. military forces were employed against the combatant forces of another nation, a guerrilla force, or a terrorist or other organization whose actions pose a threat to the security of the United States* [emphasis added].

The opinion eased concerns among soldiers in the covert ops community, including the men of Centra Spike, that their work would not someday be labeled criminal. If the Colombians were going to simply kill cartel leaders that Centra Spike found, so be it.

The situation in Colombia was clearly war. On December 6, just nine days after José Rodríguez Gacha fled his mountaintop *finca*, the second of the two bombings planned with Pablo weeks before took place. A bus loaded with five hundred kilograms of dynamite was detonated outside the *DAS* building. It carved a crater four feet deep in the pavement outside the building and tore off its front. Seventy people were killed, hundreds more injured, and the explosion caused more than $25 million in property damage. One target of the explosion was General Miguel Maza, who had miraculously survived the car bombing in May. He emerged from the ruins of the building, again unscathed.

The blasts were swiftly avenged. Centra Spike traced Gacha over the next few weeks as he fled north from *finca* to *finca*, but he never stayed in one place long enough for the Colombians to launch a raid. He settled eventually into a cabin in the *departamento* of Chocó, in a remote, heavily forested area near the border of Panama. He was picked up on a radio phone arranging for women to be trucked to this remote spot. The location wasn't precise—the portion of the intercepted call had been too brief—but elite police units were deployed to search the area. They were finally led to Gacha's *finca* by a man named Jorge Velasquez, a cocaine smuggler from Cartagena who had been working as a spy for the Medellín cartel's rivals in Cali. The Cali cartel leaders had a lot to gain by the destruction of their Medellín rivals and had begun quietly assisting the Colombian police. Once Velasquez pointed out Gacha's precise location, a coordinated assault was planned for early the next morning, December 15, 1989. Just in case, the United States readied a task force of Delta Force operators and SEALs on the USS *America*, sailing just off the coast. As the police-assault helicopters, AH-6 Little Birds armed with Israeli miniguns, descended on Gacha and his teenage son Freddy and five bodyguards, they fled the house and ran for a nearby banana grove. According to the official report, they fired on the choppers with automatic weapons and the miniguns cut them down. Their bodies were placed on display afterward. The lower half of El Mexicano's face had been shot completely away. It was a grotesque way of serving notice that this time, the drug war was for keeps.

Gacha was publicly mourned by thousands in his hometown of Pacho, about twenty-five miles north of Bogotá. At his estate there police found a working gallows, machine guns, grenades, and a gold-plated, personalized 9mm pistol with monogrammed bullets. His death would do little to curb the flood of cocaine leaving Colombia for the United States, but to the vast majority of Colombians, cowed by years of bombings, kidnappings, and assassinations, it marked a major victory for the state, for President Barco, and, quietly, for the United States.

A curious thing happened after Gacha was killed. His death prompted a torrent of phone calls to and from Pablo Escobar. One of the other things Centra Spike did, besides finding people, was track communication patterns. A fairly comprehensive chart of the power structure of any large organization can be built by monitoring the flow of electronic communication over time. None of the top people in the cartel used standard landline telephones, the central Colombian telephone network. The police and the secret police, both the *DIJIN* and the *DAS*, were both known to monitor it closely. But none of the cartel leaders apparently suspected that anyone was listening in on their cell-phone and radio calls.

It was during those days that Centra Spike got its first chance to listen to Pablo. The intercepted conversations were recorded in the Beechcrafts by Centra Spike's technicians, who would then forward the tapes to the embassy, where Jacoby and his team would study them. Unlike Gacha, who was uneducated and crude, Escobar appeared to be a man of some refinement. He had a deep voice and spoke softly. He was very articulate, and even though he could slip into the familiar *paisa* patois, he usually used very clean Spanish, free of vulgarity and with a vocabulary of some sophistication, which he was fond of sprinkling with English words and expressions. He was painstakingly polite and seemed determined to project unruffled joviality at all times, as though trying to keep things light, even though it was very clear that everyone who spoke to Pablo was afraid of him. With his intimates his standard greeting on the phone was "*Qué mas, caballero?*" or "What's happening, my man?"

Both the pattern of these calls and the content changed the unit's understanding of the Medellín cartel. Instead of scrambling to fill the leadership void or feuding between those thought to be José Rodríguez Gacha's equals or underlings, what Centra Spike heard was Pablo Escobar coolly at work, like a chief-executive officer who had lost a key associate. People called him to make decisions, and he did so calmly, redistributing Gacha's interests and responsibilities. The more Centra Spike listened over the next few weeks, the more they realized that Pablo had been the man in charge all along. Always deeply concerned about his public image, he had evidently been content to let Gacha be perceived as the chief bad guy.

What also came through was Pablo's casual cruelty. It hit home when, not long after Gacha's death, Pablo ordered his men to kidnap a Colombian officer, a commander in the army's Fourth Brigade. Angered over his associate's killing, Pablo ordered the officer be not just killed but tortured to death slowly, just to make a statement to the Colombian government.

Pablo was infuriated by Gacha's death. The government had clearly upped the stakes. In one intercepted conversation with his cousin Gustavo Gaviria, he was captured in a rare unguarded rant that offered insight into how he saw his predicament. He viewed himself as a victim, caught in a class struggle between the power elite in Bogotá and the common people of Medellín. He intended, he said, to use the public's weariness with violence to his benefit. He planned to turn up the violence until the public cried out for a solution, a deal.

"We will begin to go for the oligarchs and burn the houses of the rich," Pablo said. "It is very easy because the house of a rich person has only one watchman and one goes in with three gallons of gasoline, and with that we shit on them and make them cry and beg for mercy.... You know, brother, that is the only way. This country is asking for peace and every day there are more people asking for peace. So we have to apply much harder pressure."

A communiqué from the Extraditables not long after hammered home the point:

> We are declaring total and absolute war on the government, on the individual and political oligarchy, on the journalists who have attacked and insulted us, on the judges that have sold themselves to the government, on the extraditing magistrates . . . on all those who have persecuted and attacked us. We will not respect the families of those who have not respected our families. We will burn and destroy the industries, properties and mansions of the oligarchy.

By now Pablo was the man in Centra Spike's crosshairs. In January 1990, on a trip home to the United States, Jacoby searched out a $300 bottle of Rémy Martin cognac. He told his team in Bogotá that he had placed the bottle unopened on a shelf in his Maryland apartment and vowed that he would drink it only after Pablo Escobar was dead.

4

Trouble at once began closing in on Pablo. Three tons of dynamite planned for his stepped-up bombing campaign were seized in a police raid on a warehouse in Bogotá. Five more tons were seized at a *finca* owned by Pablo near Caldas. In February, the day before President Bush arrived in Cartagena to attend a hemispheric antidrug conference, police raided three big cocaine labs in Chocó, the state just south of Antioquia. In the two months after José

Rodríguez Gacha's death, the *PNC* seized $35 million in cash and gold. Pablo's men started falling, too.

Pablo concluded that there was a spy in his inner circle. Clearly somebody was informing the police of his whereabouts and plans. Pablo had a number of his security force tortured and executed in his presence in early 1990 to set an example. In one intercepted conversation, Centra Spike recorded the screams of a victim in the background as Pablo spoke calmly to his wife.

The U.S. embassy jealously guarded the secret of Centra Spike. Jacoby and his staff literally worked in a vault, a secure room on the windowless fifth floor of the embassy building. The vault had reinforced walls and a six-inch-thick steel door. There was strict secrecy even within the building. The Centra Spike men employed there had cover jobs on the ambassador's staff, and the entire area where they worked was off-limits to most embassy employees. So long as Pablo and the other cartel leaders didn't know anyone was listening, they would continue to talk freely on their radios and cell phones.

But Pablo did find out that his calls were being overheard. In March 1990, the Colombian government inadvertently tipped him off.

It happened because Centra Spike intercepted a phone conversation between Pablo and Gustavo Mesa, one of his *sicario* gang leaders, plotting the murder of another presidential candidate.

"What's up? How's everything going?" Pablo asked.

"Everything's going fine," said Mesa. "What you ordered to be done is going ahead well."

"But don't you do it, because you're in charge of one and only one job. Understand?"

"Yeah, I've got the people who will do the job. I'm doing well with the task and I've already presented the bill. They'll pay me Friday, everything's fine."

They went on to discuss the payment (about $1,200), promising that the young killer's family would be provided for in the event he was killed in the attempt. Mesa explained that other gunmen would take care of the bodyguards around the candidate, that the assassin need only focus on the main target. Half of the money would be paid in advance, the other half when the job was done. They mentioned the exact date and time of the hit but, maddeningly, never mentioned which candidate was to be killed or where the hit would take place.

The embassy decided that this information would have to be shared with the Colombian government, so a transcript of the tape was given to President Barco, and the government began scrambling to prevent the killing. The most likely target was assumed to be Gaviria, because he was the front-runner, he had spoken out in favor of extradition, and he was the only candidate who had publicly ruled out negotiating with the traffickers (a promise, as it happened, that he wouldn't keep). Several more attempts had been made on his life since the Avianca bombing. So Gaviria and several other likely targets were given intensive security on that day. When the appointed hour came, the victim was the least likely candidate: Bernardo Jaramillo, the minor Unión Patriótica candidate, was gunned down in the lobby of El Dorado Airport. The police immediately blamed drug traffickers for the killing, but the link was not apparent. Jaramillo had not been an outspoken opponent of extradition, nor a likely winner in the election. Through his lawyers, Pablo immediately issued a denial. But the government had the recording and it found the opportunity to publicly link Pablo to the killing too hard to resist. The transcript was leaked to the press.

There was a swift, outraged public response. Pablo was revealed to be, despite his denials, a killer, someone who was now ordering candidates killed just to sow discord. He lost whatever credibility he'd gained by his years of skillful public relations. So the leak from Barco's office had its desired effect. But it also had an undesired one. Pablo now knew that conversations on his cell phone were being overheard. His voice vanished from the airwaves. He would never again hold an unguarded conversation on a radio or cell phone.

This made life much more difficult for Colonel Martinez, who had developed a good working relationship with Centra Spike in Medellín. Over the first few months of 1990, the Search Bloc conducted raid after raid on the drug boss's suspected hideouts, but always arrived too late. The Centra Spike soldier attached to the base in Medellín was more impressed by Colonel Martinez's will than by his methods.

Clearly the colonel was different from most of those in the Colombian army and police forces. Other than the air force general who had wanted to bomb the *finca* where José Rodríguez Gacha had been staying, most of the local officers Centra Spike worked with had seemed lazy, incompetent, or corrupt—or perhaps all three. The tall, skinny colonel clearly intended to get the job done. According to some of his men, one of the first things he did at the headquarters in Medellín was line up his inner circle against a wall and tell them that if he discovered any one of them betraying their mission, "I will personally shoot you in the head." He locked down his men to prevent uncontrolled communication in and out of the compound, and perhaps most importantly, he showed genuine frustration and anger when one of his missions failed. The Americans were used to working with Colombian officers who would joke about failed missions, who took them no more seriously than getting the wrong order at a restaurant.

There were plenty of reasons why they repeatedly failed. On one occasion, approaching a suspect *finca* on a morning raid, the assault force lined up along a ridge and then simply walked toward the structure. A Centra Spike soldier accompanying them suggested that the force drop down on the ground and crawl.

"In the dirt?" asked a Colombian officer, insulted by the suggestion. "My guys don't crawl in the dirt and mud."

The occupants of the target house fled well before the raiding party arrived. The *finca* had all the hallmarks of an Escobar hideout, the giant-screen Sony TV, a well-appointed modern bathroom, a refrigerator stocked with steaks and soda, and lots of state-of-the-art radio equipment. The occupants had fled in such haste that they hadn't had time to completely burn documents, so they had urinated and defecated on them. This was enough to dissuade the national police from taking a look. When the Centra Spike man began fishing papers out of the mess, the colonel himself had objected.

"I can't believe you'd do that," he said. "That's human waste!"

"Where I come from we also low-crawl and get our uniforms dirty," the American said.

When the documents were gently cleaned and dried, they found handwritten notes from Pablo, sealed with his thumbprint. The notes promised financial security for the caretaker of the farmhouse. There were copies he had prepared for several other *fincas*, indicating that he kept a string of such safe houses stashed and ready in advance, so he always had someplace secure and comfortable to go. It was a useful insight into how Pablo recruited and nurtured assistance in the hills. While this detective work went on, the colonel's men settled in front of the television and began drinking Pablo's sodas and cooking his steaks. Two men who had stayed behind in the farmhouse, the *finca*'s caretakers, were bound and gagged. Several of the colonel's men were beating them.

"What are your guys doing?" the Centra Spike man asked Martinez.

"We're interrogating them."

"The fuck you are, you're killing them."

"We are just encouraging them to talk," said Martinez.

"If you want them to talk, why don't you take the gags out of their mouths?"

"No, no," said Martinez, ushering the American away from the farmhouse. "Leave it alone. You shouldn't be here."

After that, the Americans found that the colonel tried to keep them a safe distance from the action. Not to protect them, they deduced, but to protect their eyes. Centra Spike heard plenty of rumors about the colonel's unsavory tactics—beatings, electroshock torture, killings—but if they were happening, it was always out of sight. Centra Spike and the other Americans at the embassy were content so long as it stayed that way. Nobody wanted to be a party to human-rights abuses, but so long as the Americans didn't see them, they didn't feel obliged to report them. With all the disinformation floating around, how could the truth be known anyway? The colonel forcefully denied the accusations. But if he was playing rough, well then . . . wasn't Pablo? On March 20, 1990, two of his *sicarios* on a motorcycle threw a bomb into a crowd in the village of Tebaide, injuring seven people and killing a child. A car bomb detonated just outside Medellín on April 11, killing five police officers and agents. On April 25, two of Martinez's men were killed, seven injured, and two passersby killed when a car bomb was remotely detonated in Medellín. If the colonel's men occasionally crossed the line in response, who could fault them?

On one occasion, a Centra Spike soldier reported that two men seized in a raid had been thrown from helicopters on the flight back to Medellín. He had not seen it done but had heard several of Martinez's men joking about it. He confronted the colonel and was told, "We were concerned that they might have seen you."

When the Centra Spike man protested, Martinez waved him away. "Don't worry about it. It's not your concern."

When the soldier reported the incident to Jacoby, the major asked, "Did you actually see them thrown from the helicopters?"

"No."

"Good."

Centra Spike noted how quickly the colonel learned from his mistakes. He was candid about his unit's shortcomings and took the right steps to improve. His men did begin low-crawling, as well as fishing documents out of latrines. At first skeptical of American technology, Martinez gradually warmed up to it. When he had overheard Pablo's voice on a portable radio monitor being carried by one of the Centra Spike men on a raid, the colonel had asked that he be given the same equipment the next time out. He took suggestions, and asked for more. As a result, when rumors began to circulate that the colonel had taken money from the Cali cartel, rumors that some of the DEA guys took seriously, the embassy was not about to discard him. So long as there was no overwhelming evidence of it, such allegations could always be blamed on Pablo's sophisticated disinformation efforts. The colonel was their man. As far as the embassy was concerned, *El Doctor* had finally met his match.

Martinez may have been ruthless, but he was also relentless. Steered in part by intelligence from Centra Spike, the Search Bloc kept closing the ring around Pablo. In June 1990, they killed John Arías, one of Pablo's most trusted *sicario* leaders, and then in July they captured Hernan Henao, Pablo's brother-in-law and a trusted associate. On August 9 they killed his longtime partner in crime and play Gustavo Gaviria, his buddy from his first days of skipping school and stealing cars. These two killings were blows to Pablo both emotionally and professionally: Henao, "H.H." (Aahchey-Aahchey), had been the cartel's treasurer, its main money man, and Gustavo had been one of Pablo's most trusted confidants. The Search Bloc said he was killed in a shoot-out, which had become such a commonplace that up in the embassy vault it was greeted with winks. The expression "killed in a shoot-out with police" was regarded as a euphemism for summary execution. Pablo claimed that there had been no shoot-out, that his cousin had been captured, tortured, and then executed by the colonel's men.

Two days before Gustavo was killed César Gaviria had been sworn in as president of Colombia. He had somehow survived his candidacy. Gaviria was a low-key, pleasant man with youthful good looks and habits. He collected modern paintings, loved listening to The Beatles and Jethro Tull, played tennis avidly, and had two small children, Simon, eleven, and Maria, eight. He had entered the presidential campaign almost two years earlier as manager for Galán. The two men had shared political outlooks and interests, but Galán had been the bold one, the one with charisma and dash. Gaviria's style was milder. He was less a fighter than someone who tried to broker deals and forge consensus. That he had courage was beyond contention, but his courage was not that of a man staking himself against the tide but of one resigned to ride it out, to do his part and see it through without complaint, just as every day he marked down the "assignments" he had to complete. Gaviria was so dutiful that he had campaigned expecting he would be killed, less out of ambition than a sense of duty, a sense that it was expected of him. He arrived at Colombia's highest office somewhat astonished to still be alive. He was convinced that the only explanation why he had not been killed was that, for some reason he did not understand, Pablo had decided not to kill him.

Pablo shifted tactics after Gaviria took office. Instead of bombing, he hit upon a more devious method of fighting back. The government of Colombia had long been the preserve of a relatively small group of wealthy, powerful Bogotá families. This oligarchy owned the major newspapers and TV stations, and the presidency and top ministries seemed to cycle among the families over the generations. Pablo had long portrayed his battle against the government as a class war, wherein he represented the common folk of Medellín and Antioquia. That summer, after his cousin's death, Pablo began applying his calculated plan to "go for the oligarchs and burn the houses of the rich." He did it not by setting fire to their houses but by stabbing their hearts. On August 30, he kidnapped journalist Diana Turbay, the daughter of former president Julio Turbay, along with four members of her news team.

Gaviria had been in office only three weeks, but already he had demonstrated that his approach to dealing with Pablo would include both the carrot and the stick. Colonel Martinez's Search Bloc was the stick, and it continued its bloody work: in October another of Pablo's cousins, Gustavo's brother Luis, was killed "in a shoot-out with the police." The new president also extradited three suspected drug dealers in the first two months of his administration (the twenty-fifth suspected trafficker extradited since Galán's murder in August 1989). But Gaviria also offered the carrot. In his acceptance speech, he had drawn a careful distinction between terrorism and drug trafficking. Drug trafficking was an international problem, he said, one that Colombia could not be expected to solve alone. But terrorism was a national problem; it was *the* national problem. The two issues were separate, and he would deal with them separately. His first priority would be to end the violence, even if that meant striking a deal with the likes of Pablo Escobar. Gaviria doubted at that point if the Colombian police and judicial system were capable of arresting, trying, and punishing Pablo anyway. The nation's best hopes were to keep the pressure on and to offer the drug boss a deal sweet enough to make him surrender. Just a week after Turbay was taken, Gaviria issued a decree offering Pablo and other indicted *narcos* immunity from extradition and reduced sentences if they would surrender and confess. The decree was seen purely as a reaction to the kidnapping, which it was not. It was the first step in a plan Gaviria had thought through carefully.

Not everyone agreed with him. General Maza, the survivor of two grotesque assassination attempts, put it bluntly: "This country won't be put right as long as Escobar is alive."

Pablo answered with two more prominent kidnappings. Taken at gunpoint were Francisco Santos, the editor of the newspaper *El Tiempo* and the son of its owner and publisher, and Marina Montoya, the sister of former president Barco's top aide. He demanded that extradition be outlawed and that the government spell out exactly what kind of confession was required for surrender, provide a special prison for those who did surrender, and offer protection for their families.

The kidnappings demonstrated a shrewd understanding of Bogotá's close-knit, incestuous power structure. They literally struck home with Bogotá's elite, of which Gaviria was a part. And they produced results. A committee of powerful citizens calling themselves the Notables formed to pressure Gaviria into acceding to the kidnappers' demands. Among the prominent citizens in the group were Julio Turbay, the former president whose daughter was a captive, and Alfonso López, the former president who had met with Pablo in Panama City years before. The group began corresponding with Pablo's chief attorney in Bogotá, Guido Parra, looking for a peaceful answer.

They also met with Gaviria to plead their case, applying excruciating personal pressure. On one visit to the Presidential Palace, Turbay and Juan Santos, the owner and publisher of *El Tiempo*, found the new president in a dejected mood, weighed down by the pressure of his responsibility.

"This is a very difficult moment," said Gaviria. "I've wanted to help you, and I have been helping within the limits of the possible, but pretty soon I won't be able to do anything at all."

Turbay, who could more easily put himself in Gaviria's shoes, was sadly empathetic.

"Señor President," he said, "you are proceeding as you must, and we must act as the fathers of our children. I understand and ask you not to do anything that might create a problem for you as head of state." In García Márquez's account of the meeting, he wrote that Turbay pointed then to the presidential chair. "If I were sitting there," he said, "I would do the same."

García Márquez wrote, "Gaviria stood, pale as death."

Less empathetic was Nydia Quintero, the former wife of Turbay and the mother of the hostage. She had been in touch with Pablo through intermediaries and came to plead with Gaviria to call off Colonel Martinez, whose efforts were now forcing Pablo to run from one hiding place to the next. Gaviria explained that this was something he could not do. Law enforcement, he explained, was his duty, and nonnegotiable. Ordering the police to call off their pursuit of Pablo would be asking them to ignore their duty. Besides, the president knew what Pablo was after. "It was one thing for us to offer an alternative judicial policy, but suspending operations would not have meant freedom for the hostages but only that we had stopped hunting down Escobar," he would later explain to García Márquez. Quintero was outraged by the president's attitude. She found him cold and utterly unconcerned about her daughter's life.

The Notables, meanwhile, began issuing public statements of their own. Henceforth, one read, they alone would speak for the families of the hostages. In return for releasing the hostages, they proposed, they would urge the government to consider Pablo and the Extraditables a political movement, not a band of criminals. As such, they were entitled to the same treatment the government had given Colombia's guerrillas. The group M-19, most infamous for the Palace of Justice siege, had negotiated an agreement with the government the previous year to abandon violent struggle and become a legal political party. Its members had been granted amnesty for acts committed during their struggle against the state. The Notables wanted the government to offer the same kind of deal to Pablo. But on the same day their statement was published, October 11, Gaviria instructed his minister of justice to reiterate that the only deal awaiting Pablo was the one he had offered.

"The letter from the Notables is almost cynical," Pablo wrote Parra angrily from hiding. "We are supposed to release the hostages quickly because the government is dragging its feet as it studies our situation? Can they really believe we will let ourselves be deceived again?" Pablo wrote that there was no reason to change his position "since we have not received positive replies to the requests made in our first communication. This is a negotiation, not a game to find out who is clever and who is stupid."

Gaviria gave more ground. On October 8, he offered "legal clarifications" of the earlier decree, making it clear that Pablo or any of the others could choose the least significant charge against them and escape prosecution for all others by pleading guilty to it. It would also continue to ensure that they would not be extradited, no matter what new charges were brought against them in captivity.

Pablo was interested, but he wanted more. In a letter to his lawyer Parra, Pablo explained that he wanted the president to promise, "in writing, in a decree, that under no circumstances will we be extradited, not for any crime, not to any country." He reiterated that he wanted to control the circumstances of his imprisonment, and he wanted protection for his wife and children while he was locked away.

In November he upped the ante once more. The day after his cousin Luis was killed, Pablo's men kidnapped Maruja Pachon, the sister-in-law of the slain Galán and the wife of a prominent congressman, and her sister-in-law, the congressman's sister. An effort to abduct the granddaughter of former president Betancur failed. Defiant bulletins from the Extraditables accused Colonel Martinez's force of atrocities in Medellín. One claimed that the Search Bloc was rounding up young men in neighborhoods sympathetic to Pablo and shooting them down.

"Why have search warrants been exchanged for execution orders?" one bulletin read. "Why are search-for posters being distributed and rewards being offered for people who are not wanted by any judicial authority?"

Another acknowledged responsibility for the kidnappings and noted, in particular, that "the detention of journalist Maruja Pachon is our response to the recent tortures and abductions perpetrated in the city of Medellín by the same state security forces [Colonel Martinez's Search Bloc] so often mentioned in our communiqués."

Pablo's tactics were paying off. His bombing campaign had terrified the public, and polls showed growing support for striking a deal to end the violence. Just weeks before Christmas, he ordered three of the hostages released, part of the news team who had been taken with Diana Turbay. Gaviria responded immediately, again sweetening the terms for surrender. In return for releasing the hostages unharmed and working to end the plague of violence in the country—fifteen hundred deaths had been attributed to the drug traffickers in the previous two years—the president now offered the *narco* kings, in the words of Gabriel García Márquez, "the gift of imprisonment." The president promised that those who confessed to even a single minor crime would serve only a reduced prison term. Fabio Ochoa turned himself in on December 18, the day after the new decree was issued. "I feel the same happiness on entering jail as someone else feels when leaving it," he said. "I only wanted to end the nightmare that my life had become." Over the next two months his two brothers, Jorge and Juan David, did the same.

By the end of 1990 Pablo's life was also a nightmare. Colonel Martinez had come close to catching him several times and had chipped away at the people around him. The deaths of his cousins and brother-in-law, the surrenders of the Ochoas . . . his organization was falling apart. The man who just a year earlier had dozens of luxurious estates to chose from was now sleeping some nights in the woods in the mountains, running to stay ahead of his determined pursuers. He dared not speak by radio or telephone, so he sent messages by courier. He had neither the time nor the means of controlling his cocaine business, so every month that he spent on the run he lost money and standing. By the end of 1990 he saw only one sure way out of his predicament. He would escape—into the arms of the Colombian government.

But not until he had arranged the terms exactly as he wanted them. Gaviria had once promised never to negotiate with the *narcos*, but he was now dealing regularly through intermediaries with Parra. The lawyer was despised, distrusted, and feared by many in Bogotá for representing Pablo. Just days after warning the government publicly that it should not trust Parra, the president of the Colombian Association of Journalists, Alejandro Jaramillo, disappeared. But as much as people now feared him, Parra evidently lived in fear of his client. Delivering a message from the hostage Francisco Santos to his family, Parra broke down and wept.

"Remember," he told them. "I won't be killed by the police. I'll be killed by Pablo Escobar because I know too much."

Pablo still had good reason to hold out, even though life on the run was miserable. Gaviria had called an assembly to rewrite the Colombian constitution, which presented Pablo with a chance to have a prohibition on extradition written into the founding document of the state. Extradition had never been that popular, and with Pablo's bombings, his kidnapping, and his *plata o plomo* strategy, there were more than enough votes. If he could hold out until the assembly formally drew up and enacted the document, it would crown his biggest victory.

So the dying continued. In the first two months of 1991 there was an average of twenty murders a day in Colombia, and in Medellín a total of 457 police had been killed since Colonel Martinez had started his hunt. Young gunmen in that city were being paid 5 million pesos for killing a cop. When the Search Bloc shot two more of Pablo's top *sicarios* in January 1991, Pablo announced that two of his prize hostages would be executed in return. Marina Montoya was murdered on January 24. Her kidnappers placed a bag over her head and marched her from the place where she had been held captive for four months, a woman of sixty with long white hair, and shot her six times in the head. Her body was found in an empty lot north of Bogotá. Someone had stolen her shoes. Diana Turbay was killed ten days later when police forces found where she was being held and tried to rescue her. She was evidently killed in the crossfire. The deaths of these women, well known and loved in the social circles of Bogotá's elite, had exactly the effect intended.

Nydia Quintero, the mother of Diana Turbay, asked for an audience with Gaviria.

"They killed Diana, Señor President, and it's your doing; it's your fault," she said. "It's what comes of having a soul of stone."

Monica de Greiff, the minister of justice, resigned. She had received chilling phone calls from would-be kidnappers, who had detailed for her the progress of her young son on his way home from school, just to let her know they could take him at any time. Gaviria responded by extending his offer of immunity from extradition. If Pablo turned himself in and confessed to something, anything, he would not have to worry about facing justice even for these fresh outrages. The new president was all but begging Pablo to stop.

The drug boss's lawyers continued to negotiate. Pablo insisted on being seen not as a criminal but as a revolutionary. He was not seeking a role in the government, but in return for putting down his arms he expected significant concessions. It was simple power versus power, his guns, bombs, and *sicarios* against the state's. By now the issue was only incidentally connected to drug trafficking. Pablo was playing a dangerous game, because if the colonel and Centra Spike succeeded in finding him first, he would most likely be killed or, if not, extradited immediately. He had been indicted in three states in the United States. The alternative being worked out by his lawyers may have been the most generous plea bargain of all time, but it did represent a significant compromise. If he could hold out and continue to evade Colonel Martinez, whatever prison time he agreed to serve would be a far cry from the unparalleled luxury he had enjoyed for the last fifteen years. He would have his own special "prison," which would be built in his hometown of Envigado on a hill called *La Catedral,* on land that he owned. He would pay to have it built. The guards in the prison would work not for the Bureau of Prisons but for the government of Envigado, which Pablo effectively controlled. The only inmates would be his closest associates and *sicarios.* The PNC—most particularly the Search Bloc—would not be allowed within twenty kilometers of its gates. Prison would give Pablo a comfortable, safe place to settle down and reestablish his dominance of the cocaine-trafficking business. If his lawyers managed to limit his term, he would emerge in a few years cleansed of his sins in the public eye, a fabulously rich, powerful Medellín citizen, Don Pablo, exactly what he had always wanted to be. Who could say where his ambition might take him from there?

Just as Gaviria applied both a carrot and a stick, so did Pablo. On April 30, his *sicarios* killed Enrique Low, a former justice minister who had spoken out in favor of extradition. Earlier Low had been delivered a small wooden coffin with a tiny Colombian flag attached, soaked in blood. Pablo also struck a blow to the president by having one of Gaviria's cousins and oldest intimates, Fortunato Gaviria, abducted from a *finca* in Pereira and killed. The autopsy showed that he had been buried alive. The president's boyish manner was by now nearly crushed. He looked defeated, moving through the Presidential Palace heavy with sadness and frustration, increasingly alone and blamed for the country's tribulations. "I was the only Colombian who didn't have a president to complain to," he would say later.

But his efforts finally paid off. Over the spring Pablo began gradually releasing the remaining hostages, the final two, Santos and Pachon, on May 20. Then, after all these months of uncertainty and death, Pablo surrendered.

5

Pablo orchestrated the endgame through a popular Catholic televangelist. He claimed he had chosen the date for many reasons, but the most telling one was that on that day, June 19, 1991, over the loud protests of U.S. Ambassador Thomas McNamara and DEA chief Robert Bonner and the opposition of Gaviria's government, the Constitutional Assembly voted to formally outlaw extradition by a vote of fifty to thirteen.

The surrender had been arranged by Pablo's lawyers, after hammering out the last of the terms with the government. His specially built Envigado prison, *La Catedral*, was still under construction but habitable. His celebrity hostages—those who had survived—were home with their families, trying to resume normal lives. Word leaked that Pablo intended to surrender, and the country collectively held its breath. The news seemed too good to be true.

He awakened early that morning, which was not his custom. He ate breakfast with his brother Roberto and his mother and sisters in Medellín. They were happy to see him. In the months he had been on the run, he had not dared to spend time with them. Pablo was still negotiating the final details on the phone at nine in the morning.

He emerged from hiding like a man expecting to be shot. To secure the short helicopter flight from the agreed-upon rendezvous point to the new prison, high in the hills beyond the southern edge of the city, his lawyers had negotiated a ban on all other flights—"Not even birds will fly over Medellín today," Defense Minister Raphael Pardo wrote in his diary. At midafternoon, a twelve-seat Bell helicopter took off for the prearranged spot, a mansion with a private, impeccably groomed soccer field on the grounds to its rear. Aboard was Father Rafael García and Congressman Alberto Villamizar, a man Pablo had once tried to kill. Villamizar's wife and sister had been among the ten prominent hostages Pablo had taken the year before. Both had been released unharmed. Villamizar had been instrumental

in working out the details of this moment. With the priest and the congressman was the drug boss's old associate Jorge Ochoa, who had been released
from prison temporarily at Pablo's request. As described in García Márquez's
book *News of a Kidnapping,* there were about thirty armed men waiting on the
soccer field as the chopper set down. About half of the gunmen moved forward, surrounding a short, chubby man with black hair to his shoulders, a
leathery suntan, sunglasses, and a thick black beard that reached to his chest.
He wore a light blue cotton jacket, an Italian shirt, blue jeans, and his trademark new white tennis shoes, and he carried a portable phone and battery
pack in a briefcase. Pablo stopped to quickly embrace several of his bodyguards. Then he gestured to two of the men to board the helicopter and
climbed up himself.

He extended a hand to the congressman.

"How are you, Dr. Villamizar?"

"How's it going, Pablo?" Villamizar said, shaking the prisoner's hand.

Pablo looked over and smiled at his friend Ochoa, whom he had not
seen for months.

"And you," he said. "In the middle of this right to the end."

The group sat silently for a few moments until the pilot asked, "Do
we take off now?"

"What do you think?" said Pablo. "Move it! Move it!"

Minutes later, the chopper landed on the prison soccer field, which
was not yet planted with grass. The newly built prison was set on
the top of Mont Catedral, a green peak with a commanding view of the
valley and the entire city of Medellín. Pablo had overseen construction of
the prison, which was still under way. So far there were fences, a cinder-
block-roofed home for the warden, a collection of larger prison buildings on a lower clearing, and another, larger structure higher up the
hill to house prisoners. It looked austere, appropriately prisonlike. But
Pablo had plans for the place and he had also taken precautions. He and
his brother had visited *La Catedral* weeks earlier and had buried an arsenal
of rifles and machine guns on the slope uphill from where their "cells"
would be.

"One day we will need them," he'd assured Roberto.

As Pablo stepped off the helicopter, he found himself facing fifty
armed prison guards in new blue uniforms, each pointing a rifle.

"Lower your weapons, damn it!" Pablo ordered, and they did.

He was escorted to meet the prison director, and there he raised his left pants leg and withdrew a 9mm SIG-Sauer handgun with a gold monogram inlaid on a mother-of-pearl handle and theatrically took out the rounds one by one, flicking each to the ground before handing over the gun. It looked like something Pablo had rehearsed, a symbolic end to years of war. He then called his brother on his portable phone to tell him the surrender was complete.

Pablo talked to some of the reporters who had been invited to the prison. He told them his surrender was "an act of peace."

"I decided to give myself up at the moment I saw the national Constitutional Assembly working for the strengthening of human rights and Colombian democracy."

Starstruck journalists swooned. Already forgetting Pablo's campaign of terror, even his war on their own profession, all the editors and reporters he had kidnapped and killed, a Medellín TV reporter gushed: "I had thought that he was a petulant, proud, disciplined man, one of those who is always looking over his shoulder. But I was wrong. On the contrary, he is educated, he asks permission if he walks in front of a person and is agreeable when he greets someone."

"You can see that he is someone who worries about his appearance," said another. "Especially his shoes. They were impeccably clean."

"He had a bit of belly," said another, "which makes him look like a calm man."

"He walks as if he had no hurry in the world. He is very jovial and he laughs a lot."

Before leaving, Villamizar chatted with jovial Pablo, who apologized to him for the suffering he had caused his family. He explained that the war had been hard on both sides. In their conversation, Pablo denied any responsibility for the death of Luis Galán.

"A lot of people were involved in that," he said. "I didn't even like the idea because I knew what would happen if they killed him, but once the decision was made, I couldn't oppose it."

He also said he was happy that his men had never killed Villamizar, even though he had been told that the congressman was a stubborn enemy.

"In that war we were fighting, just a rumor could get you killed," he explained. "But now that I know you, Dr. Villamizar, thank God nothing happened to you."

He promised that no further harm would come to his family.

"Who knows how long I'll be here," Pablo told him. "But I still have a lot of friends, so if any of you feels unsafe, if anybody tries to give you a hard time, you let me know and that'll be the end of it. You met your obligations to me, and I thank you and will do the same for you. You have my word of honor."

It was over, or was supposed to be. Pablo's "confession," part of his deal with the state, would ignore the kidnappings, the murders of Turbay and Montoya, the thousands of car-bomb victims, political victims, murdered judges and police officers. In keeping with President Gaviria's decree, Pablo acknowledged only one crime: acting as a middleman in a French drug deal arranged by his dead cousin Gustavo. In purely legal terms, he did not even admit he was guilty of that. He had been tried and convicted in absentia by French authorities, and, according to Pablo's carefully crafted statement "That country's penal code . . . gives one the right to apply for a revision of their case, when they appear before their national judge, in this case a Colombian judge. This is precisely the objective of my voluntary presentation to this office, in other words, to have a Colombian judge examine my case."

To satisfy the requirement of his plea, Pablo agreed to appear before a judge in Bogotá and confess. He did so months later, in February 1992, in a revealing session in which the drug boss lied fluently but displayed his usual wit and pugnacious patriotism, turning the session into his own indictment of the authorities. Everyone in the room knew, of course, that Pablo Escobar was the world's most notorious drug trafficker and the most prolific killer in Colombian history, but he understood that the court was obliged to assume his innocence of crimes for which he had not been convicted, and he played the role with cynical aplomb. He identified himself as "a livestock farmer," noted his one semester of accounting after high school in 1969, and added, "I have no addictions, don't smoke, don't drink." He emphasized his innocence, that he was surrendering only to enable an appeal of the conviction against him in France, and announced his intention of pursuing a college degree while in jail. Pablo presented himself as a victim. "I wish to clarify that there may be people who might try to send anonymous letters, make phone calls, or commit actions in bad faith under my name, in order to harm me. There have been many accusations, but I've never been convicted of a crime in Colombia."

This was demonstrably untrue, but there were few living who would stand up in court to dispute it, and the records of those earlier convictions had all been destroyed. Pablo confessed to setting up a meeting for his cousin Gustavo that had led to a four-hundred-kilo cocaine transaction.

"Do you know where they got the four hundred kilos of cocaine?" the judge asked.

"I think Mr. Gustavo Gaviria was in charge of that."

"Who is Mr. Gustavo Gaviria?"

"Mr. Gustavo Gaviria was a cousin of mine."

"Do you know how Mr. Gaviria died?"

"Mr. Gaviria was murdered by members of the national police during one of the raid-executions which have been publicly denounced on many occasions."

"Let's talk," the judge later suggested, "about your personal and family's modus vivendi and the economic conditions you've had throughout your life."

"Well, my family is from the north-central part of Colombia, my mother a teacher at a rural school, and my father is a farmer. They made a great effort to give me the education I received, and my current situation is perfectly defined and clear before the national tax office."

The judge asked Pablo to explain how he had been employed throughout his adult life.

"I have always liked to work independently, and since my adolescence I have worked to help sustain my family; even when I was studying I worked at a bicycle rent shop and other less important jobs to support my studies. I repeat, since I was an adolescent. Later on, I got into the business of buying and selling cars, livestock, and land investment. I want to cite Hacienda Nápoles as an example of this, that it was bought in conjunction with another partner at a time when these lands were in the middle of the jungle. Now they are practically ready to be colonized. When I bought land in that region, there were no means of communications or transport and we had to endure a twenty-three-hour journey. I say this in order to clarify the image that people have, that it's all been easy...."

The judge asked Pablo if anyone had helped him get started in business.

"No. It all began from scratch, as many fortunes have started in Colombia and in the world."

"Tell the court what disciplinary or penal precedents appear on your record."

"Yes, there have been many accusations, but I've never been convicted of a crime in Colombia. The accusations of theft, homicide, drug trafficking, and many others were made by [*DAS* head] General Miguel Maza, according to whom every crime that is committed in this country is my fault."

Escobar denied knowing anything about cocaine, owning airplanes, clandestine airstrips, or boats, and explicitly denied being involved in *narco* trafficking. Pressed by the exasperated judge if he knew *anything* about such things, Pablo said, "Only what I see or read in the media. What I've seen and heard in the media is that cocaine costs a lot of money and is consumed by the high social classes in the United States and other countries of the world. I have seen that many political leaders and governments around the world have been accused of *narco* trafficking, like the current vice president of the United States [Dan Quayle], who has been accused of buying and selling cocaine and marijuana. I have also seen the declarations of one of Mr. Reagan's daughters in which she admits to taking marijuana, and I've heard the accusations against the Kennedy family, also accusations of heroin dealing against the shah of Iran as well as the Spanish president; Felipe Gonzáles publicly admitted that he took marijuana. My conclusion is that there is a universal hypocrisy toward drug trafficking and narcotics, and what worries me is that, from what I see in the media, all the evil involved in drug addiction is blamed on cocaine and Colombians, when the truth is that the most dangerous drugs are produced in labs in the United States, like crack. I've never heard of a Colombian being detained for possession of crack because it is produced in North America."

"What is your opinion, bearing in mind your last few answers, on *narco* trafficking?" the judge asked.

"My personal opinion, based on what I've read, I would say that cocaine [will continue] invading the world . . . so long as the high classes continue to consume the drug. I would also like to say that the coca leaf has existed in our country for centuries and it is part of our aboriginal cultures. . . ."

"How do you explain that you, Pablo Escobar, are pointed out as the boss of the Medellín cartel?"

Pablo declined to comment directly, but he referred the judge to a videotaped statement he had turned over to the court, adding, "Another explanation I can give is this: General Maza is my personal enemy.... [He] proclaimed himself my personal enemy in an interview given to *El Tiempo* on the eighth of September, 1991. It is clear then that he suffers a military frustration for not capturing me. The fact that he carried out many operations in order to capture me, and they all failed, making him look bad, has made him say he hates me and I am his personal enemy...."

The judge read Pablo a list of names of known traffickers who had publicly identified him as their boss, including an American named Max Mermelstein.

"I don't know any of these people," Pablo said. "But through the press I know about Mr. Max Mermelstein. I deduce that he is a lying witness which the U.S. government has against me. Everyone in Colombia knows that North American criminals negotiate their sentences in exchange for testifying against Colombians.... I would like to add to the file a copy of *Semana* magazine which has an article about Max Mermelstein, to demonstrate what a liar this man is. I want to read an excerpt from this interview: 'Escobar was the chief of chiefs. The boss of cocaine trafficking wore blue jeans and a soccer shirt, was tall and thin.'"

Short, chubby Pablo then stood up.

"I ask you to tell me, am I a tall and thin person? For a gringo to say that one is tall, you would suppose that man to be very tall."

So ended the first war. Pablo had tumbled from a great height. He was still one of the richest men in the world, but Colonel Martinez's pursuit had cut him off from his wealth. He had been reduced to bargaining for a place for himself in Colombia, but he had still bent the country to his will. It was now written into the constitution that he could not be removed from his country to face trial for his crimes. And within his own country, Pablo had little to fear from the authorities, even in jail, as time would tell. President Gaviria had achieved peace, albeit at the cost of wounding his country's dignity in the eyes of the United States and much of the rest of the world. His hope now was that Pablo would remain contained at *La Catedral* long enough for the country's judicial system to heal and, it was also hoped, bring more serious charges to bear on the imprisoned drug boss. Then he might lock him up for the rest of his life.

In time, Gaviria would realize that this had all been wishful thinking. In striking this deal, he had badly underestimated Pablo. He had failed to understand how deep the man's influence reached in Colombian government and society, and how hard it would be to contain him. Pablo was going to make a fool of him.

Pablo's public standing rebounded immediately. On his surrender, the fickle public, relieved to see an end to the war, swiftly forgave him the bombings, assassinations, and kidnappings—after all, hadn't most of his famous hostages been released unharmed? Shortly after taking up residence at *La Catedral,* Pablo granted a number of cheerful interviews to reporters, always protesting his innocence and displaying his impressive knack for public relations. He told a reporter from the newspaper *El Colombiano* in July 1991 that he intended to study journalism while serving his term, which prompted a wit at the U.S. embassy to point out that he might want to reconsider, given how dangerous that profession had become in Colombia.

IMPRISONMENT
AND
ESCAPE

June 1991–September 1992

1

Pablo had fallen from a great height, but he had fashioned himself a comfortable place to land. Ensconced inside the walls of *La Catedral,* he was confident that his French conviction would eventually be overturned by a friendly Colombian judge. Under the terms of his deal, he would then be a free man, with an amnesty for all the other crimes he was suspected of having committed before the date of his surrender. Meanwhile, he was in a safe place while things cooled off, and he had a chance to begin putting his cocaine empire back together.

During the months he had been running, hiding, and fighting the government, dozens of his associates had been killed or arrested. Through the first half of 1991, the Colombian police, steered by American technology, had seized about sixty thousand kilos of cocaine and all but destroyed the cartel's infrastructure. In February they had taken one of the cartel's converted DC-3 cargo planes. All of this made little more than a dent in the amount of the drug reaching the United States, but it did have an effect. Wholesale prices for cocaine in New York were rising, and purity levels were down—a sure sign that the supply was being cut back at its head. Mostly it was hurting Pablo's competitive position against the Cali cartel. With Colonel Martinez off his back, he would have a chance to regroup.

He went to work rebuilding. Knowing that the police and the Americans were still listening to his radio and phone calls, Pablo raised pigeons for private communications; he even had little personalized leg bands that read:

PABLO ESCOBAR
CÁRCEL MÁXIMA SEGURIDAD
ENVIGADO

Not long after Pablo moved into *La Catedral,* the purity levels of cocaine on the streets of New York were restored and the prices dropped.

Lawyer Roberto Uribe visited him weekly and found the place growing cozier. At first the living quarters, gymnasium, and cafeteria had seemed
like a real prison, but gradually the furnishing became more lavish. Pablo
had grown accustomed to his life on the run, and at first he'd wanted little.
But the men with him, his brother Roberto and some of his top *sicarios*,
began importing luxuries and, not wanting to outshine *El Doctor,* whatever they ordered for themselves they also ordered for him. Anything could
be brought in. The prison guards were no more than Pablo's employees,
and the army checkpoints just waved Pablo's trucks through. The inmates
facetiously referred to the regular truck route as the "tunnel." To have
plenty of cash on hand, Pablo shipped in tightly rolled American hundred-
dollar bills in milk cans, which would be buried in the fog of dawn at places
around the prison. Two of the cans, each containing at least $1 million,
were buried under the soccer field. A bar was installed, with a lounge and
a disco. For the gymnasium there was a sauna. Inmates' "cells" were actually more like hotel suites, with living rooms, small kitchens, bedrooms,
and bath. Workmen began constructing small, camouflaged cabanas uphill from the main prison. This is where Pablo and the other inmates intended to hide out if *La Catedral* was ever bombed or invaded. In the
meantime, the cabanas made excellent retreats, where the men entertained
women privately. Brightly colored, surrealistic murals were painted on the
walls and ceilings of the cabanas, as in classic sixties-era dopers' lairs, complete with black lamps and Surround Sound. Food was prepared for them
by chefs Pablo hired away from fine restaurants, and once the bar and disco
were up and running, he hosted many parties and even wedding receptions.

He had a powerful telescope placed on the balcony overlooking
Medellín, which opened up beneath his feet like a personal fief, so that he
could see his wife and children at any of their various homes below. They
visited him often at the prison. A small play area was built for Manuela,
with a big playhouse stuffed with toys and dolls. On his forty-second birthday, December 1, 1991, they threw a party. His mother presented him with
two big Russian fur caps, which Pablo announced would henceforth be his
trademark. Just as Che Guevara had worn a beret and Fidel Castro was
know for his beard and cigars, Pablo would be known for his big fur caps.
Family and friends dined on stuffed turkey, caviar, fresh salmon, smoked
trout, and potato salad. Pablo posed for pictures at the table with Maria

Victoria and their two children, with his mother standing proudly behind them.

It was not a normal prison in other ways. Pablo, for instance, did not feel obliged to actually stay. He rarely missed an important pro soccer game in Medellín—police would block off traffic to allow Pablo's motorcade easy access to and from the stadium he had built years before—and he was sighted shopping in a fashionable Bogotá mall over the Christmas holidays. In June 1992 he celebrated the first anniversary of his imprisonment with his friends and family at an Envigado nightclub. Pablo considered such excursions minor . . . he did, after all, always come back. He had made his deal with the state and intended to honor it—even if he did put one over on his jailors now and then.

To pass time, the inmates lifted weights, rode exercise bikes, and played soccer. Pablo would play for hours at a time. He always played center forward, even though he wasn't the quickest or most skilled player and he had a bad knee. His men always let him win, sometimes arranging for him to kick the winning goal. If Pablo grew winded, which was often, he would wave in a replacement until he caught his breath, and then he'd plunge back in. Uribe once waited four hours for Pablo to finish playing before they could talk. Prison guards served drinks to the inmates on the sidelines and doubled as waiters in the bar afterward. Despite the long hours of play, Pablo and the other men were growing fatter by the week. They liked to dine on the typical Antioquian fare of beans, pork, eggs, and rice. Pablo and the others had entered the prison intending to use the time to lose weight and get in shape, but after the first few months this resolution crumbled and most of the exercise equipment stood idle. They still played soccer, but they drank a lot and smoked dope. Pablo grew talkative when he was stoned. He told Uribe once that he had been terrified of the stories of killings, bombing, kidnappings, and torture from *La Violencia* as a boy, but that as he grew older he realized that terrorism, as he put it, "was the atomic bomb for poor people. It is the only way for the poor to strike back."

Pablo still identified himself with the poor. He said he had been forced to turn violent because of government persecution, but he was confident that he remained popular with most Colombians, especially *his* people, the poor of Antioquia. He received letters from supporters every day. Women wrote, offering to visit him at the prison; supplicants wrote, asking for money to pay their debts. Pablo read and saved the letters, and he often responded, sometimes sending money. At night, after the other inmates were asleep, Pablo would pace on the veranda outside the living quarters almost until dawn, and then he would sleep until midafternoon.

Prison was a welcome hiatus for nearly all concerned, but it was not without risks. So long as he remained at *La Catedral,* his enemies knew where to find him. That was why he had selected this site on a steeply sloping mountainside, built the cabanas uphill, buried an arsenal, and scouted out avenues of retreat up and over the top of the hill. He had looked at several locations in Antioquia for the prison, and he'd liked the layout of this one best. On a visit there months earlier with his brother Roberto, Pablo had said, "This is the place, brother. Do you realize that after six in the evening it fogs over and is foggy at dawn, too?" That would discourage a surprise aerial assault and give them ample cover if they decided to flee. He had his men string wires high over the soccer field to prevent helicopters from landing on the prison's one flat piece of ground.

There were also legal concerns. While Pablo was imprisoned, the government was working to build criminal cases against him. Just days after his surrender, he had been charged with being the "intellectual author" of the assassination of Galán. In September one of his top *sicarios,* Dandeny Muñoz, was arrested in New York City and charged with arranging to have a bomb placed on the Avianca airliner and with more than a hundred other killings. Weeks later, police found evidence at one of Pablo's estates linking him with the murder of newspaper editor Guillermo Cano. There was plenty for him to talk about with Uribe on his regular visits.

President Gaviria assigned the "Escobar problem" to a young lawyer on his staff who had been begging for something more important to do. Eduardo Mendoza had handled security for Gaviria during his presidential campaign, and as a reward had been appointed to a position in the Justice Ministry. He was inexperienced and naive, but he was honest, kind, and idealistic. His work in the campaign had earned him a place in the palace's inner circle, a group of advisers so young the press dubbed them Gaviria's *Jardín de Infancia,* or "kindergarten." Mendoza himself, a principled vegetarian, was particularly unimposing, a very slight man with thin brown hair that tended to flop across his forehead. Even in his well-fitting gray suit and with a bulky leather briefcase, he could be mistaken for a secondary school student. After naming him a vice minister of justice, the president had assigned him the task of *doing something* about the imprisoned Pablo Escobar.

Apart from finding a charge that could be made to stick, Mendoza was also instructed to build a real prison for the drug boss. The question of where such a prison could be built was already answered. The agreement with Pablo dictated that it must be at *La Catedral,* where Pablo and his men were already living. The new real prison would have to be constructed around the existing flimsy one, with Pablo inside. That was the plan. But who would build it? Mendoza knew that the Bureau of Prisons was thoroughly untrustworthy. It had a small engineering unit specifically charged with such tasks, but that group was the most corrupt of all. They stole everything. Mendoza was in the process of building a case against them when he hit on the idea of the Americans. They were the ones so eager to get Pablo seriously locked down. The Americans would be perfect. Mendoza began imagining an ideal prison that relied extensively on TV surveillance and electronic systems, which would minimize human contact with the prisoners, hence opportunities for intimidation and bribery. He had read about such high-security jails in the United States and seen stories about them on TV. So he flew to Washington, D.C., and presented his case at the State Department and at the National Bureau of Prisons, only to learn that the Americans were prohibited by law from helping to build prisons overseas. When he approached construction companies in Colombia directly, no one wanted the job. Everyone was terrified of Pablo. One major Colombian contractor told him, "We are not going to build a cage with the lion already inside."

He finally found a firm called General Security, owned by an Israeli "security expert" named Eitan Koren, who was willing to take the job. Blueprints were made, but before any money could be dispersed the project had to be approved by the controller's office. Mendoza's request languished there for months. The controller and his staff would not take calls from him or the minister of justice, failed to return calls, and refused to meet with them. Gaviria had to intervene personally to secure the necessary authorizations. When the work started, with laborers recruited from distant parts of Colombia so they were not linked to Pablo's Medellín empire, some of the new men refused to proceed after seeing Pablo's men sitting at the fence taking notes, writing down the license-plate numbers of vehicles entering and leaving the area. Then some of Escobar's men came out and challenged the work crews, knocking a few of the laborers down, and workmen resigned in droves. This caused another long delay. A squabble erupted in El Congreso when Mendoza revealed his plan to hire an elite workforce for his new high-tech prison. Recognizing the special difficulties of incarcerating the drug lord, Mendoza envisioned attracting a team of professional guards to run *La Catedral*, men with special training and technical skills. This would call for a higher pay scales, pensions, and medical benefits, which immediately ran afoul of the guardians of Colombian bureaucracy, civil service administrators. The whole matter bogged down like a tractor in a sinkhole. Watching from their embassy, the Americans interpreted all the confusion and delay as further evidence that Pablo was calling all the shots. When Mendoza thought about it from their perspective, how could they not think so?

Pablo was like a phantom. Even though he was ostensibly locked up, his power and menace were everywhere. Every once in a while, when he was displeased, like after construction work began around him, one of his army of lawyers would call the ministry to report that their client wished to turn over a large quantity of dynamite. They would direct the authorities to a truck, which would be found outside the home of a minister or beneath the windows of a government office, loaded with enough explosives to obliterate a city block. The press always found out, of course, and the story would come across as a munificent gesture by the imprisoned, reformed Don Pablo. But this was not disarmament. Mendoza and everyone else in the building knew very well that their "prisoner" had just delivered an unsubtle reminder that he, Pablo Escobar, held their lives in his hands. It was his way of saying, *Let's not hurt each other.*

Although Mendoza was frustrated by all these obstacles, he remained undaunted. Colombia was an old country but in some ways was still very young, one of the oldest democracies in the western hemisphere but one whose great institutions still rested on shaky ground. It remained a place that was largely unformed, where the idealism and industry of a young man could—or so Mendoza thought—still make a difference.

He had finally gotten construction started by the summer of 1992. The first new fences were slowly going up, much to Pablo's consternation, and new evidence against him mounted. The *PNC*, barred from the vicinity of *La Catedral*, set up electronic listening stations just beyond the

proscribed twenty-kilometer perimeter. Pablo was careful about his communications, using the pigeons for his most important messages, but others
in the prison talked freely. The police quickly established that *La Catedral*
was, in the words of the police major who ran the unit, "a grand business
center." The police monitored the steady flow of contraband into the
prison, the liquor and drugs and whores, but did nothing to stop it. They
merely observed, taped, filmed, and filed reports. Month after month, nothing happened. The police units responsible for this surveillance were disgusted by the weakness of their government. As they saw it, the Gaviria
administration was afraid to confront Escobar directly, so they hid behind
excessive concern for personal freedoms. This gave Pablo and his associates plenty of room to maneuver.

2

Throughout the first year of Pablo's imprisonment, the United States
embassy, the press, and many government officials—including Mendoza—
had urged Gaviria to end the charade. Everyone knew *La Catedral* was no
prison. Effectively, it was a state within the state. The surrender agreement had been a capitulation to violence, pure and simple, a deal with the
devil. Still, most of official Colombia were happy to live with it. Pablo was
like a dangerous snake that had been driven into a hole. The prevailing
attitude was: *Before, Pablo Escobar ruled Colombia; now he rules Envigado, so leave
him alone.*

The gringos were the only ones fixated on the drug trade. The new
U.S. ambassador, Morris D. Busby, kept pushing for action against Pablo
and the other cocaine exporters, but this was nothing new. The Americans wore blinders. They toiled behind the high walls of their fortress
embassy in north Bogotá, a modernist gray four-story structure that looked
like a bunker, shuttling back and forth to their secure apartments in armored cars, walled off from the general whirl of Colombian life. Between
the two peoples was envy, disdain, and a century-old grudge. The gringos
made things worse by suspecting all Colombians of corruption. Every
month that went by with Pablo camped on his mountaintop reinforced this
suspicion. Even the cheerful idealist Mendoza, when he visited the em-

bassy to ask for help building new criminal charges against Pablo, was treated with undisguised suspicion, as though he were a defense lawyer for the drug boss instead of his determined prosecutor.

Few in the U.S. embassy understood how hard it was to get things done. Even if Gaviria had wanted to act against Pablo, it would not have been easy. In America, perhaps, the president could order a thing and it would simply happen. In Colombia, everything was a fight. On paper, the president had power over all his ministries, but in reality, as Gaviria and all Colombian presidents before him discovered to their frustration, his authority was hopelessly diffuse. The army and the police and the secret police and the Justice Ministry were all fiefs, each made up of a multitude of smaller fiefs, all of them feuding and conspiring and plotting against one another.

In the case of Pablo, all were united in their unwillingness to get involved. The police, locked out by Pablo's deal, were eager to see the whole thing discredited. The judiciary wanted no part of prosecuting a man who had ordered the murder of every cop, judge, and jailer who had ever crossed him. The army was even worse. Mendoza had been cursed and thrown out of offices by generals who refused, in their own words, to become jailers.

Another fief eager to embarrass the president was the office of the attorney general, an independently elected position headed by a pipe-smoking former law professor named Gustavo de Greiff. The attorney general embarrassed the president in early 1992 by producing photographs of Pablo's scandalous luxuries in *La Catedral*—the waterbeds, Jacuzzis, expensive sound systems, giant-screen TVs, and other goodies.

When Mendoza investigated, however, he discovered that all of Pablo's furnishings were legal. They had been stamped and approved in efficient triplicate by his very own Bureau of Prisons. The bureaucrats had protected themselves well. The regulations allowed each prisoner a bed but gave no description of what kind. Likewise with bathtubs. Who could argue that a Jacuzzi was not a bathtub? Under the rules, a prisoner could be allowed a TV set for good behavior, and where did it say that the TV set couldn't have a wall-sized screen with a satellite hookup, VCR, and stereo speakers? The prison system had created a parallel world for Pablo. He lived in the equivalent of a resort, while on paper he was in a maximum-security prison.

Gaviria was furious.

"I want all of these things taken out immediately," he told Mendoza. "Tell the army to go in there and take everything out. Escobar has to know we're not kidding."

That was one of the times Mendoza had driven over to the Defense Ministry to seek help from Rafael Pardo, the minister of defense. Mendoza showed him the pictures and explained the president's order.

"No way," Pardo said. "I cannot do it because I don't have the people."

"But you have a hundred and twenty thousand men under arms!" said Mendoza.

Pardo and his generals were stubbornly indifferent.

The national police were out because of the deal, so Mendoza went next to the *DAS,* the secret police. They told him—*Perdon, Señor Vice Minister*—that unfortunately they were not allowed to intervene in a prison unless there was a riot. As comfortable as Pablo and his men were, that seemed an unlikely event.

Eventually, in desperation, Mendoza hired a truck and assigned a lawyer on his staff to drive up to the prison with a crew of men, load up all the TVs, recorders, and stereos, and drive them out.

"Eduardo, you are my friend," the lawyer pleaded with him. "What have I ever done to you? Why do you give me this assignment?"

Mendoza figured the truck would simply be turned away at the gate by Pablo's men, and he would have new ammunition to urge the army or secret police to act.

Instead, the gate to *La Catedral* swung open, and Pablo himself waved the crew in.

"Certainly, Doctor," said the drug boss, with his characteristic good manners. "I didn't know these things bothered you. Please, take everything out."

Pablo's men even helped to load the truck. Pictures were taken of the denuded quarters, which Mendoza proudly showed the president.

All of the goods, of course, were quietly replaced at *La Catedral* that evening.

But as time passed, the electronic communications started to reveal problems within Pablo's happy new kingdom. The walls that protected him also stood between him and normal hands-on management of the cartel.

For that, Pablo had to rely increasingly on a few powerful lieutenants, about whom he began to form suspicions.

Entrusted with a large portion of his cocaine empire were two families, the Galeanos and Moncadas, who were longtime players in Medellín. Both families had grown fabulously rich, even more so after Pablo's surrender, despite paying Pablo's "war tax" of $200,000 per month. Suspicious of the families' growing prosperity and of their loyalty, Pablo reportedly hiked their tax to $1 million a month, and then authorized some of his men to steal $20 million from the families' secret stash houses. When the heads of the two families, Fernando Galeano and Gerardo Moncada, visited *La Catedral* in the summer of 1992 to complain, they were lectured by the boss about his importance to the industry, about how he had established the early trade routes "so that others could benefit," and about how he, Pablo Escobar, had once and for all defeated the U.S.-Colombian extradition treaty. Then he had Galeano and Moncada killed. Days later, Pablo's *sicarios* tracked down the brothers of both men, Mario Galeano and William Moncada, and they, too, were killed.

The extended families of these four men geared up for war. Some of the less hard-core members went to the police, complaining that because the first two men had vanished after visiting *La Catedral*, the government of Colombia was complicit in their disappearance and evident murder. So it was that an exasperated President Gaviria was finally forced to act.

3

Mendoza was in his office at the Justice Ministry in Bogotá late Wednesday afternoon, July 21, 1992, when President Gaviria's chief of staff phoned to ask that he stop by the Presidential Palace. The vice minister of justice was helping to redraft the nation's criminal-procedure code, and he already had a meeting scheduled at the palace after lunch. He was working on a section of the proposed new constitution that would restore jury trials to Colombia; they had been stopped some years ago when *narco* assassinations had made it too dangerous to serve on a jury.

"That's perfect," Mendoza said with typical enthusiasm. "I'll get two things done at once."

When he arrived at the palace that afternoon he checked in on the drafting session and told the others he had to look in on the president.

"I'll be right back," he promised.

But he didn't return. Something big was happening upstairs. In the waiting area outside Gaviria's office there were generals in their crisp green uniforms and ministers in their well-tailored suits, staff people bustling, servants in white jackets offering hot coffee and tea on silver trays, phones ringing. Mendoza was ushered into a room with his own newly appointed boss, Justice Minister Andrés Gonzalez. With him was the dapper defense minister, Rafael Pardo, and one of Pardo's generals.

"Eduardo, we are at this moment attacking *La Catedral*," said Pardo. "You just missed it. We are attacking it with everything, and we are going to bring Escobar back to Bogotá."

Pardo knew this would be welcome news to Mendoza, of all people, who had begged him several times in vain for help with the Escobar problem. Pardo had always insisted that the military would not get involved. So his announcement was a significant capitulation. Mendoza tried not to show his pleasure.

Then Pardo surprised him.

"We want you to go there," he said.

"To legalize," said Gonzalez.

"Legalize?" Mendoza asked.

"You know, formalize the transfer," said Pardo.

This was typical. Little happened in Colombia that didn't require the presence of a lawyer. In a nation of such sweeping uncertainty, where the government itself could be toppled by a strong enough push, everyone was obsessed with self-protection. Just as one always traveled with bodyguards and built walls around his house, one made no official move without first digging a legal moat. Mendoza sensed that he was being handed the shovel. By dispatching a vice minister of justice to the scene, the officials in Bogotá would be shielded from blame if anything illegal or untoward occurred.

Still, Mendoza was excited. Something bold was afoot. At last the army was moving against Escobar, this monster, this menace to Colombian society. Real power was being flexed here, the legitimate power of the people. For once action had shouldered aside caution. It was heady, and for that moment everyone seemed pleased to be playing a part. Shrewd enough to know he was being used, Mendoza was nevertheless eager to accept a leading role.

Gaviria meant business. The president had seen reports of the executions Pablo had carried out from inside the jail. The bodies of one set of Moncada and Galeano brothers, Mario Galeano and William Moncada, had been found. For now, the discovery of the bodies remained a secret—not even Mendoza knew about them—but the president knew it would leak. His critics in the press would use the killings to prove all the rumors about Escobar and would claim that the Gaviria administration was in the pocket of the imprisoned *narco* king. The government would be further discredited in the eyes of the United States and the world, for whom it relied on assistance to combat the guerrillas. There would be inquiries and investigations. Gaviria had been embarrassed enough.

So he had decided. Pablo would be moved that day to a real prison. He had ordered the army to enter the sanctum, by storm if necessary, and take him. This step would violate the agreement he had made with Escobar, and Pablo's army of lawyers and their civil-libertarian allies would descend like a pestilence, but the drug lord had certainly violated the agreement himself by committing capital crimes in the "jail." Still, there were bound to be legal complications. That's where Mendoza came in.

He was instructed to fly to Medellín with Colonel Hernando Navas, the military director of prisons, to represent the administration on the ground.

"What exactly do you mean by formalize?" he asked again before he left.

"Look, everything is under control," said Pardo. "You just ask the general there for instructions. He'll know what to do."

"Am I to bring Pablo back to Bogotá?"

"Yes. We're moving him to a military base in Bogotá," answered the defense minister. "Now, run." Pardo said that one of the army's rapid deployment planes was waiting for him at the airport.

So Mendoza took off in his car, stopping to pick up Colonel Navas on the way. When he explained what was happening, the director of prisons shook his head.

"This is totally crazy," he said. "This is totally, absolutely crazy. You cannot do this to Escobar and get away with it."

Navas complained that they were just asking for more trouble. They had their agreement with Pablo, and so far he had honored it. Breaking it meant nothing short of going back to war. "This is going to kill lots of people," Navas said.

"Colonel, this is not my decision," said Mendoza. "We have been ordered to go and we are going to put him on a plane and bring him back."

As certain as he sounded to Navas, Mendoza was still unclear about what exactly he was supposed to do. They arrived at the airport to discover that the "rapid deployment" plane had no fuel. So while they waited for that to be remedied, Mendoza phoned the president's office again to ask for clarification. He asked to speak to his boss, the new justice minister.

"Andrés, I really don't understand what's going on. Tell me again, what exactly am I to do?"

"Look, if the prisoners give you any trouble, you tell them it is because of the construction. Tell them we are having problems because they have been bullying the workers. So we've had to move them temporarily out of the way."

As the wait for fuel stretched absurdly on into the evening, Mendoza called Defense Minister Pardo. Again he was told to report to the general in charge of the Fourth Brigade. "Just do whatever he tells you," said Pardo.

The flight to Medellín in the little Cessna took about forty minutes. It was still daylight when they took off, and Mendoza watched the land fall away as they flew northwest out of the Cordillera Central. The green mountains dropped suddenly to sea level, where the Magdalena River coursed through the valley between ranges. The river was already in darkness. Mendoza watched the sun ease slowly toward the snowcapped peaks of the Cordillera Central. Far to the south rose the towering peak of Nevado del Ruiz.

It was nearly dark when they landed outside Medellín. A jeep was waiting for them at Olaya Herrera Airport, and they drove east through the suburbs outside Medellín and then began climbing the hills toward the exclusive neighborhoods of Envigado. Past there the paved roads ended, and they wound their way up a steep, dirt road higher still into the mountains. This was Pablo's country, Mendoza realized. He noticed that with nightfall it had suddenly grown very cold. Mendoza turned up the collar of his business suit and listened for gunfire. He heard nothing. *It must all be over.* The jeep came to a halt on a dirt road just a short walk uphill from the outer prison gate. General Gustavo Pardo (no relation to the defense minister) strode up to the jeep as Mendoza and Navas stepped out. The general was wearing his neatly pressed green camouflage fatigues with a green jacket and cap, and he looked very determined and industrious. Mendoza had met him on several occasions and had always found him to be a serious, businesslike man. He liked him and was happy to see him there. The general greeted him warmly, but seemed less than his usual efficient self.

"Eduardo, what are your orders?" he asked.

"General, my orders are to take Escobar back to Bogotá."

"I have different orders," said the general. He explained that he had been told only to surround the prison and make sure no one entered it or left it. Mendoza was shocked. Nothing had happened! As far as he could see in the dark, there were soldiers milling around, waiting. So much for hitting *La Catedral* with everything.

"We have to check this out with Bogotá," Mendoza said.

When the orders were read again over the radio, they were entirely different from what Mendoza had been told that morning. He was disgusted. It was the worst thing about this government he served, exactly the thing that drove the Americans crazy and made Colombia seem so inept and corrupt. Orders might begin with great purpose and enthusiasm, but by the time they made their way down the chain of command, with everyone backing away from responsibility, pushing it off on someone else, the great machine of state always wound up confused, impotent, mired. Back in Bogotá, Gaviria's office had already issued a press release saying that Escobar had been transferred to another prison. Yet not a thing had happened at *La Catedral.*

"If they want Escobar, I'll go in there myself and get that *bandido* and tie him up and bring him out!" boasted the general. "But until my orders change...."

Mendoza explained the scene at the president's office that morning, when the top officials in the government believed the raid on the prison was under way. He said they would be angry to learn that nothing had happened.

"This is very, very confusing," the general said, and he startled Mendoza by asking, "Do you think we should do this tonight, or should we wait until tomorrow morning?"

"General, look, I have no idea," said Mendoza. "I was sent to do this immediately. I thought it had already been done. I don't have the authority to tell you to wait until tomorrow. Maybe if it would be easier for you to do it in daylight, maybe we should wait, but I'm not a military officer. I don't know. Let's call Bogotá."

The general got back on his radio phone. Mendoza was annoyed when he heard him say, "I'm here with the vice minister, and he wants me to do this thing tomorrow." Then the general hung up the phone and invited Mendoza to join him for a nice dinner at a restaurant in Medellín.

The president's office called back, for Mendoza. The caller, a presidential military aide, told Mendoza that the president was furious. He had been sent to observe; why was he interfering with a military operation? Mendoza didn't have time to defend himself or explain. He said he would try to get something done. It was clear that no one wanted to assume responsibility, so he decided to take charge himself.

"You must do it tonight," he instructed the general. *"Immediately."*

But the general again delayed. He seemed determined to do nothing. He phoned his own superiors again, and together they came up with the idea of sending Mendoza's companion, Colonel Navas, into the jail to check things out, gather intelligence. By now, of course, because of radio and TV reports, Escobar and the rest of the country knew that armed forces were massing around his prison. Any hope for surprise was gone. For the first time Mendoza began to worry that Escobar was going to escape. The hunt for Pablo had consumed years and thousands of lives and many millions of American dollars and Colombian pesos. Escobar was the most famous prison inmate in the world. His incarceration was vital to Colombia's standing as a modern, law-abiding nation. Mendoza could just imagine the embarrassment if he were somehow to get away. Any faith he might have had in General Pardo and his four-hundred-man Fourth Brigade was fast eroding.

Mendoza argued with Navas for a moment about going in. "I should be the one to go in, not you," he said, since he was nominally Navas's superior.

"No, no, no, Doctor. Don't worry about it. We have control."

Mendoza felt relieved when the colonel started downhill toward the main gate and disappeared into the darkness. Navas shouted, "Open up!" and they heard the squeak of the gate.

It was forty-five minutes before Navas returned.

"Well, the situation is under control, but these people are very scared," he said. "They told me that they will start blowing the place up if the army tries to come in and take Escobar, which is what they hear on the radio is about to happen." Then he turned to Mendoza. "Doctor, if you were to go in there and explain what is going on and calm them down, we may be able to save a lot of lives."

Mendoza decided to go in. He was tired and cold and frustrated. Maybe he could force this thing to happen, and without bloodshed. So he walked with Navas down the hill toward the gate. When it swung open for them, the guards, all technically Ministry of Justice employees, lined up and snapped to attention.

"Señor Vice Minister, welcome to *La Catedral*," said the captain, reeling off with practiced formality the number of inmates and the number of prison guards and what weapons they had, and concluding with a reassuring, "All is quiet."

Mendoza noticed that he was trembling, and not just because of the cold. He was about to meet the notorious outlaw Pablo Escobar face-to-face, and he knew Pablo would be angry. The slender young lawyer reasoned sternly with himself. He was a vice minister of justice for the Republic of Colombia. With him was Hernando Navas, the director of the Bureau of Prisons, and surrounding them were fifteen armed prison guards. They were here representing the power of a nation. And what was Pablo? A prison inmate. A criminal. Mendoza's job was to inform him that he was being transferred to a different prison. It was a simple matter, and, as Mendoza saw it, he had all the power. He stuck his hands in his pockets to stop them from shaking.

The dirt road wound downhill in blackness. Up ahead he saw light. It was from a single bulb, suspended from a wire attached to another stretched across the road, and it threw a big circle of light on the ground. Just to the left of the circle, at the edge of the shadow, stood a short, fat man. A group of about a dozen other men stood arrayed behind him like, Mendoza thought, the chorus in a Greek play. The fat man, who looked to be about forty years old, had to be Pablo, but he seemed much shorter, fatter, and less imposing than Mendoza had imagined. He wore jeans, bright white Velcro-strapped sneakers, and a thick dark jacket. His black hair was wet and slicked back, as though he had just showered. He was clean-shaven. In most pictures, even those going back to the earliest arrests in Medellín, Pablo had a mustache. Before Mendoza now was just a round little man with a fleshy face and broad double chin. Prison food must have agreed with him, Mendoza thought. Nearly all the men behind him were fat, too, like men with nothing to do but eat. None of them appeared to be armed, which made Mendoza relax. He felt he was in control of the situation.

"Good evening, Doctor," said Pablo, softly, calmly, but without a smile.

Mendoza introduced himself and shook the prisoner's hand. He had rehearsed many times that evening the speech he would make when he finally met Pablo, but now when he tried to speak, his voice squeaked. He swallowed and forced out the words as authoritatively as he could. "As you have no doubt heard, you are going to be transferred—"

"You have betrayed me, Señor Vice Minister," Pablo interrupted. He spoke softly but was clearly angry. "President Gaviria has betrayed me. You are going to pay for this and this country is going to pay for this, because I have an agreement and you are breaking the agreement."

Mendoza did not know what to say to this, so he resumed the statement he had rehearsed. "You have nothing to fear for your life," he said.

"You are doing this to deliver me to the Americans," said Pablo.

"No, we—"

"Kill them!" shouted one of Pablo's men.

"Sons of bitches!" shouted another. Mendoza glanced at the guards who had escorted him in. They all looked away.

"You are going to deliver me to Bush so that he can parade me, before the election, just like he did with Manuel Antonio Noriega," Pablo said, "and I'm not going to allow that, Doctor."

"We should have killed this one during the campaign!" one of the men shouted. "It would have been easy!"

"Look," said Mendoza. "It would be unconstitutional for us to send you to the United States." This was true. The new constitution forbade extradition.

"Then you are going to kill me," Pablo said. "You are going to take me out of here and have me killed. Before I allow that to happen, many people will die."

"Let us kill them, *patrón!*" one of his men pleaded.

"Do you really think they are going to send someone like me to kill you?" Mendoza said. "There are hundreds of soldiers outside and other officials—do you think we would send for this many witnesses if we were going to kill you? This is just not reasonable. I will stay with you, if you want, all night. Wherever you go, you are a prisoner and we are obligated to guarantee your safety. So you don't have anything to worry about."

Escobar just glared at him silently.

"All we have to do is finish the prison, and we can't do that with you here."

"No, no, no, Doctor," said Escobar. "That problem we had with the workers, that was just a misunderstanding."

Mendoza could see that Pablo did not want his deal with the government to break down. The vice minister again felt as if he had some leverage.

"Look, I'm going to walk out of here; I will be right out there," said Mendoza, pointing back up the road he had walked in on. "We are going to deliver the prison to the army, and I will be out there and I will stay with you guys wherever you are going."

Pablo said nothing. He looked away toward the fences, as if trying to see through the night whatever forces were arrayed against him. He seemed to be thinking hard, calculating.

Mendoza decided he had said everything that needed saying.

"I'll talk to you later," he said, and turned with Navas and the guards and started walking back toward the gate. It surprised him, but it appeared as though Pablo was going to let them go. Behind him he heard the drug boss's men pleading, "*Patrón!* That son of a bitch is going to betray us. We should kill them all! Are you going to let them walk out?"

Mendoza did not turn around. They were almost to the gate when they heard the men running to overtake them, and then they were surrounded. Pablo's men now had automatic weapons, which Mendoza realized must have been hidden under their jackets. When Mendoza looked to his armed guards, urging them to do something, the men drew up their weapons and pointed them . . . at *him!* The moment struck Mendoza with the force of revelation.

Welcome to the real world. What a fool he had been! *He* wasn't the authority here! Mendoza turned to Navas, who made a pained, helpless expression.

"*Patrón,* look! Look! They are sending messages to each other!" screamed a round-faced thug with slightly crossed eyes, a man shorter than Pablo who, unlike the others, looked lean and wild. This was the one they called Popeye, the notorious Medellín *sicario* Jhon Jairo Velasquez. Popeye bounced in agitation from foot to foot and screamed, "Kill him! Kill him, the son of a bitch!"

Pablo's men began pushing them back downhill. Mendoza looked at the ground as he walked. His mind raced, trying out different scenarios for how this would turn out, none of them good. He would reflect on this later, on the cliché that a condemned man in his last moments sees his life pass before his eyes, and it wasn't true. He thought of nothing except his next footfall. He had never felt so completely focused on a particular moment in time. He was scared, very scared, but also oddly calm. He wasn't angry, not even at the guards who had just betrayed him. Who was he to them? Some pampered son of Bogotá, an effete rich kid—he felt as powerless as a child—come to order them around with his important title and his fancy business suit. He knew they couldn't do otherwise. The best word for how he felt was impotent. Utterly impotent. And foolish, for having believed that his words would carry some weight inside this prison. There was nothing he could say or do to help himself. What was going on now was just about power, about who had the most guns at this place, at this time. He was now in the hands of the most notorious killer in Colombian history, a man who had ordered the deaths of thousands, including generals, judges, presidential candidates, Supreme Court justices—what chance did he have of coming out of this alive? His eyes searched the path as they walked, and he wondered, *At what spot along this path will I die?*

At the door to the warden's house, Popeye suddenly grabbed Mendoza and threw him through the entranceway and into a wall, pressing the barrel of an automatic pistol to the side of his face and screaming, "I'm going to kill the guy! I've always wanted to kill a vice minister!" Then, thrusting his face right into Mendoza's, he yelled, "You son of a bitch. You motherfucker. You have been trying to get us for years, and now I will get you." Popeye used a peculiar Medellín euphemism for killing. The term he used was *despegue,* or "takeoff," in the sense of launching someone into the grave, or the afterlife. Mendoza was so frightened that he felt removed, as if he were

watching the scene outside himself, as though it were happening to someone else. Popeye moaned and pleaded like a psychopath.

Roberto Escobar, Pablo's brother, intervened, speaking to Popeye
calmly, respectfully. "Popeye, you know, not now. Maybe later. Relax. He's
worth more to us alive at this moment."

They sat Mendoza down on a sofa in the warden's living room, and
Pablo addressed him. The drug boss now had a pistol in his hand. "Señor
Vice Minister," he said. "From this moment you are my prisoner. If the
army comes, you will be the first to die."

"Don't think that by retaining me you will stop them," Mendoza said,
believing his argument. "If you take us hostage you can forget about everything. They have heavy machine guns, loads of them. They'll kill everybody here! You can't escape!"

Pablo laughed.

"Doctor," he said, speaking softly, leaning in close to Mendoza. "You
still don't understand. These people all work for me."

Then everyone began to make phone calls. There were so many phones
it was comical. There was a whole bank of regular phones connected to wires,
and most of the men had cell phones. Mendoza remembered all the memos
that had crossed his desk in the past year requesting authorization for one
or two new phone lines for *La Catedral*, arguing that without the new lines
they would have no way of calling for help in an emergency.

"Why was I getting all these requests for phones?" he asked Navas.
"This place looks like a Telecom center."

Again Pablo laughed. Moments later he was on the phone with someone, evidently a lawyer. Others were talking to family members who had
been seeing the reports on TV. Mendoza heard Pablo talking to his wife,
calming her.

"We're having a little problem here. We're trying to solve it. You
know what to do if it doesn't work."

Then he handed Mendoza the cell phone.

"Call the president," he demanded.

"The president will not take the phone," Mendoza said.

"Get somebody to take the phone, because you are about to die."

Mendoza dialed the president's office, and the phone was answered
by Miguel Silva, a staff worker for the president and a friend of Mendoza's.

"You are being held hostage?" Silva asked.

"Yes."

Silva abruptly hung up.

"Let me kill him, *patrón*," pleaded Popeye.

Then Escobar disappeared, and Mendoza waited. How had he gotten himself into this fix? Look what a mess he had made of the assignment given to him by his friend the president, who had asked him to solve the problem of Pablo Escobar. Ha! What a fool he had been to believe in the power of the state. Mendoza had always known that the *narcos,* and particularly Pablo Escobar, wielded tremendous influence, but the ultimate authority, he had always assumed, rested with the state. Once the government roused itself, he felt sure, it would throw off these evil, violent men. That's why he had never lost heart in the years of battling with everyone to do something about Pablo, and why he had stepped forward tonight to confront the man himself in the jail. Surely once Escobar saw that the government really meant business, that an entire brigade of the army had him surrounded, he would realize that he was outgunned and would back down. But now it was clear that the opposite was true. Mendoza had sat in the Presidential Palace that morning and felt the enthusiasm and energy of a nation deciding to act. They had confronted Pablo and . . . who had backed down? The troops outside seemed frozen in place. Suddenly General Pardo's reluctance to move in seemed less the product of bureaucratic confusion and more the posture of a man who was too frightened to act. And that was the kind interpretation. Perhaps it was corruption; perhaps the general had been paid not to act. Mendoza felt so stupid. *These people all work for me.*

Still, he did not feel angry with himself. He, Eduardo Mendoza, had done what he could. All through that year he had pushed for a crackdown on Pablo, and he had entered this prison with the hope of saving lives. Remembering Pablo's dynamite trucks and assassination squads, he reflected, *I tried to save as many people as I could.* With that thought he resigned himself to his fate.

The drug lord returned after about five minutes. The pistol he had held in his hand was now tucked in his pants. Mendoza had the distinct impression that Escobar had talked to someone, probably a lawyer, because his manner was different. He plopped down beside Mendoza on the sofa.

"Doctor, you are detained, but you are not going to be killed," he said. "If anyone touches you, he will have to answer to me."

"You cannot escape from here," Mendoza said. "The army has the prison surrounded."

Escobar smiled at him patronizingly.

"You had an agreement with me, and you are breaking it."

Mendoza had decided not to argue with him. Then Escobar said something that Mendoza didn't understand. "Doctor, I know you guys are worried about those killings. Don't worry. These are problems among mafioso. They do not concern you."

Then Escobar stood up and left the room, and Mendoza did not see him again.

He and Navas were taken back out into the prison and marched up to wait in Pablo's "cell," a spacious suite, handsomely furnished. Mendoza noted that all the items that had supposedly been removed months ago were back in place—stereo equipment, big-screen TV, giant bed. He wondered if they had ever been removed.

Popeye and another gunman kept watch over them. Popeye had exchanged his automatic pistol for a shotgun. Now and then he would strut up to Mendoza, pump it once or twice, and grin. Mendoza just sat and waited. He no longer worried as much about being killed by Popeye, but was certain that he would die when, and if, the army invaded.

They sat like that through the night. Mendoza wrapped a poncho around his shoulders, but it didn't do much to ward off the chill.

4

At the Presidential Palace, Gaviria didn't hesitate when he heard his friend had been taken hostage. *Why in the world had Eduardo gone into the jail? What a stupid, stupid thing to do!* The president had planned a trip to Spain for that evening to take part in celebrations marking the five hundredth anniversary of Columbus's arrival in the Americas. He had postponed the trip in the afternoon, as this crisis at *La Catedral* had worsened. Now he demanded that the general outside the prison attack immediately—and the general refused.

He refused!

Gaviria ordered Defense Minister Rafael Pardo to send a special forces unit to Envigado immediately to make the assault. Speechwriters at the palace began working on a draft of a statement the president would make to the nation the following morning. In the statement, the president would say, unfortunately, Eduardo Mendoza, his friend and vice minister of justice, and Hernando Navas, the national director of prisons, had been tragically killed in the shoot-out.

When the special forces units arrived at El Dorado Airport in Bogotá, there were no pilots on hand to fly the C-130 transport. So they waited for pilots. It was 4:30 A.M. when the strike force finally descended toward José María Córdova Airport in Rionegro, outside Medellín. The dense fog prevented them from landing for a time, and it was early in the morning before they could start up the mountain in trucks. On the way up, regular army units steered them along the wrong road, which took them back down to the airport.

The blundering progress of this strike force was being reported on radio and TV nationally, and observed by the prisoners inside *La Catedral,* and their hostages. They all waited in a state of anxious boredom.

"How do you manage to keep so slender?" Mendoza was asked by one of the gunmen, a thick, dark-haired man with a wide belly.

"I'm a vegetarian."

"What should I eat to lose weight?" he asked.

Mendoza told him to try eating more fruits and vegetables.

At about two o'clock in the morning the man left; he reappeared carrying a plate filled with apple slices.

"Now I am going to start a healthy diet," he said.

"What are you going to do that for?" asked Popeye. "We're all going to be dead by seven o'clock."

Mendoza certainly thought so. He could hear the preparations on the shortwave radio. He heard when a special forces unit finally arrived and relieved the reluctant general outside. Then he heard the various units readying themselves, calling in with their bizarre code names, checking off their readiness.

Mendoza was familiar with this unit, and what he knew scared him. It had been created after the debacle in 1985, when the guerrilla group M-19 had stormed the Palace of Justice and taken three hundred hostages, including most of the nation's Supreme Court. When the government took the ministry back by force, the raid killed more than one hundred people, including eleven justices. This disaster had prompted the creation of an American-trained special forces unit recruited from both the army and the national police. Shortly after the unit was formed, Mendoza was at his office in Bogotá when he got an emergency phone call telling him that the U.S. embassy nearby was being violently attacked. He phoned a friend at the embassy who told him all was quiet there.

"Then could it be the ambassador's residence?" Mendoza asked.

"I'll check," his friend said.

He called back seconds later.

"No, Eduardo, the ambassador's residence is quiet; it's *your* building that's under attack!"

The police were conducting a raid at his own apartment building nearby. Months later, when it was all sorted out, it was revealed that the new special forces unit had been hired by a rich Bogotá emerald and drug dealer to assassinate a rival and make it look like a government operation. The plan had backfired because the primary target of the hit had crawled through the ceiling and escaped. Every other person in the suite had been killed. In the ensuing scandal the unit had been disbanded, its leadership fired. It had only recently been reconstituted, and this mission, here at *La Catedral*, was the first time President Gaviria had ordered them into action. Mendoza was now terrified to be on the receiving end of its assault. He knew that, unlike the timid army brigade, these men would attack, furiously.

"Can I go outside for a look?" he asked his captors.

They let him step out on the porch. Sunlight had begun to illuminate the fog, but he still could not see for more than a few feet. Beside him, just outside the door to Escobar's room, was a table covered with machine guns and ammunition. He took off the poncho, even though he was freezing, and stood out in the cold, hoping that the attacking forces would see his business suit and not shoot him. As he stood there shaking, he heard the first shots of the assault. There were explosions and screams.

His captors pulled him inside and began to plead with him.

"Doctor! Please! They are going to kill us! Help us!"

"I've been telling you that all night!" Mendoza shouted at them. "Now it's too late!"

He crawled toward the bathroom and tried to curl himself up behind the toilet, the sturdiest fixture, but then decided it was too dangerous there because there was so much glass that would shatter. He crawled back out to the living room, where Navas and one of the prison guards were crouching. Mendoza was terrified. The sound of shooting and explosions was louder now. In a kind of trance, he stood and tried to walk out of the room, hoping to see the attacking forces and speak to them, but a prison guard screamed at him to get on the floor unless he wanted to be killed.

He tried to move Pablo's mattress to get behind it, but it was too heavy. Even with one of the gunmen helping, they couldn't budge it. So Mendoza, exhausted and numb with cold and fear, gave up. He stretched prone on the floor and waited. He looked at the gunmen arrayed around him in the room and thought, *This is how I'm going to die.*

But he did not die. A concussion grenade exploded just outside the room, and as he instinctively recoiled, a gun barrel was jammed against his forehead. The invader, a black Colombian special forces sergeant, didn't shoot. A powerful man, he threw the vice minister against the wall and sat on him. Mendoza stayed pinned under the man through shooting and explosions. When it was clear that Pablo's gunmen had surrendered the room without a fight, the sergeant turned to him. Mendoza saw a kind face, with deep wrinkles at the eyes.

"We're going to try to get out of here," the soldier said. "Just look at my boot. Don't think of anything. Just look at my boot."

He began crawling, and Mendoza followed. They crawled out to the porch and behind a short brick wall, past a row of doors.

"When I tell you to run, run," the sergeant ordered. On cue, Mendoza leapt up and took off uphill for the main gate as fast as he could go, arms churning, blinded by the smoke, confused by the explosions and gunfire. The officer ran behind him shouting, "Run! Run! Run!" and Mendoza sprinted faster than he ever had. He ran so recklessly and hard that he careened into a wall, breaking two ribs, but kept on running in such a lunging panic that he felt no pain and would discover the broken bones only later. He ran out the main gate and up the hill to where General Pardo and his men were positioned, right where he had left them hours before.

"General, is Escobar dead?" Mendoza gasped.

Pardo said nothing. He stared at him with a vacant, slightly amused expression and shrugged. It instantly dawned on Mendoza what had happened.

"Oh, my God!" Mendoza cried. "He got away? How could he get away!"

5

Morris D. Busby, the U.S. ambassador to Colombia, was awakened by two phone calls early on Wednesday, July 22, 1992, at a house in Chevy Chase, Maryland, where he and his wife were staying with friends. Both calls were from the embassy in Bogatá. The first was welcome news. Colombian President César Gaviria had finally decided to move Pablo Escobar to a new prison, something Busby had been urging for some time, and the transfer was under way. Shortly after that call came another, telling him that Pablo had somehow escaped through an entire brigade of the Colombian army, roughly four hundred men. The ambassador had spent too much time in Colombia to be surprised by that. He cut short his vacation and flew back to Bogotá later that morning.

This embarrassing turn of events for Colombia might be just the break he needed. Ever since he had been assigned to the embassy in Bogotá the previous year, handpicked for the assignment in large part because it had become such a dangerous one, Busby had been eager to make an example of Escobar, but was frustrated by the drug boss's deal with the government. Here was the most notorious drug trafficker in the world perched on a spectacular Andes mountaintop, running his cocaine business surrounded and protected by the Colombian army. Current estimates were that seventy to eighty tons of cocaine were being shipped from Colombia to the United States every month, and Pablo controlled the bulk of it.

At the Presidential Palace later that same day, Busby found President Gaviria furiously pacing in his office. Gaviria had been up all night receiving one outrageous report after another. The whole episode illustrated his powerlessness. It had taken more than two years, hundreds of lives, and hundreds of millions of dollars to hound the murderous drug billionaire into his surrender. Now, in one night, it had all come undone. Waiting through the president's lamentations were Joe Toft, the flinty DEA Country Attache, and Bill Wagner, the "political secretary" who was in fact Bogotá's CIA station chief.

Gaviria was fed up. He had been living with the threat of Pablo Escobar for years. All the time he'd campaigned for president he had *expected* to be killed by the drug boss. He had seen him in person only once, in 1983, the day Pablo had taken his seat in Congress. The short, mild-mannered economist's fondest hope on taking office two years before was for Pablo to just go away, at least for a while. Colombia was in the midst of rewriting its constitution, an enormously important and historic task that could establish a stable undergirding for the nation for the first time since *La Violencia*. The rebels in the mountains and jungles were on the run. The government had ended, at least temporarily, the raging *narco* violence by striking their deal with Pablo. A new constitution, assuring democratic representation and addressing some of the long-simmering land-use issues at the heart of the civil war, would strengthen the state and further disarm the guerrillas, and would assure an impressive legacy for Gaviria. The last thing he needed was for this damned outlaw to be running loose again, setting off his truck and car bombs and unleashing his *sicarios*, sowing fear, corruption, and dissent. That Pablo had been able to simply vanish from his "maximum-security prison" was a huge international setback, confirming all of the worst assumptions about the country. It made Colombia look like a narcocracy.

The president was sure of one thing. This was the last time he and the country would be humiliated by Pablo Escobar. There would be no more deals, no more special prisons. Pablo would be hunted down and killed. It was a terrible thing to hunt down a man as you would an animal, but now there was no other way. Pablo was a criminal with no restraints, no boundaries. He could do anything; he *would* do anything.

The president continued to pace and vent. Who had ever had to face down a criminal like this? What country had ever been held hostage like this by one terrible man? What leader of a nation of twenty-seven million people had ever felt his own life was at stake in the pursuit of a criminal? Someone with the power to walk right out of prison and through an entire brigade of the army. An entire brigade!

Busby was used to the president's gusty temper. He admired Gaviria's courage, but he did not find him an especially charismatic man. Squeaky-voiced, moody, and introspective, Gaviria didn't convey much that was obviously impressive or presidential to the ambassador, even though he was almost classically handsome, with his dark hair and strong chin. Busby found the president and the others in his administration to be pleasant, well educated, idealistic, and hopelessly naive. They tended to be polite upper-middle-class sophisticates who trusted that everyone down deep

was basically decent and well-meaning. They hadn't stood a chance bargaining against a tough, streetwise gangster like Pablo Escobar, who was
as well-meaning as a scorpion. To someone like Pablo, the trusting nature of a man like Gaviria was an invitation. The *narcos* played with these
effete Bogotá boys.

Still, Busby had hopes for Gaviria. He had nice manners, but he was
also powerfully ambitious. He had risked his life to get this job, braving
intense, real danger daily. To do that required principled toughness, and
this was what gave the ambassador hope. A man like that, if he was frustrated and angry enough, could turn cold and calculating.

"An entire brigade!" Gaviria shouted in amazement. "And the general
allows two officials inside the prison to talk to him! For what? To *notify*
him that he was going to be taken? What did he expect would happen! Such
a stupid thing! I mean, such a stupid thing!"

The scene at *La Catedral* remained chaotic. One guard had been killed
in the raid, a sergeant who had been employed by the Bureau of Prisons.
Two Bureau of Prisons guards had been wounded. Five of Pablo's men
had been captured. The army was insisting that Pablo must still be inside
the jail in a carefully prepared hiding place, so their forces were tearing
the place apart. Hoping to collapse a tunnel, they were detonating explosives out on the soccer field. Mendoza, the hapless vice minister Pablo had
held captive the night before, was back in Bogotá and, at Gaviria's insis-
tence, telling his story to all who would listen. "We must hide nothing in
this," the president had told him. "Don't take time to prepare a response;
just get out there and tell people exactly what happened."

It hadn't dawned on Mendoza yet how bad this was all starting to look
for him. So he did as instructed. After briefing the generals and the Americans
he went before microphones and cameras and told his story on national TV.

Wagner then invited the shaken vice minister over to his house, and
Mendoza told the story of the whole episode again while it was still fresh
in his mind. Unshaven, haggard, and up for nearly two days without sleep,
he still had a sense of humor. He told the CIA man that he would be surprised by how much of a man's body could be hidden behind a toilet. He
said that while he waited for the raid to begin, he had heard the steady
sound of a pickax being used in an adjacent room, which supported the
theory that Pablo had escaped by way of a tunnel.

Bogotá was in a frenzy of blame. Defense Minister Rafael Pardo was arguing that despite the abysmal performance of the army, if Pablo had escaped through a tunnel, the escape was the fault of the Justice Ministry, which supervised the Bureau of Prisons. Meanwhile, Mendoza's boss the justice minister was blaming the army for failing to act until Pablo got away, and for apparently looking the other way as he walked off. Journalists were asking if the escape had resulted from corruption or incompetence or both, and how high up it went. There would be investigations, indictments, heads would roll, and people were going to go to jail. Everyone assumed the *narco* violence was about to resume.

At the U.S. embassy the night before, while the standoff at the prison had still been under way, DEA chief Toft had been more excited than alarmed by these events. Bolivian by birth, he was a tall, lean man with a leathery, deeply lined face. An avid tennis player with short-cropped, spiky hair, he cultivated a flashy, tough-guy look, with his leather jacket and his handgun strapped to his belt. Toft had grown up in the Bay Area of California and had started out as a customs agent. He had been one of the first men assigned to the DEA when it was established in 1973. He was one of the administration's first foreign agents, having worked in Rome and Madrid before coming back to the States to take over the Latin America desk. He was known to be fearless and ambitious, someone who welcomed dangerous work, so he was a natural choice for the job in Bogotá. It was the world capital of cocaine, the front line of the war on drugs. Toft embraced the risk. He had been divorced and then remarried just before he left for Colombia, but for security reasons had left his new wife and stepchildren behind. So he plunged into the work alone, sleeping behind steel-reinforced doors with an automatic pistol by his side. For the bureaucrats in Washington, the drug war was an abstraction, a game of tons seized and traffickers indicted. For Toft and his men, it was real war, with bullets and blood. He recognized Pablo's escape as an opportunity. The drug boss would be fair game again, and the DEA chief was a man who thrilled to the chase. So long as Gaviria didn't capitulate, this time they would hunt Pablo down. In a cable to headquarters in Washington, D.C., hours before he had gotten confirmation of Pablo's escape, Toft had written:

The BCO [Bogotá country office/ the U. S. embassy] feels that Escobar may finally have overstepped his self-perceived illegitimate boundaries and has placed himself in a very precarious position. Escobar's gall and bravado may lead to his ultimate downfall. But then again, the GOC [government of Colombia] has always bowed to Escobar's demands in the past. This current situation again provides the GOC with an opportunity to demonstrate its dedication to bring all narco-traffickers to justice, including the most notorious and dangerous cocaine trafficker in history, Pablo Escobar.

Gaviria seemed insulted and embarrassed enough to see the effort through this time, no matter how rough or distasteful. He told the Americans that as far as he was concerned, the door was now open. Despite constitutional barriers to foreign troops on Colombian soil, Gaviria said he would welcome any and all help the Americans could give:

"This is critical, please," he told the ambassador. "Help us get this guy as soon as possible."

Pablo had done his enemies a favor. There were three indictments awaiting him in the United States. President Bush's Justice Department had determined that U.S. military forces had the authority to arrest foreign nationals and bring them back to the States for trial. They had done it with Manuel Noriega. For several years Colombia had now accepted military training and eavesdropping assistance from the United States, including Centra Spike, but the U.S. military had always been kept at arm's length, and very low-key. There was enough historical resentment of U.S. power and interference in Latin America to cause serious political consequences for Gaviria if a major American presence became public.

The help requested would be needed fast. If Pablo was not apprehended soon, before he had a chance to securely set himself up as a fugitive, the search might drag on for months, or years. He had spent a lifetime building criminal associations, and he had virtually limitless resources. His wealth and reputation for violence ensured loyalty where his popularity did not. Ensconced in his home city of Medellín, in his home state of Antioquia, he was king of the mountain.

Like Toft, Ambassador Busby relished the opportunity provided by Pablo's escape. It was the kind of task he was cut out for. He originally had been a military man, joining the navy after graduating from Marshall College with a degree in physical education. Busby had served with a navy special forces unit that predated the SEALs, but he was often described as a "former SEAL," a mistake he was always quick to correct but that nevertheless added to his mystique. Busby did have close connections with

American special forces, but they stemmed not from his service in uniform as much as from the years he had served as ambassador at large for
counterterrorism in the State Department, a job that involved coordinating American diplomatic and covert military action throughout the world.
He was a military man who had adopted diplomacy as a second career,
which made him a new kind of diplomat.

To Colombians he looked like Uncle Sam himself, minus the white
goatee. He was tall and tan, with graying sandy hair and the long, powerful arms and hands of a man who was a skilled carpenter and who loved to
sail the waters of the Chesapeake Bay. In his first week in Bogotá, the
newsweekly *Semana* ran an article about him with a full-page photograph
showing the new ambassador from head to toe, eyeing the camera as if he
meant business. The story said that America had sent not a diplomat but a
warrior. It was not meant as a compliment, but Busby took it as one.

So did the new president, who asked Busby in their first meeting if
he had seen the piece. Busby said he had.

"Let me tell you something," said Gaviria. "You're just what we need."

The president and the article had Busby pegged right. Diplomacy
and war spring from different philosophical wells. The underlying premise
of diplomacy is that people, no matter what their differences, are well-
intentioned and can work together. Warriors believe in intractable evil.
Certain forces cannot be compromised with; they must simply be defeated. Busby could go either way, but he had the stomach for a fight if
it came to that. There was something about him that responded to the
moral simplicity of confrontation. He was an American patriot, a true
believer, and few circumstances in his career were more clear-cut than
the challenge posed by this man he considered a monster, Pablo Escobar.

6

On the day Pablo Escobar walked out of jail, the men of Centra Spike were
back in the United States. They had all been living off and on in Bogotá
under assumed names for more than two years. Ever since Pablo had retired to *La Catedral* the year before, the pace of the *narco* violence had
slowed, and the urgency of their mission had temporarily throttled back.
So after years of shuttling back and forth to work, along deliberately var-

ied routes in armored unmarked cars, shifting residences every few months, climbing back stairs to barren apartments locked down like bunkers, Major Steve Jacoby had used the slack time to pull most of his men and equipment out. Marriages and machines were in need of repair.

Word came as it usually did, on one of the bulky black phones they hauled everywhere like a ball shackled to their ankles, the STU-3, which was for secure calls.

"Get your act together and get back down to Bogotá."

The call came, you packed, you apologized, and you drove to the airport.

This time, though, Centra Spike was just a small part of the summons. Once word was relayed to Washington that Gaviria had opened the door to *anything,* everyone and his dog wanted in on the chase. Ever since Pablo's men had blown that Avianca flight out of the sky, the drug boss had been among the most wanted men in the world. There were fears that Pablo's *sicarios* planned a bombing campaign in America, and even that he had targeted the president of the United States.

Apart from these direct concerns, combating drugs had become a top national priority. In September 1989, Defense Secretary Dick Cheney had sent a memo to all top military commanders directing them to define counterdrug efforts as "a high-priority national mission" and requesting them to submit plans for increased military involvement. This was an invitation for various commands to define their relevance in the changing world. With the threat of worldwide communism evaporating, America's military and espionage community had become a high-priced, highly skilled workforce in search of a role. Not every general at the Pentagon or executive at the CIA was eager to get involved in combating narcotics, which many regarded as an expensive, difficult, and ultimately futile endeavor, but going after someone like Pablo Escobar was another story. He was a new kind of target for a new world, a *narco* terrorist. It didn't take a genius to foresee that big budget cuts loomed at the Pentagon, CIA, and NSA. One way to ensure survival in the era of deficit reduction was to prove how vital you were to this new struggle. Every overt and covert intelligence unit in the arsenal would want to prove that it was flexible and smart enough to be effective against this new kind of target. Pablo offered a test case, an opportunity for these agencies to prove themselves—the CIA, the

NSA, the FBI, the Bureau of Alcohol, Tobacco, and Firearms (ATF), the DEA, and the army, navy, and air force. All would want a piece.

Major Jacoby was back in Bogotá the next day, July 23, 1992. He joined a meeting in the fifth-floor vault with the ambassador. Busby looked like he hadn't slept.

"How long do you think it's going to take for you to find him?" the ambassador asked.

It had never taken Centra Spike long. Jacoby said maybe a day or two. Remembering the first war, they knew that the hard part wasn't finding Pablo; it was getting the Colombians to act. The Americans had little respect for the Colombian police or military. After the escape, the joke at the embassy went: "How many Colombian prison guards and soldiers does it take to let Pablo Escobar escape?" Answer: "Four hundred. One to open the gate and three hundred and ninety-nine to watch."

"No matter how good our intelligence is, and how hard they try, they just can't close the last thousand meters," said Jacoby. "With these guys, it just ain't gonna happen."

Busby pondered the resources at his disposal. The CIA was good at long-term intelligence gathering, not special ops. The DEA was law enforcement; they were good at street work, recruiting snitches, and building cases. The FBI in foreign countries did mostly liaison work. What they needed for this mission were manhunters, Delta Force, the army's elite and top-secret counterterrorism unit. Busby was familiar with the unit from his years as ambassador for counterterrorism. Nobody in the world could plan and perform a real-world op better than those guys. Colombian law forbade foreign troops on their soil, and it would really be pushing Gaviria's invitation, but the ambassador felt it was doable on the Colombian end. Delta was stealthy enough that the Colombian press would never find out they were involved. But he wasn't as sure about the American side of things. He felt it was unlikely that General Colin Powell, chairman of the Joint Chiefs, was the man to order such a move.

"What we need is Delta, but we could never get them," Busby said.

"Why not?" asked Jacoby. "I think you're wrong. If you ask, I think you'll get what you ask for."

In fact, General Wayne Downing, who headed the army's Special Operations Command, had expressed interest in such a mission several years earlier. In a meeting at Fort Bragg in 1989, he had asked one of Centra Spike's men to describe the kind of missions Delta might be able to perform in Colombia.

"What are our chances of going in and not getting anybody killed?" Downing had asked.

"Almost zero," he was told.

So the general had backed off. A dead American sergeant from Delta would provoke a major shit storm in Washington, bringing down all sorts of scrutiny he was not prepared to accept.

"None of these *narcos* is going to surrender peacefully," he was told. "If you go in you either have to take them all or kill them all."

But Downing had remained interested and had asked to be kept apprised of opportunities. At the meeting in Bogotá, Jacoby's response encouraged the ambassador.

"I guess there's no harm in asking," he said.

"Don't say you want them to come in here and go after Pablo themselves," Jacoby suggested. "That will never fly. Say you want them to offer training and advice."

They all agreed that Delta was the answer.

7

When Pablo walked out of jail, the hopeful Gaviria administration began to splinter. Every day a new official investigation began. The Ministry of Justice accused the army of accepting bribes to allow Pablo's flight; one widely circulated report held that Pablo had paid huge sums to the soldiers around *La Catedral*, and walked out dressed as a woman. President Gaviria had already fired all the guards and army officers associated with the disaster, as well as the air force general whose pilots had kept the assault force waiting for hours on the ground in Bogotá after they were ordered to attack the prison, but now the generals were demanding that heads also roll in the executive branch.

And whose head was stretched out and waiting on the block? Eduardo Mendoza was in shock. The eager young vice minister of justice suddenly found every finger of blame pointed at him. Hadn't he been in charge of Pablo's imprisonment from the start? Didn't it seem fishy that it was

Mendoza who had flown up to *La Catedral* to tip off the drug boss? Wasn't he the one who told the general outside the prison to wait, to raid the prison the next day, and then had gone in to confer with Pablo?

The accusations started in the press, and soon there was a new official probe announced every day, with him as the prime target. First there was the Senate investigation. That would last for four months, with Mendoza on TV every day along with all the generals and prison guards who let Pablo go. Then the comptroller's office announced that he was going to investigate all of the contracts Mendoza had handed out to build a new prison for Pablo; somehow the difference between the existing "prison" and the real one Mendoza had hoped to build got twisted together, and in the press he became the architect of Pablo's luxurious accommodations. Then the *Procuraduria*'s office (a kind of internal-affairs unit for the government) decided to investigate him on allegations of negligence. Then came the scary one. Gustavo de Greiff, the attorney general, announced that he was beginning a criminal investigation and named Mendoza a target. In a land of suspicion, the vice minister of justice suddenly looked like the most guilty character of all.

Less than a week after his escape he got a call from President Gaviria's chief of staff.

"Eduardo, the time has come," his friend said sadly.

Mendoza was asked to resign, as was the general who had refused to storm the prison and the chief of the air force, which had taken hours to find planes to fly the strike force to *La Catedral.* The jail guards who had turned on Mendoza and Navas were arrested on suspicion of having accepted bribes.

Mendoza was now jobless and unhirable. He had become a pariah. He felt as though all of the country's anger and embarrassment over Pablo's escape was focused on him. It was worse than his experience at *La Catedral.* Every day for months he and his lawyer showed up before the Senate committee and listened to the elected officials hurl insults and accusations. Before his family and all his friends he was disgraced, humiliated. He began mentally preparing himself to go to jail.

Pablo had, in fact, walked out. He and his brother Roberto had led a small group of his men uphill, past the camouflaged cabanas, cut a hole in the wire fence, and walked over the top of the hill—and right past soldiers either too friendly or too intimidated to stop them. The "tunnel" spoken of in the intercepted phone conversations was, of course, the inmates' sarcastic term for the covered truck that had been used to roll contraband—women, weapons, money, bodies, alcohol—up and down the mountain, right under the studiously disinterested noses of prison guards and army patrols.

In a taped statement he had delivered to select TV and radio reporters two days after his escape, Pablo offered his own version of the night he escaped, and the reasons for it. He complained that he and his men (the *inmates*) had generously agreed to "lose control over more than half of the jail and our rights" when the government had started construction of the new fence around *La Catedral,* and he was shocked when a large army force suddenly showed up at the jail on July 22. He denied having taken Mendoza and Navas hostage and that the two officials had been threatened, calling Mendoza "a liar." His statement concluded: "As for the aggression carried out against us, we won't take violent actions of any nature yet and we are willing to continue with the peace process and our surrender to justice if we can be guaranteed to stay at the Envigado jail, as well as handing control of the prison to special forces of the United Nations."

The statement was signed, "Colombian jungle zone, Thursday, July 24, 1992. Pablo Escobar and comrades."

The day after his disappearance, Pablo's lawyers presented the government with a surrender offer, which basically called for him to be returned to *La Catedral* under the same terms, with no additional charges against him. Much to the satisfaction of the U.S. embassy, Gaviria had flatly refused, but then de Greiff muddied the waters by promptly announcing that *he* was willing to bargain.

The following day an odd explanatory communiqué was broadcast by the national radio station Caracol, from someone calling himself "Dakota," who claimed to speak for the Extraditables. The enumerated items included the claim that a bribe of one billion pesos had been paid to the army to allow Pablo's escape. The threatening statements made by Popeye (statements like "I've always wanted to kill a vice minister," reported by Mendoza after his release) were "the result of nervousness," and while there would be retaliation against high officials, there would be no acts of violence against the public. The statement said there were no tunnels beneath *La Catedral,* that seventy armed men had met Pablo when he left the prison early in the morning. It said that the murders that had prompted Gaviria's decision to move Pablo to a different prison (the Moncada and

Galeano brothers) were nothing more than an "internal war" within the Medellín cartel and that Pablo could not understand why the government was "involving itself."

Adding to the mix was a fax received at the U.S. embassy on the day of Pablo's escape. It was vintage Escobar: The ugly threat issued politely:

> We, the Extraditables declare: That if anything happens to Mr. Pablo Escobar, we will hold President Gaviria responsible and will again mount attacks on the entire country. We will target the United States Embassy in the country, where we will plant the largest quantity of dynamite ever. We hereby declare: The blame for this whole mess lies with President Gaviria. If Pablo Escobar or any of the others turn up dead, we will immediately mount attacks throughout the entire country. Thank you very much.

Trying to cut through all this noise—it was hard to tell what was true and what wasn't—the embassy was lucky to have Centra Spike in the air high over Medellín. Any lingering doubts about a tunnel were erased when the unit picked up Pablo talking at length on a cell phone and pinpointed his location to an area about four miles from the prison, in a wealthy suburb of Medellín called Tres Esquinas. Evidently assuming that the government was not yet geared up enough to have gotten surveillance units on his tail, Pablo was doing a lot of talking, using as many as eight different cell phones.

Predictably, he saw himself as the victim in all this. He had been very content with the deal he had struck with the government. The last thing he wanted was to be back out of jail and on the run once more. It was clear from his phone conversations that he desperately wanted back in. He explained as much in a long lecture (intercepted by Centra Spike) to his lawyers, just two days after his escape.

Pablo didn't believe that the government had intended only to transfer him to Itagui, a maximum-security prison in Medellín, just as he had disbelieved the reassurances of Vice Minister Mendoza on the night of his escape. He felt Gaviria's stated reason for this supposed transfer was a ruse—he viewed the Galeano and Moncada murders as a strictly private, business affair. What was really behind the move on *La Catedral,* he insisted, was an American-backed assassination attempt.

"[Let us] give this a little bit more clarity," Pablo explained. "The situation arose because they went in there shooting and all, and we were defending our lives, but our intention was to comply with the government until the end. . . . It is possible that one or two persons were smuggled into the jail. I won't deny it . . . that happens in jails all over the country and the world, and, in reality, I am not to blame. The person to blame is the person who lets them in. . . . So that if people entered [*La Catedral*] shooting and all and we had information that Americans were participating in the operation, we have to put our lives first, we have families!"

Accepting imprisonment anywhere other than *La Catedral* would compromise their safety, Pablo explained.

"Yes, yes," said one of the lawyers. "That was the first issue that I explained to the president."

Pablo objected to Mendoza's efforts to build a new prison around the existing one. "There was a delineation of the jail," he said. "It had been arranged. We made the design, we reworked the map, so the only thing that we didn't bargain for was a jail different from that one. And we need a public guarantee from the president that he will not take us out of the country."

"No, he already said that . . . we'd be protected, that the same protection guarantee would be maintained," said one of Pablo's representatives. "He continues to reiterate that."

"The problem is, I have some information . . . that there were some gringos," said Pablo. "So what happens is that there's a combined force. The army and the gringos [are] looking for Bush's reelection, so we need their [Gaviria's administration's] guarantee in this respect. . . . Do me a favor. Tell Señor President that I know he is misinformed. Now, they say that I am perpetrating crimes from jail." Pablo explained that if he was convicted of committing another crime while in jail, "[The government can] make me stay here all of my life. But they can't move me from there because that's the deal I made with the government."

"Perfect," said the lawyer.

"Anyway, accept my apologies," said Pablo, winding up the oration with typical deference.

"No, sir. It is my pleasure. And we'll see that all this works out. We are very interested in working this out."

"We are well disposed to come back," said Pablo. "There will be no more acts of violence of any nature, although some resentful people have been making some phone calls. People want to create chaos. But anyway, we are well disposed and we want to get this thing resolved. . . . Tell the president that we were very uneasy because the gringos were going to be a part of the operation."

"We saw the tapes of the gray uniforms and all that," said another of the lawyers. Pablo and his men believed that the CIA employed agent-soldiers who wore gray uniforms.

"Of the gringos?" asked Pablo. "And how many were there?"

"Well, we could see some uniforms on TV. This afternoon we asked for tapes from the evening news program."

Pablo knew that the accusation that American soldiers had been involved would create big political problems for Gaviria.

"There are two things that are very important," said Pablo, now addressing Santiago Uribe (no relation to lawyer Roberto Uribe). "When you have a chance of making a statement, say that what caused the biggest concern to us was the presence of the gringos. The fact that the army would be going along with the gringos. What explanation can be given for that?"

"Yes. The press is already after that. We're on top of that."

"Okay. And another thing. The president has to say it officially and make an official commitment. Everything is a contract. Now it's going to be a contract signed by the minister who makes the commitment that if tomorrow or the day after tomorrow I kill the warden and get thirty more years, they don't transfer me from here. That this is a commitment."

"Yes. Yes," said Uribe.

"Okay, gentlemen, good luck then."

8

There is no evidence that American soldiers and CIA agents—gray-uniformed or otherwise—had been involved, but if that was one of Pablo's fears, his escape would make it come true. Four days after he left *La Catedral,* a team of Delta Force operators led by Colonel Jerry Boykin arrived in Bogotá. Ambassador Busby's request for Delta, much to his surprise, had sailed through Washington. The State Department had approved it and passed it up to the White House, where President Bush had consulted with Joint Chiefs Chairman Colin Powell and then instructed Secretary of Defense Cheney to give Busby anything he needed.

Eight very fit men dressed in civilian clothes were met at El Dorado Airport by midlevel embassy officials and driven downtown, moving swiftly along roads that in daylight would be choked with traffic. Busby, Toft, and Wagner were waiting in the vault. Busby and Boykin were old friends, and after a few minutes of getting caught up, the ambassador began briefing Boykin on the situation. It was, to say the least, confusing.

Boykin's team had taken the assignment hoping to go after Pablo themselves, especially given the clumsy track record of the Colombians in the months before his surrender. Delta specialized in this kind of quick, dirty strike. They trained constantly and could move rapidly on any target anywhere, day or night. Their official orders typically explained the what and why of the mission without spelling out the how. Their commanding officer, General William F. Garrison, was a veteran at these kinds of covert ops, ever since his work on the Phoenix program in Vietnam, where suspected Vietcong leaders were assassinated in retaliation for killings of village leaders who were less than enthusiastic about communism. Garrison was not one to shy away from an assassination mission. But Delta's plan had been vetoed emphatically by U.S. Army Southern Commander, General George Joulwan when he'd met with Boykin before the men flew down.

"No, you're not going to do it yourself," he had instructed Boykin. Joulwan knew how easy it was for these "black" special ops guys to fly beneath the army's command radar, and he knew they wanted to do the job themselves. As far as he was concerned, the potential political and legal fallout of such a mission would eclipse its benefits.

But if the Colombians took all this training, intelligence, and guidance and went out and shot somebody while trying to arrest Escobar, the U.S. mission stayed comfortably within the law. Officially, the Delta operators were not to participate in raids. Joulwan wanted them to get out there and show the Colombian police how to track this son of a bitch down.

Busby also conveyed the urgency of the situation. He and the staff at the embassy had been working around the clock ever since Pablo's escape. Steve Murphy, the DEA agent with the well-worn Spanish-English dictionary, had subsisted on coffee and donuts for so long, without sleep, that when he felt his heart fluttering oddly in his chest he took a break to go have his heart checked at the embassy dispensary. He thought he might be having a heart attack. He was advised to cut down on the sugar and caffeine.

Pablo had been free for four days. He was already assembling the support system he would need to live underground. If they didn't catch him quickly—specifically, in the next few days—they were going to face a much harder task.

The following day, Monday, Boykin and the ambassador went off to meet with President Gaviria, to tell him the United States was putting up a $2 million reward for information leading the authorities to Pablo. Two high-ranking Colombian officers came to the embassy to meet with the remaining newly arrived Americans, Colonel Luis Montenegro and Lieutenant Colonel Lino Pinzon, the man assigned to head the search effort.

"You're going back with these guys, and they're going to help you locate Escobar," Colonel Montenegro told Pinzon.

Members of the Delta team inflated their rank to avoid embarrassing the higher-ranking Colombians. Gary Harrell, one of the largest line officers in the American army, was a lieutenant colonel with an aggressive personality to complement his lineman's physique. He was a country boy with a very direct, forceful style, and a handshake that people warned you about. He was introduced as a general, and he managed to fill the room with his take-charge, can-do personality. This was a mistake, aggravated when the Americans refused to allow Pinzon to see the command center in the vault. It didn't bother Montenegro, a slender, dark, nervous man, who was delighted to have this American support. Montenegro kept repeating, *"No me dejes solo"* (Don't leave me alone), but Pinzon was insulted. He was a dignified man with a crisp salt-and-pepper crew cut. He was regarded as something of a ladies' man, played a good game of tennis, and kept a manicurist and pedicurist on his staff. The DEA agents who had been working with him regarded Pinzon as a clever dandy with more ambition for rank than actual accomplishment, but they liked him. These same traits were anathema to the Delta operators. They sized up Pinzon as a "ticket puncher," the kind of officer who was content merely to appear as though he were doing his job. Harrell was strictly a results man, with Delta's legendary disdain for rank or privilege. If ever two men were designed to conflict, it was these two.

Pinzon and Montenegro were told that the embassy had found Pablo at a hilltop *finca* in Tres Equinas. Pinzon was unconvinced. His own intelligence indicated that Pablo was still near the prison, probably someplace underground, but Montenegro agreed that if another call came from the same place, Pinzon's forces should be ready to move in. Four members of the Delta team would travel to Medellín the next day to assist with the assault.

One of the first two operators to leave for Medellín was a man who the Colombians would know as Colonel Santos. None of the men who stayed in the country used their real names. While Boykin was the commander and Harrell was initially in charge in Medellín, it was Santos, whose real rank was sergeant major, who would end up staying on for most of the hunt, supervising the Delta operators and SEALs who rotated in and out. Santos also acted as liaison between the embassy and the Search Bloc. He was a slender, exceedingly fit former track star who had grown up in New Mexico speaking both Spanish and English. He had been one of the first men selected for Delta when it was formed in 1978, and its first Hispanic recruit.

In what had proved to be his final interview for the unit, Colonel Charlie Beckwith had tried to bait him.

"Why, shit, Sergeant, you're a wetback, aren't you? What makes you think we'd be stupid enough to select someone like you for a sensitive unit like this? You're no American, you're a fucking *Mexicano*."

Even though Santos knew he was being goaded deliberately, the insult got under his skin.

"I was born and raised in the American system and I am an American citizen, sir," he said calmly.

"All right, Sergeant," said the squadron commander, Lieutenant Colonel Lewis H. "Bucky" Burruss. "What if I were to tell you that you did okay but we've decided not to select you? If you want to get into this unit, you'll have to do the whole thing all over again. Would you do that?"

"Yes, sir."

"Why?"

"Because I want to be here, in this kind of unit."

"Okay, Sergeant Wetback, we have three days before the next class comes in," said Beckwith. "You better get ready to do it again. You're excused."

Santos had exited the room, silent but horrified. The physical-selection process had been the most difficult experience of his life. The prospect of having to go through it again was daunting and clearly unfair. He was still standing in the hallway wrestling with those feelings when the door opened and he was invited back in.

"Okay, Sergeant," said Beckwith. "You are accepted. You will not have to go through it again."

Santos and another operator boarded a plane to Medellín the following evening, laden with top-secret high-tech equipment, portable GPS satellite positioning devices, microwave visual imagery platforms, and video cameras with powerful lenses for remote ground surveillance (both day and night). The idea was to link up with Colombian forces; pinpoint the target where Pablo's phone calls had originated, using coordinates supplied by Centra Spike; put the camera on it; and begin watching for signs of the fugitive's presence. The microwave transmitter would send real-time images back to the Colombian police, so there would be no mistaking the target.

They unloaded all this gear at one end of a runway at Rionegro, a remote landing strip outside Medellín. There were supposed to be police officers waiting for them there, but the landing strip was empty. Santos and his partner sat on their classified cargo and waited.

About a half hour after their plane had taken off to return to Bogotá, the two operators grew concerned. This was hardly an auspicious beginning. Here they were, two American secret operatives laden with some of their unit's fanciest gear, unarmed, unescorted, sitting out in the heartlands of *narco* territory with no radio. They hadn't even worked up a good cover story. It was hours before members of the Search Bloc came to pick them up—the Colombians had gone to the wrong airport.

The Carlos Holguin School, an old police training academy, had a broad green campus surrounded by high fences and barbed wire, set on a residential hillside overlooking the city from the west. They slept that night in sleeping bags on the floor of one of the school's storehouses.

Santos met the following morning with Pinzon, who, it was immediately apparent, was not happy to see him. The Colombian lieutenant colonel appeared to regard Delta's arrival as an insult to his leadership and a threat to his career. When Harrell arrived later that day, things got really bad.

Javier Peña, a DEA agent who was a veteran in Colombia and who had dealt often with Pinzon, pulled Santos aside that first day. Peña was a fearless, cheerful busybody, a man who kept his finger in everything, a Mexican-American from Austin, Texas, who at one time had served as the only hispanic DEA agent in that city. "Man, was I busy," he says. A short man with glasses and a big mustache, Peña loved his undercover work and was a sponge for information. The more dangerous his job was, the more he seemed to enjoy it. He and Santos hit it off immediately, at least partly because they were the only two Americans at the Holguin base who spoke fluent Spanish.

"Santos, it's not working out, man, because as soon as you guys got here, you acted like you wanted to rule," he said. "Then you want things done your way, and Pinzon and this colonel [Harrell] are already butting heads."

Pinzon and Harrell were stuck with each other. Delta positioned two operators in Pablo's own observation tower up at *La Catedral* because of its panoramic view of the entire urban valley. One of them was Sergeant Major Joe Vega, a "captain" in Colombia, a broad-shouldered weight lifter with long, thick black hair. The Colombian police had moved in and were living in comfort, with the commander ensconced in Pablo's own luxurious suite. Vega had a satellite phone, a laptop computer to help him rapidly correlate Centra Spike's coordinates on the map, an 8mm video camera with several high-powered lenses to focus in on the target, and a microwave relay to transmit the image back to Harrell and Santos at the Holguin school. They waited for Pablo to make another phone call.

He didn't that night, but early the following evening Centra Spike picked up another phone call from Tres Esquinas. Up in the observation tower, Vega quickly found the coordinates on his map, focused his camera, and shot the image to Harrell, who tried to rouse Pinzon and get his men moving. The Colombian commander responded to the news offhandedly, as if it were just another bit of information to be added to the mix—dozens of leads were reported every day, he told the Delta commander. Despite Harrell's urgency, Pinzon pointedly made it clear that he gave this tip no more weight than any other.

When the embassy in Bogotá learned that Pinzon had not moved, calls were placed to the Presidential Palace, and Gaviria himself ordered the Search Bloc to get going. Angered that the Delta team had gone over his head, the Colombian lieutenant colonel took hours to assemble his men. It wasn't until early next morning that he launched the "raid," sending about three hundred of his men creeping up the side of the hill, to Harrell's horror, in a caravan of pickup trucks and cars that could be seen and heard from miles away. Advice from the Delta operators to send a smaller, stealthier unit was ignored. It was like stalking a deer in a bulldozer. From

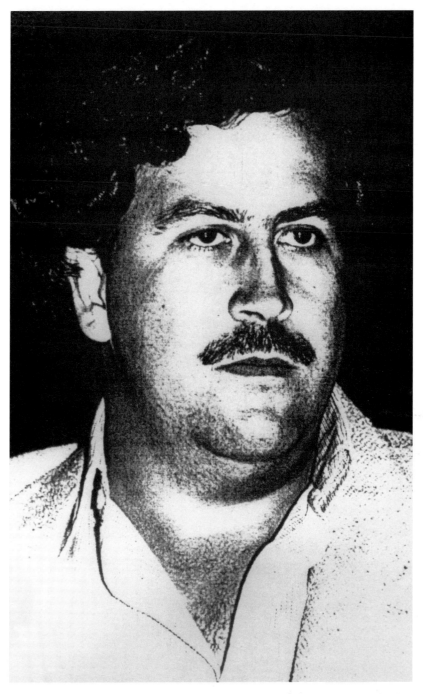

Pablo as he appeared in 1983, one of the richest men in the world and a newly elected alternate to Colombia's congress. He was thirty-three years old and at the height of his wealth and power.

Map of
Colombia.

Colombia

MAGDALENA
ATLANTICO
BOLIVAR
CORDOBA
PANAMA
SUCRE
LA GUAJIRA
CESAR
NORTE DE SANTANDER
VENEZUELA
ANTIOQUIA
SANTANDER
ARAUCA
• Medellin
CHOCO
BOYACA
CASANARE
CALDAS
RISARALDA
CUNDINAMARCA
⊛ Bogota
VICHADA
VALLE DE CAUCA
TOLIMA
• Cali
META
CAUCA
HUILA
GUAINIA
NARINO
GUAVIARE
GUAINIA
PUTUMAYO
CAQUETA
VAUPES
ECUADOR
Area of detail
SOUTH AMERICA
AMAZONAS
BRAZIL
N
PERU
MILES
0   100

WILLIAM NEFF / Inquirer Staff Artist

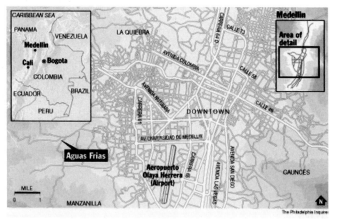

CARIBBEAN SEA
PANAMA
VENEZUELA
Medellin
Cali
⊛ Bogota
COLOMBIA
ECUADOR
BRAZIL
PERU

LA QUIEBRA
CARRERA 64 D
CALLE 73
AVENIDA COLOMBIA
CALLE 58
Medellin
Area of detail
DOWNTOWN
CALLE #9
AV. UNIVERSIDAD DE MEDELLIN
CARRERA
AVENIDA SAN DIEGO
AVENIDA LAS VEGAS
Aguas Frias
Aeropuerto Olaya Herrera (Airport)
CAUNCES

MILE
0   1
MANZANILLA
N

The Philadelphia Inquirer

Map of
Medellín.

Pablo and his wife, Maria Victoria, in 1983. She married the up-and-coming crime boss when she was just fifteen and bore him a son and daughter.

Pablo embraces his wife, Maria Victoria, and his daughter, Manuela. His son, Juan Pablo, stands behind them. The drug boss was devoted to his family despite his sexual interest in teenage girls.

President Bush with Colombian president Virgilio Barco in September 1989 after Barco requested the help of U.S. Special Forces in the hunt for Pablo and other Medellín drug traffickers.

Morris D. Busby, the U.S. ambassador to Colombia, steered the secret U.S. military and law enforcement effort to track down Pablo after he walked away from prison in July 1992.

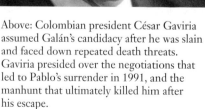

Above: Colombian president César Gaviria assumed Galán's candidacy after he was slain and faced down repeated death threats. Gaviria presided over the negotiations that led to Pablo's surrender in 1991, and the manhunt that ultimately killed him after his escape.

Left: Luis Galán was a charismatic Colombian politician and front-runner in the race for president of Colombia when Pablo's assassins killed him in August 1989. It was after Galán's death that Delta Force joined the hunt.

Above: Fernando Galeano, shown here in 1989, was murdered by Escobar's men in 1992 at *La Catedral* prison after being accused of stealing from the drug boss. Galeano's death and that of his brother, Mario, and the murders of Kiko and William Moncado, forced the Colombian government to act and led to Pablo's decision to leave prison.

Top left: A dinner party in the mid-1980s. Pablo is surrounded by family and associates. His wife, Maria Victoria, is to his right; his son, Juan Pablo, stands behind him. To his left is Carlos Lehder, who would blame his arrest and extradition to the United States in 1987 on Pablo.

Middle left: A view from the comfortable living room of Pablo's suite at *La Catedral* prison, where he managed his cocaine empire during his imprisonment from June 1991 to July 1992.

Bottom left: DEA agents Steve Murphy (left) and Javier Peña clown on the bed of Pablo's living quarters at *La Catedral* days after the drug boss's "escape." The agents are wearing hats Pablo had worn in famous photographs, including the one on the cover of the *Semana* magazine held by Peña.

Agent Joe Toft ran the DEA operation in Colombia throughout the bloody years of battling the Medellín cartel. Toft was troubled by the involvement of criminal gangs in the manhunt for Escobar, and months after the drug boss was killed, Toft retired from the DEA and leaked information linking the newly elected Colombian president Ernesto Samper with the Cali drug cartel.

José Rodriguez-Gacha, or "The Mexican," was considered the most violent and powerful of the Medellín cartel leaders until his death in 1989 revealed that Pablo had been the man in charge all along.

Eduardo Mendoza, appointed vice minister of justice by his friend President Gaviria, found himself held hostage by Pablo on the night of the drug boss's escape from *La Catedral*, and was later falsely accused of collaborating with him and even orchestrating the escape.

Colonel Hugo Martinez, shown in a recent photograph, rejected bribe offers from Pablo and lived with death threats against himself and his entire family. Despite accusations of brutality and corruption, U.S. embassy officials stood behind the colonel and admired his courage and tenacity.

An exhibit at the *Policía Nacional de Colombia*'s museum in Bogotá displays the mug shots and (in some cases) morgue photos of Pablo's top associates who were killed by the Search Bloc during the manhunt.

The third page of a handwritten letter by Pablo just days before he was killed. The letter denounces the government for allowing *Los Pepes* and Pablo's rivals to commit crimes against him with impunity and accuses Colonel Martinez of leading the death squads. It is signed with Pablo's thumbprint.

The Colombian government and U.S. embassy printed thousands of posters and handbills encouraging citizens to help with the manhunt. This handbill is targeted directly at Pablo's former associates in Medellín, offering cash rewards, "absolute confidentiality," and forgiveness for past crimes. "You set *all, all* of the conditions," it reads.

A victim of *Los Pepes* photographed by a Colombian TV station. The cardboard sign around the man's neck is signed *Los Pepes*. In the spring of 1993, the vigilante group was killing as many as six people associated with Pablo every day.

Members of Colonel Martinez's Search Bloc celebrate over Pablo's body on December 2, 1993, in a photograph taken by DEA agent Steve Murphy. Pablo's death ended a fifteen-month effort that cost hundreds of millions of dollars. It was the deathblow to the Medellín cartel.

Pablo's grave in Medellín is a popular tourist attraction. His casket was carried through the streets by thousands of angry mourners.

his perch at *La Catedral,* talking by phone to Major Steve Jacoby back at the embassy, Vega noted the procession of headlights as this giant convoy began moving up the hill.

"Wait a minute," he told Jacoby. "Now there's another set of headlights moving down the hill on the other side of the mountain."

Pablo would not have even needed to be tipped off. Everyone on the mountain could see and hear the approach of this colossus. Pinzon's men spent about four hours searching the hill to no avail, then withdrew. They found the suspected *finca* to be typical of an Escobar hideout, luxurious furnishings far beyond the norm for that neighborhood, including a sparkling new bathroom with a deep tub (Pablo was finicky about his toilet). A records check showed he had used the place as a hideout during his first sojourn as a fugitive.

More calls were intercepted early the next morning, these from Pablo's men arranging to move him to a new hideout, discussing the need to collect identity documents and weapons. Pinzon answered the summons at the door of his quarters in his silk pajamas.

"How do you know he's there?" Pinzon asked.

Harrell was not at liberty to explain.

Again, it took pressure from Bogotá to force Pinzon to move, and again he sent the caravan up the hill. This time they spent the rest of the morning and most of the day searching door to door, and found nothing. Pinzon remained convinced that it was all fruitless and he complained to Peña, "These Delta guys are trying to get me fired in Bogotá."

By the end of the week, the search force was empty-handed and Pablo had clearly moved on. There was now little chance that he would be found quickly. Harrell brought back the horror story of Pinzon's attitude, effort, and tactics. Pinzon complained to his superiors about Delta. At the embassy, the Colombian colonel would henceforth be known simply as "Pajamas."

9

Busby had his own problems back in Bogotá. As expected, once the Colombian government's invitation for help had been broadcast at the Pentagon, it had prompted an overwhelming response. By the end of the first week the ambassador had people camped out on the floor in the embassy conference room. Every direction-finding, surveillance, and imagery team in the arsenal descended on Medellín. The air force sent RC-135s, C-130s adapted for sophisticated imagery, U-2s, and SR-71s. The navy sent P-3 spy planes. The CIA, which already had its own two-prop De Havilland over Colombia, now sent Schweizer, a remarkable machine that looked like a big glider and could stay silently aloft over a target for hours on end. It could provide highly detailed imagery over a target with FLIR, an infrared technology that could peer through clouds and darkness. Anything that had a potential capability was shipped south. It was like a sweepstakes: see who could demonstrate the most effectiveness first. Target-acquisition units were using their equipment to do surveillance. There were so many American spy planes over Medellín, at one point seventeen in the air together, that the air force had to assign an AWACs, an airborne warning-and-control center, to keep track of them. It took ten C-130s just to deliver the contractors and maintenance and support staffs for all this stuff.

Toft had spent years learning his way around Colombia, and his initial excitement over all this military help quickly soured. Data is only as good as the people who collect it. There were lots of false alarms. Some surveillance teams would pick up a phone call in which one caller referred to the other as "Doctor" and would assume that it was Pablo on the line, even though the informal honorific was commonplace in Colombia.

This eagerness, along with the sudden influx of hardware and manpower, also spooked Centra Spike. The unit relied on blending in quietly with the surroundings. Now it was hard just finding airspace for their little Beechcrafts. Major Jacoby prevailed on Busby to give everyone else a flight ceiling of 25,000 feet. The U-2 stayed up above 60,000 feet. Centra Spike kept its planes at about 30,000 feet.

This sudden full-court press was meant to cause problems for Pablo, but instead it provoked a crisis in Bogotá. One night, during the same week Delta was trying to prod Pajamas Pinzon into action, one of the new arrivals, an RC-135, caught sight of something interesting and moved down below 1,000 feet for a closer look. The jet flew so low that the Colombian press was able to photograph it clearly at night.

The outcry forced Defense Minister Raphael Pardo into the hot seat before the same congressional committee grilling Mendoza—many in that body were calling for both his and Gaviria's immediate resignations. The Colombian press had proclaimed all the activity an American military "invasion" of Medellín. Pardo admitted that the Americans had been invited to help but argued that planes flying overhead did not violate the prohibition against foreign troops on Colombian soil. He volunteered nothing about Delta Force.

It was the journalistic equivalent of war. Radio Medellín started broadcasting the tail numbers of American planes, including one of the CIA planes, which was promptly flown out of Colombia.

CIA station chief Wagner was furious, Jacoby was frustrated, and President Gaviria, mindful that he had invited this help, was now complaining to the ambassador, "This is nuts!"

By the end of the week Busby had ordered home everything except Centra Spike, the CIA, and Delta. The first look at Pinzon's effectiveness had made it clear that Pablo was not going to be caught, even with the most sophisticated targeting information, until Colombia could muster a mobile, elite strike force that would be trustworthy, determined, stealthy, and fast. Clearly what they needed was something like a surrogate Delta Force.

Pajamas Pinzon would have to go. And whether it was quid pro quo or not, Harrell was shipped back to Bragg.

"Captain" Vega stayed camped out up at *La Catedral*, and "Colonel" Santos stayed on at the Holguin school, awaiting the arrival of the one man everyone felt was needed to make the effort come together: Colonel Hugo Martinez.

10

The colonel was delighted when he got the news, in Madrid, that Pablo had walked out of jail. No one knew better than he did what a charade that imprisonment was. After his two years on Pablo's heels, he viewed the infamous "surrender" as the evasive drug boss's cleverest escape.

For the colonel, it had been a defeat. His friends in the police command had teased him that he would not be promoted to general until he got Escobar, which at first had sounded like a joke. But as each succeeding year had passed without the promotion, the colonel had realized it was true. Martinez had been a colonel for six years while others of equal tenure and experience had already been promoted. His future, his life, was now inextricably mixed with Pablo's. With the son of a bitch in jail, there was no telling when, if ever, he could get on with his life. It wasn't that the police didn't appreciate his efforts. He had been rewarded with a post in Madrid, as military liaison to Spain.

Under ordinary circumstances this would have been a coveted assignment, an extended posting to safety, relative luxury, and the high culture of the mother country. The best part of it was that he and his wife, their daughter, and their two younger boys (the oldest, Hugo Jr., was a student at the police academy in Bogotá) would at last step out from the chilling shadow that had fallen over them when Martinez had been given the assignment in 1989.

But Pablo's reach proved as long as his memory. A bomb had been placed on the plane that flew the colonel's family to Spain in 1991, set to explode when they reached a certain altitude. The airline found out about it from a phone tip only after the plane was airborne. The pilots had held a very low altitude to the nearest airfield, landed, found the bomb, and removed it. In the spring of 1992, in Madrid, a car bomb was discovered on the street outside the Colombian embassy, right where Martinez passed each day on his way to work. The embassy was so sure that the bomb had been meant for the colonel that they asked him to stay away from the building.

So when word reached him that Pablo was once again at large and that his superiors wanted him to come back and resume the hunt, Martinez was grateful. So long as Pablo Escobar was alive, the colonel knew he and his family were in danger. The two men's destinies were connected. He made plans to fly back to Bogotá immediately.

Now they would finish this thing.

Four days after Pablo's "escape," Steve Murphy, Javier Peña, and several other DEA agents spent the day touring *La Catedral*. The mountaintop "prison" was now a hot tourist attraction for top-ranking American and Colombian officials. CIA chief Wagner would tour it days later with a video camera, accompanied by several members of his staff. It confirmed all of the worst suspicions and stories about Pablo's supposed imprisonment, but it also gave the agents a rare glimpse into the life and mind of the world's most famous fugitive.

Although the agents suspected the Colombian army of destroying or carrying off most of the documents, including floppy disks and the hard drives from Pablo's computers, there was much of interest left behind. First there was just the luxury of the place, which they had heard about but still found hard to believe. If there had ever been a doubt about who was in charge at the prison, it was put to rest by a small table with telephones and a metal box mounted on the wall just outside Pablo's "cell." It was the main circuit box for all the communications lines to the prison.

One of the rooms in Pablo's suite had been his office. On a shelf over his desk was a neat library of news articles, diligently clipped, pasted, and sorted in a row of file boxes. There was also Pablo's collection of fan mail. One was from a local beauty queen, who referred to Pablo as her boyfriend and lover. One pathetic letter was from a man pleading with Pablo not to kill any more members of his family, as he had already done away with nearly all of them. There was a letter from the wife of a prison guard, thanking him for her husband's recent promotion. Pablo had copies of all his indictments, going back to his youth in Medellín, and had framed on his office wall a collection of the mug shots taken at each of his arrests, showing the tousle-haired teen with a thinner face who was arrested for stealing cars in Medellín, and a fuller-faced, mustachioed shot from his first and only drug bust in 1976. The agents also found a handwritten draft of a letter from Pablo to President Gaviria, requesting armor-plated cars for his wife and children. Pablo had saved a complete transcript of the U.S. indictment of Ivan Urdinola, a heroin trafficker from the Cauca region, and kept files on his Cali cartel rivals, complete with photographs, addresses, descriptions of their vehicles, and license numbers. On the wall he had a photograph of Ernesto "Che" Guevara, the famous Argentine Marxist revolutionary, alongside an illustration from *Hustler* magazine depicting Pablo and his associates cavorting in an orgy behind bars (throwing darts at a picture of President Bush on a TV screen) and a photograph of himself and a young Juan Pablo posing before the front gate of the White House. Among his collection of videotapes was, predictably, a complete set of the *Godfather* films, Chuck Norris's *The Octagon*, Steve McQueen's *Bullitt*, and Burt Reynolds in *Rent-a-Cop*. There were five Bibles in his personal library, and books by Graham Greene and Nadine Gordimer. It was not the book collection of an avid reader but of someone who bought in bulk. Among the collection were works by Colombian Nobel Prize winner Gabriel García Márquez and, curiously, a complete collection of the works of the Austrian writer Stefan Zweig. The closet in his bedroom was stacked with identical pairs of Nike sneakers and a neat pile of pressed blue jeans.

Over his gigantic bed was an ornate, gold-framed portrait of the Virgin Mary painted on inlaid tile. Beside the bed were hundreds of bound copies of a book Escobar had had privately printed, in which were reproduced hundreds of newspaper cartoons about him.

There were photographs of Pablo, his family, and his fellow inmates from the lavish Christmas dinner in the prison's disco and bar, and pictures of him posing with some of Colombia's biggest soccer stars. One framed photo showed Pablo posing in full costume as Pancho Villa, clearly enjoying himself, and another showed him and Popeye dressed as Prohibition-era American gangsters, complete with tommy guns.

The DEA agents itemized all they found and took turns posing for snapshots, happy as high schoolers invading a rival gang's clubhouse. They posed sitting on Pablo's bed, taking turns wearing one of the thick fur caps that the drug boss's mother had given him for his birthday, and that he had worn in a photograph that had run on the cover of the weekly news magazine *Semana*.

These were all just scraps left behind by the Colombian investigators, but they added up to a fascinating portrait of a man who clearly relished his celebrity outlaw status, even though he was known to protest his complete innocence at every public opportunity. Here was a man who went to vicious bloody lengths in a vain effort to wipe out evidence of his criminal past, who repeatedly argued his innocence of drug exporting, yet who posed for photographs dressed as a famous outlaw and hung framed copies of his mug shots on his office wall. The effects left behind at *La Catedral* exposed the cheerful cynicism behind Pablo's public pose of wronged innocence. It suggested a man who viewed criminality as a normal, healthy outlet for his ambition, just as he remained devoted to his family while employing teenage whores and beauty queens to satisfy his wider sexual appetites. Pablo clearly saw government and law enforcement as nothing more than power rivals, earnest opponents in an ongoing chess match.

Drawing on this information and its own files, the CIA prepared a brief "personality assessment" of the infamous fugitive. The summary attempts, with thinly veiled contempt, to sketch the internal life of this complex new military target. Anyone familiar with Pablo would have found it amusingly obvious—"Escobar has difficulty containing his extreme aggressiveness" certainly rang true—but it concluded with a chilling suggestion for how he might be lured into the open:

Escobar does seem to have genuine paternal feelings for his children, and the young daughter Manuela is described as his favorite. His parents were once kidnapped by a rival group, and Escobar apparently spared no effort or expense rescuing them. Whether his concern for his parents or his children would overcome his stringent security consciousness is not clear.

A week after Pablo escaped, a Colombian court rejected an appeal by his lawyers to have his flight ruled a legitimate action taken in fear for his life. So there would be no putting things right. Pablo's comfortable deal had come completely undone.

Instead, Pablo was back on the run, only this time the search would be conducted with the full cooperation of the United States. Over the next six months, the secret American operation in Colombia would swell to nearly one hundred personnel, making the Bogotá embassy the largest CIA station in the world.

The men involved in this manhunt knew that it had only one likely end. Escobar knew it well himself. It was the one thing that everybody understood but no one said out loud. None of this effort was about arresting Pablo anymore. The Colombians had no further patience for trying to put him on trial or lock him up; he had shown how pointless that was. They couldn't extradite him and try him in the United States; Pablo's own bullets and bribes had made extradition unlawful. No, this time the hunt was for keeps.

When they found him, they were going to kill him. It was a practice so commonplace throughout South America that there was even an expression for it: *la ley de fuga,* the law of escape.

11

The American soldiers, agents, and spies, the pilots, technicians, and analysts were just getting acquainted, late in the summer of 1992, with a personality that had preoccupied Colombia now for nearly a decade. In September, more than a month after his escape, Pablo felt secure enough to grant a rambling and defiant interview with Radio Cadena Nacíonal. Once again, he denied being a criminal. The interviewer began by asking tough questions but was quickly disarmed by Pablo's manner. The broadcast degenerated into a fawning celebrity interview. Pablo lied fluently and good-naturedly. Philosophical, self-deprecating, witty—he didn't sound like a man running for his life. The tone was infuriating to his pursuers, as if he were taunting them.

"Do you regret having surrendered a year ago?" he was asked.

"At least, I regret having escaped," he said. He explained that he had left the prison only because he feared for his life. "Does one seek escape alternatives when you have arrived at a jail to which you have voluntarily surrendered?" he asked.

"Were you the man in charge in the prison?"

"I wasn't in charge . . . [but] I was not just any prisoner. I was the product of a peace plan whose cost was not high for the government. . . . They simply gave me a dignified prison and special conditions previously agreed to by the government, with the lawyers and with me."

Pablo downplayed and defended the luxuries in *La Catedral,* the parties. "Even if it is the most beautiful mansion in the world, if you are limited in your movements and watched by tower guards with weapons, and soldiers, then that is a prison," he said. "But I am not going to evade responsibility in the sense that I permitted some curtains and some special furniture and I am willing to pay for that error in accepting the most humble cell in any jail in Antioquia, as long as my rights are respected and I am guaranteed that I will not be moved for any reason."

"Is your head worth more than the one billion pesos offered by the government and more than the two and a half billion pesos offered by the government of the United States?"

"It seems my problem has become political, and could be important for the reelection of the president of the United States."

"At this moment, you have become once again the most sought-after man in the world. The Colombian authorities, other secret services, DEA agents, the Cali cartel, former accomplices of your activities, deserters of your organization, indirect or direct victims of terrorist acts. Whom do you fear the most? How do you defend yourself from them?"

"I don't fear my enemies because they are more powerful. It has been my lot to face difficult circumstances, but I always do it with dignity."

"For you, what is life?"

"It is a space of time full of agreeable and disagreeable surprises."

"Have you ever felt afraid of dying?"

"I never think about death."

"When you escaped, did you think about death?"

"When I escaped, I thought about my wife, my children, my family, and all the people who depend upon me."

"Do you believe in God and the hereafter? In heaven and hell?"

"I don't like to speak publicly about God. God, to me, is absolutely personal and private. . . . I think all the saints help me, but my mother prays a lot for me to the child Jesus of Atocha, and that is why I built Him a chapel in Barrio Pablo Escobar. The largest painting in the prison was of the child Jesus of Atocha."

"Why have you been willing to have yourself killed?"

"For my family and for the truth."

"Do you accept that you have ever committed a crime or had someone killed?"

"That answer I can only give in confession to a priest."

"How do you think everything will end for you?"

"You can never foretell that, although I wish the best."

"If it depended on you, how would you like to end your life?"

"I would like to die standing in the year 2047."

"Under what circumstances would you commit suicide?"

"I have never thought about those types of solutions."

"Of all the things that you have done, which are the ones of which you are most proud, and of which are you ashamed?"

"I am proud of my family and of my people. I am not ashamed of anything."

"Whom do you hate, and why?"

"In my conflicts I try not to end up hating anybody."

"What advice have you given your children? What would you do if either of them dedicated themselves to illegal or criminal activities?"

"I know that my children love me and understand my fight. I always want the best for them."

"What do your wife and children mean to you?"

"They are my best treasure."

"Do you accept that you are mafioso? Does it bother you that someone says that about you?"

"The communications media has called me that thousands of times. If it bothered me, I would be in an insane asylum."

"What is it that most angers you and gets you out of control?"

"You can get angry, but you cannot lose your control. I get angry at hypocrisy and lies."

"Do you accept that they say you are a drug dealer or a criminal, or don't you really care?"

"My conscience is clear, but I would respond as a Mexican comedian once said, 'It is completely inconclusive.'"

"People say that you always get what you want . . ."

"I have not said that I have always gotten what I wanted. If I had always gotten what I wanted, everything would be rosy and I would calmly be drinking some coffee in the Rionegro Plaza or the park at Envigado. I fight tirelessly, but I have suffered too much."

"What is the key to your immense power?"

"I don't have any special powers. The only thing that gives me strength to keep on fighting is the energy of the people who love and support me."

"Corruption. To what extent has it gotten in the government?"

"Corruption exists in all the countries of the world. The important thing would be to know the causes of corruption in order to avoid it and stop it."

"Of what do you repent?"

"All human beings make mistakes, but I don't repent of anything because I take everything as an experience and channel it into something positive."

"If you were born again, what would you do? What would you repeat and what would you dedicate yourself to?"

"I would not do those things that I thought would turn out right but which came out wrong. I would repeat everything that has been good and nice."

"What did your wife and children say when you were in prison and what did they think of your activities?"

"They have loved and supported me always. And they accept my cause because they know it and understand it."

"Do you consider yourself an ordinary man or someone of exceptional intelligence?"

"I am a simple citizen, born in the village of El Tablazo of the municipality of Rionegro."

"Have you, personally, ever taken drugs?"

"I am an absolutely healthy man. I don't smoke and I don't consume liquor. Although, with respect to marijuana, I'd have the same reply that the president of Spain gave when he was asked about it."

"Do you consider it a mistake on your part to have entered politics?"

"No, I do not accept it as a mistake. I am sure that if I had participated in other elections, I would have defeated everyone in Antioquia by an overwhelming majority."

"Why so much money? What do you do with it? Is your fortune as large as the international magazines say it is?"

"My money obeys a social function. That is clear and everyone knows about it."

"If you had to make a profile of yourself, what would you say? To you, who is Pablo Escobar?"

"It is very difficult to portray one's self. I prefer that others analyze me and that others judge me."

"Why did you enter drug trafficking?"

"In Colombia, people enter this type of activity as a form of protest. Others enter it because of ambition."

"Do you feel yourself bigger than Al Capone?"

"I am not that tall, but I think Al Capone was a few centimeters shorter than I am."

"Do you consider yourself to be the most powerful man in Colombia? The richest? One of the most powerful?"

"Neither one nor the other."

"Did you feel complimented when the magazine *Semana* presented you as Robin Hood?"

"It was interesting and it gave me peace of mind."

"By temperament, are you violent and proud?"

"Those who know me know that I have a good sense of humor and I always have a smile on my face, even in very difficult moments. And I'll say something else: I always sing in the shower."

LOS PEPES

October 1992–October 1993

1

On January 30, 1993, a car bomb exploded in Bogotá, blowing a crater several feet deep in the street and sidewalk and taking a savage bite out of a bookstore. Even by the capital city's weary standards this was a nightmare. The bookstore bomb was estimated to have contained 220 pounds of dynamite. Inside the store, crowds of children and their parents had been buying school supplies for a new semester. Torn body parts were strewn about. In all, twenty-one people were killed, seventy more injured. Bill Wagner, the CIA station chief, recoiled when he stepped past the police barricades into the horror of the bombing's aftermath. In a gutter running with blood he saw the severed hand of a child.

He thought: *We are going to kill this son of a bitch if it's the last thing I do on this earth.*

Despite the determination of the United States and Colombia, the loss of hundreds of lives, the expenditure of hundreds of millions of dollars, and the deployment of elite U.S. military and espionage units, the half-year-old hunt for Pablo Escobar had so far yielded little but frustration. Colonel Martinez's discipline and Delta Force training had vastly improved the speed and efficiency of the Search Bloc, which was headquartered at the Holguin school in Medellín. It now felt almost like home to Colonel Santos, the Delta sergeant major in charge, and the other Delta operators who regularly rotated through. There had been some successes, most notably October 28, 1992, when Brance "Tyson" Muñoz, one of Pablo's most notorious *sicarios,* was killed in the proverbial "gun battle with national police." But that was about all they had to celebrate.

The Search Bloc had learned Tyson's whereabouts thanks to the U.S. embassy's reward program. Ambassador Busby had tried to get the Colombian government to offer money for tips but it had refused, pointing out that whatever reward money it put up would likely be topped by Escobar—"If we put one million dollars on his head, he'll just put ten million on ours," an official had explained. So the embassy had gone ahead on its own, offering a $200,000 reward and relocation to the United States for any useful information. Ads for the rewards ran on television and displayed photos of Pablo and some of his top people. The Tyson tip was the first time it had paid off.

A notorious killer whose nickname came from his resemblance to the American fighter Mike Tyson, he was renowned for his ferocity and loyalty to the boss, whom he had known since childhood. He had gained weight and grown his hair long in an effort to disguise himself. The informant was a friend of someone who worked for Tyson. He lived in a building across from the house where the infamous *sicario* was staying, and he told police he could see him coming and going.

Ten days after the tip, the raid was launched at one in the morning with the whispered radio code "The party has begun." The Search Bloc found Tyson's apartment secured with a heavy steel door, which they blew off its hinges. The breaching charge was a bit overdone. It blasted the door across the apartment and punched it completely through an outer wall, sending it crashing to the street nine stories below. Twenty-six officers followed the blast into the apartment. Tyson tried to flee out a back window to a fire escape, but there were iron bars on the window, and he was trapped. He took a bullet right between the eyes.

By the end of 1992 twelve major players in Pablo's organization, including Tyson, had been killed in "gun battles" with the Search Bloc. There was always a steep price to pay for these victories. On the day Tyson was killed, four police officers were gunned down in retaliation. Five more were killed over the next two days. Through the first six months of the hunt more than sixty-five police officers had been killed in Medellín, many of them Search Bloc members whose identities were supposed to be a state secret. Often these men were killed in their homes or traveling to and from the academy, which demonstrated that Pablo knew not only their identities but their work shifts and home addresses. Pablo was offering a $2,000 bounty for killing Medellín policemen, and it was working.

Death wracked the enterprise. DEA chief Toft was so depressed by all the funerals that he stopped attending unless the officer killed was high-ranking enough that he couldn't get out of it. They were grueling. Colombians were not fastidious embalmers, so the special chapel the national police had built in Bogotá to handle the grim tide often reeked of death. The Colombians, men and women, tended to be more demonstrative than

Americans, so the funerals produced wrenching outpourings of grief and anger. The women would wail, and the men would gasp and weep and then retire to get staggeringly drunk. After attending a funeral where a pregnant widow clutching a small child threw herself on her husband's casket and refused to let go until she was pulled away, the normally stoical Toft went back to his secure apartment and cried.

Pablo kept up excruciating pressure. On December 2, a huge car bomb exploded near a Medellín stadium, killing ten policemen and three civilians. Ten days later, a top police intelligence officer was assassinated. At the end of the month, police discovered a car loaded with three hundred pounds of dynamite parked outside the national police's Antioquian headquarters.

There was impatience in Washington, D.C. The previous September, the U.S. Justice Department had indicted Tyson's brother, Dandeny Muñoz, for the bombing of the Avianca airliner in 1989 (in the attempt to kill then-presidential candidate César Gaviria). With the drug war in full swing, there is little doubt President Bush would have liked to have seen a headline noting the drug lord's demise before Election Day, November 3, 1992, as tangible evidence of progress. But election day came and went, Bush lost to Bill Clinton, and Pablo remained at large. Clinton took office in January with ballooning deficits and promptly began cutting government spending. The new president was less inclined to approach the drug war militarily, and Bush's defeat meant that Ambassador Busby's days in Bogotá were likely to be numbered. Few in Bogotá believed that the new administration would long share their enthusiasm for a protracted, seemingly futile pursuit of Pablo Escobar.

There was a growing weariness in Colombia, too. The public's immediate response to Pablo's renewed bombing campaign had been anger. They wanted him caught and punished. But as the months wore on and the blood toll mounted, anger gave way to resignation, and then to impatience. If the government could not catch Pablo, and if the cost of the hunt was so high, then why continue?

All of these factors combined to create a feeling in the embassy vault that time was running out. It seemed that Colonel Martinez's Search Bloc could not close the last one hundred yards.

This was the assessment delivered by Santos, who had spent most of the last six months living at the Holguin base. It had been a large training school for the national police until commandeered for this manhunt. It had big classroom buildings, barracks, a training range, a soccer field, and a track. The Delta operators based there occupied a small room, where they slept on cots or air mattresses. Adjacent to it they set up their office, with a desk, some chairs, and a fan. They covered the walls with giant photo-maps of the city of Medellín and the surrounding areas. Whenever Centra Spike would forward the latitude and longitude coordinates for a target, Santos and his men would locate the exact spot on their maps. The colonel was always glad to receive the information and usually acted upon it, but he was too proud to permit the Americans to help plan his assaults.

For Santos and the others, usually a squad of six who rotated in shifts that lasted about a month, it was a challenge to avoid drudgery. They spent most of their time working out on the school grounds, holding classes for Search Bloc assaulters, or holed up in those small rooms playing cards or video games and counting down the days until they got to go home. There were usually two CIA agents and a Centra Spike technician sharing the space. Whenever Murphy or Peña rotated through, they stayed there as well. The academy grounds were girded by two layers of fences and barbed wire. Just outside the outer fence, a few blocks downhill toward the city, was a checkpoint on the road that let only authorized vehicles pass. The Americans were allowed to wander beyond the outer fence to a few small stores or restaurants inside the checkpoint but were otherwise strictly forbidden to leave the compound.

They left anyway, and not just for Search Bloc assaults. Embassy officials received undeniable evidence of this when a young woman arrived at their door from Medellín with a baby and the name of the red-haired Delta sergeant she said was its father. The baby's red hair lent credence to her story. The operator was sent home and kicked out of the unit. That these men were straying outside the fence should not have come as a surprise. Delta operators were handpicked for their independence and war-fighting skills. They were daring, highly trained men used to accomplishing what they set out to do. There was little chance they would happily sit around playing games for weeks on end while there was action just a few miles away. Given a new set of coordinates for an important target, they became forward observers, heading off into the surrounding city or hills to find a convenient observation post where they could watch the suspected hideout, sometimes for days. Often they accompanied the Search Bloc on raids, operating global positioning system devices that they were far more familiar with than were the Colombians. Going along also earned them the respect of Martinez and his men. The raids were dangerous. How could they push the Colombians to take risks that they would not run themselves?

Even DEA agents Peña and Murphy felt compelled to go along on raids. They would ride in choppers with Martinez or whichever of his men was leading the assault. Sometimes the Search Bloc would ask the agents to accompany them with a video camera to record payoffs to informants. There was such suspicion about corruption that the agents were asked to keep the camera running on the bag of money from the minute they left the base until it was handed over to the informant. On one occasion, when word got back to the embassy that Murphy had left the compound, he was told, "If you do it again, you will be back in the United States before your luggage arrives."

There was stiff competition among all the American agencies in Medellín. Each organization was out to prove that its men, equipment, and methods were the most useful. The winner in this chase would likely become a prototype for such deployments—and funding—in the future. The two groups most directly pitted against each other were the CIA and Centra Spike. The spy agency operated two kinds of aerial surveillance: it flew the wide-winged, silent Schweizer to provide imagery, and it had its own version of Centra Spike, code-named Majestic Eagle, to electronically eavesdrop on targets and pinpoint their locations. Centra Spike's Beechcrafts performed the same service. At the Pentagon and in the White House, the unit that got credit was usually the one that delivered fresh intelligence first.

Peña remembers seeing the CIA and Centra Spike men actually racing to telephone back new information. And sometimes on its way to Washington, the source of new information got confused. Centra Spike's Major Jacoby got angry on one occasion when data collected by his unit showed up in a CIA report as agency-developed intelligence. He complained about it bitterly to the ambassador. As far as Centra Spike was concerned, the CIA radiotelemetry was inferior. Its equipment had cost far more to develop and deploy, and had been designed to find secret *narco* and guerrilla airstrips in the jungle. Centra Spike's system had been perfected by actually tracking individual targets. In 1990, when Pablo had started using digital cell phones with scrambling devices, it had taken Centra Spike just fifteen days to adapt. Now, with Pablo at large again, the two systems were competing head to head. Since budget dollars would grow much scarcer in 1993 and the years ahead, it was more than just galling to see the CIA taking credit for Centra Spike's success. It was a threat to the army unit's survival.

So Busby authorized a competition. The two units ran field trials to see which could do a better job of pinpointing targets. They set up phony targets over Medellín and flew a series of missions in late 1992. The contest wasn't even close. Centra Spike pinpointed the signal to just under two hundred meters. The best the CIA plane could do was seven kilometers, even after allowing the agency team to try three separate telemetry methods. That settled things, and the CIA backed off its claims for Majestic Eagle. Centra Spike got another boost in congressional funding, and could look forward to getting new equipment in the coming year that would double the system's accuracy.

There was little that Centra Spike's operators missed. Up in their Beechcrafts over Medellín, they monitored dozens of communications channels simultaneously, and sometimes they were shocked by what they heard. On one occasion, after picking up a brief radio transmission from Pablo, they sent the coordinates they plotted for him on a secure line down to the teams at the Holguin base. Within minutes, after the new data was shared with the colonel and he had huddled with his top commanders, they picked up a phone call *from* the base. Someone was calling from the Search Bloc headquarters to alert Pablo that he needed to move. There was evidently what the Colombians called a *soplo,* or snitch, within Martinez's inner circle.

The operators recorded the *soplo*'s phone warning—"They're on their way, they're coming for you"—which went to an Escobar associate called Pinina. Several days later, after the raid failed, a Centra Spike technician visited Martinez at the base and played him the tape. The colonel didn't recognize the voice, but he knew it had to be one of the men on his command staff. So he dismissed all but his two or three most trusted men, sending the others back to Bogotá for reassignment. Eight days later, after briefing only his top commander, Major Hugo Aguilar, about a pending raid, Martinez was again called by the man from Centra Spike. They had picked up another telephone warning to Pinina from the base!

"If it isn't you," the American said, "it has to be one of the men who are right there with you."

Martinez was angry and frightened. It had only been two minutes! He knew he could trust Aguilar . . . or could he? He summoned the major to his office and confronted him. Aguilar looked like he was in shock. He swore he had made no such call and was wounded to be accused. Martinez felt wounded, too. Aguilar said that he had conveyed the colonel's plans to three other top officers, but that was it. The information had not traveled outside the Search Bloc's newly proscribed inner circle.

The colonel was spooked and bewildered. If he couldn't carry on a conversation with his most trusted officer in his office at Holguin without Pablo finding out about it minutes later, what hope did he have of ever catching the man? Within the half hour he was on a helicopter to Bogotá, where he once again turned in his resignation. He explained to the generals that the situation was completely out of his control and hopeless, and that he wanted out. The generals refused his resignation and ordered him back to Medellín to straighten things out.

When he returned the following day, Aguilar met him at the helicopter and said they had found the *soplo*. When Martinez had left, Aguilar had stormed out to confront the officers he had spoken with. All three had angrily denied the betrayal, but as they spoke they'd noticed that an auxiliary policeman, one of the regular force assigned to guard the perimeter of the base, was standing near enough to overhear them. He had been standing at the same spot when they had spoken earlier.

"That's got to be him," said Aguilar.

Before accusing the man, they set a trap. With the colonel back in his office the next day, they ran through the same scenario. Aguilar emerged from Martinez's office and consulted with his three officers, standing close enough for the guard to overhear. Sure enough, minutes later Centra Spike recorded another phone call forwarding the false information. The guard was confronted, and he confessed. In a panic, fearing for his life, he explained that he had been recruited by a second lieutenant, one of the men Martinez had banished from Holguin nine days earlier. He said he had even been paid to kill Martinez. He had been given a pistol with a silencer and had actually climbed a tree several nights before, outside the window where the colonel often sat reading late into the evening. The guard was too far away to feel confident of his aim and, fearing that an errant shot would prompt return fire and his death, he had resolved to spend a few days practicing with the pistol before his next attempt. He had planned to try again the night before, but the colonel had not returned from Bogotá.

Martinez knew that the Americans distrusted all Colombians, even him, so the phone calls had distressed him. When the *soplo* was discovered, Martinez was more relieved at being able to shift suspicion from himself and his top men than he was to learn how closely he had escaped an assassin. Still, the incident reinforced how insidious Pablo's influence was, even within his own ranks.

After this *soplo* was uprooted, there was still reason to believe that Pablo had sources inside the Holguin base. A massive raid on November 5 in an area just west of the old Nápoles estate had turned up nothing, even though the colonel believed Pablo had been there, and another one two days later likewise came up empty. During the same period, raids on some of the cartel's midlevel management routinely got results. The successes confirmed the accuracy of the intelligence and telemetry, yet when it came to Pablo, the raids were always too late.

Over the Christmas holidays at the end of 1992, Pablo made another surrender offer in a letter to two sympathetic Colombian senators. He offered to turn himself in if the government would agree to house him and sixty members of the "military and financial arms" of his organization at a police academy in Medellín, to be supervised by an integrated group of Colombian army, navy, and air force personnel. He also demanded that all members of the Search Bloc be fired. In the letter, he accused Colonel Martinez of routinely torturing those he arrested in an effort to gather new information. Pablo the humanitarian demanded an investigation of these "human-rights abuses," and then made a threat: "What would the government do if a 10,000 kg bomb were placed at the Colombian prosecutor general's office?" He concluded by promising a new wave of kidnappings, threatening members of the "diplomatic community," and warning that he would plant bombs at the government-owned radio and television stations, the national tax offices, and the newspaper *El Tiempo*.

Gaviria responded in early January by calling the demands "ridiculous" and dismissed Pablo's charges of human-rights abuses as a public relations ploy. Still, the warnings spread fear throughout official Bogotá. Attorney General Gustavo de Greiff asked Busby to help relocate his family to the United States for safety.

For all the misery Pablo had caused, Colonel Martinez could not help but admire the man's talents. His enemy never seemed to lose his temper, especially when he was in danger. At those moments, in secretly recorded conversations with his associates, Martinez noted that Pablo seemed to radiate calm. He had a talent for managing several problems at the same time, and never made a move that had not been carefully thought through. Pablo was flexible and creative. During the months when Martinez imposed a blackout on all cellular-phone use in Medellín, hoping to make it more difficult for Pablo to contact his organization, the drug boss just switched over to radio or communicated by messenger through a series of couriers so that recipients would have no idea where they originated. To ensure that there would be no mistake about the message's author, Pablo signed with his thumbprint. He had a good feel for human nature. He was able to anticipate how others would react, and to plan accordingly. The colonel also admired Pablo's mind. Conversing on open lines with his family or friends, he employed elaborate impromptu codes that required remembering specific dates, places, and events. Often Pablo's fluency with these facts tripped up his associates, who couldn't keep up with their boss's agile memory.

There was another thing about Pablo that everyone noticed, when reading his messages and listening to his radio and phone calls. He was comfortable. He clearly believed he could play this game indefinitely. He would stay one step ahead of the colonel for as long as it took until the Gaviria administration, or Attorney General de Greiff, or maybe the next administration, capitulated to his demands. Despite all the resources arrayed against him, Pablo didn't even seem rattled. It was galling, that comfort. Maybe there was something that could be done about that.

2

In January, one day after the terrible bookstore bombing in Bogotá, *La Cristalina*, a hacienda owned by Pablo's mother, Hermilda, was burned to the ground. Then two large car bombs exploded in the *El Poblado* section of Medellín in front of apartment buildings where Pablo's immediate and extended family members were staying. A third bomb exploded at a *finca* owned by the drug boss, injuring his mother and his aunt. Several days later, another of Pablo's country homes was torched. All of these acts were against the law, and they targeted individuals who, while related to Pablo, were not themselves considered criminals. No one was killed or even seriously injured, but the message was clear. In the timeless hammerlike prose of the police teletype, DEA agent Javier Peña explained:

> The CNP[Colombian National Police] believe these bombings were committed by a new group of individuals known as "*Los Pepes*" (Perseguidos por Pablo Escobar) [People Persecuted by Pablo Escobar]. This group . . . has vowed to retaliate against Escobar, his family, and his associates, each and every time Escobar commits a terrorist act which injures innocent people. . . . Obviously the CNP and the GOC [government of Colombia] cannot condone the actions of "*Los Pepes*," even though they may secretly applaud these retaliatory acts.

Officially, the embassy was silent on the appearance of *Los Pepes*, but the gang in the vault on the fifth floor—Busby, Wagner, Jacoby, and Toft, the DEA agents, Centra Spike, and Delta Force operators—were not displeased. And why should they have been? What could be better than a homegrown vigilante movement against public enemy number one? All along, Pablo's official pursuers had fought at a disadvantage. Pablo had long hidden behind the law and his "rights," which he vigorously policed. Why not spread a little fear on Pablo's side for once? Hit *him* where it hurt most?

What was needed was some extralegal muscle, some hands-on players who didn't mind crossing the lines of legality and morality that Pablo so blithely ignored. The drug boss certainly didn't lack for bitter enemies, but they had no commonality. They ranged from some of the wealthiest and most powerful families in Bogotá to rival street thugs in Medellín and Cali. What if someone were to give them a push, some organization, some money, some intelligence, some training, planning, and leadership . . . ?

Los Pepes were so perfect they were . . . well, too perfect.

After the frustrations of the first six months, the manhunt needed to shift gears. If Pablo stood atop an organizational mountain that consisted of family, bankers, *sicarios,* and lawyers, then perhaps the only way to get him was to take down the mountain.

The bookstore blast had just about finished off what was left of Pablo's popular following outside Medellín. The government, responding to public outrage, officially declared him "public enemy number one." They dropped their reluctance to post a reward and offered the unprecedented sum of 5 billion pesos ($6.5 million) for information leading to his capture. DEA agent Peña felt a definite shift in mood at the Holguin base, where he was doing one of his regular monthly rotations. On the day of the blast he encountered a group of Martinez's top men emerging from a meeting with the colonel. They told Peña that "things have changed now." The hunt, already bloody and terrible, was about to take an even darker turn.

In the weeks following the bookstore blast, bodies of Pablo's associates began turning up all over Medellín and Bogotá. Sometimes they were victims of *Los Pepes*, sometimes of the Search Bloc. Some of his closest partners had already managed to give up. On October 8, Pablo's brother Roberto and "Popeye," Jhon Velasquez, had surrendered and were promptly locked up at Itagui, the nation's conventional maximum-security prison. But in most cases, where the police were involved, the reports read, "Killed in a gun battle with the Colombian police."

The official forces arrayed against Pablo were not always at pains to disguise their preference for killing him rather than taking him alive. Santos, Vega, and the other Delta operators at the Holguin base were not distressed by this attitude; they embraced it. The debacle of Pablo's first imprisonment had illustrated the futility of bringing him to justice. As they saw it, there was a race going on between Attorney General de Greiff, who had hopes of negotiating surrenders for all the country's *narcos*, and the embassy and the police, who wanted Pablo dead.

No one would say that, of course. In the DEA memos over these months, the agents employed an amusing kind of doublespeak. A September DEA memo noted that both the national police and the U.S. embassy hoped that somehow Escobar would be "located" before he struck another deal with the government, "which could amount to the beginning of a new farce." In a memo drafted by DEA agent Murphy in October, he wrote, "It should be noted that the CNP remains optimistic in their effort to capture Escobar if they can 'buy' some time by preventing his surrender. The BCO will continue to offer any and all assistance available."

If the hunt was going to turn ugly, the Americans in place knew how to get the job done. CIA chief Wagner was no stranger to the dark underside of South American affairs. He had begun his service in 1967 in Chile, leaving shortly before the agency-backed overthrow of socialist president Salvador Allende by Augusto Pinochet in 1973. Wagner had served in Uruguay battling the sophisticated Tupamaro urban guerrillas, and had then opened a CIA station in Haiti before becoming acting chief of the agency's Miami office, where he'd helped supervise operations in twenty-six nations, including Cuba. During his tenure in Miami, there were bloodless coups in Grenada (1979) and Suriname (1980). He was a reticent but worldly man, an avid gun collector and outdoorsman who didn't look the part, with his pale complexion, glasses, and easy, informal manner. But beneath his laid-back style, there was nothing passive about Wagner. He knew how to play hardball, both in the field and in Washington. He had been assigned to antinarcotics work up at headquarters in Langley, Virginia, back in the early eighties, before the agency got very interested in it, and in a few short years he had shepherded the effort into one of the agency's primary missions. One of his goals in Colombia was to establish a link between cocaine trafficking and the *FARC* and *ELN,* links that would justify pushing antinarcotics work from the realm of law enforcement into the realm of war. This was the bigger picture Wagner had had in mind when he arrived in Colombia in January 1991, and Pablo's escape a year and a half later had hastened the transition. Now Wagner had the kind of resources in Colombia needed to wage war against the *narcos,* and for him the hunt had become a full-time job.

He was not alone. General William F. Garrison, head of the Joint Special Operations Command and the direct authority over Delta Force and Centra Spike, had a long history in covert U.S. operations. He had been involved with the Phoenix program in Vietnam and was known throughout the army as an officer who could navigate beneath the radar. Counterinsurgency had always flirted with extralegality, whether in the Congo, El Salvador, or Nicaragua. The death squads were horrible, but nothing equaled them for striking fear into the hearts and minds of would-be Marxists. Ambassador Busby was no stranger to this world, either. He had been the State Department's ambassador-at-large for counterterrorism. He believed that virtuous goals sometimes demanded hard methods, and he had seen the advantages of playing ugly. It was always a temptation. There would always be powerful, well-intentioned men who believed that protecting civilization sometimes required forays into lawlessness.

Killing Pablo was one very specific goal, by now only indirectly related to cocaine. Justice demanded it. He was "too big for his britches," in the words of one of those involved. He had to be stopped. If that could not be done within the strict language of a deployment order, then there were other ways. If it was handled discreetly, who would know except those who had much to lose by revealing the truth?

When *Los Pepes* surfaced, there was no shortage of likely suspects. Pablo had been warring with other drug exporters and crooks all of his adult life. His years-long campaigns of intimidation and murder had left hundreds, if not thousands, of aggrieved family members, some of them from very wealthy and powerful families. And fratricidal violence was a way of life in Colombia. Homicide there enjoyed an overlapping abundance of motive; every corpse could claim a dozen authors. If a bomb went off or a beloved cousin was kidnapped or one of Pablo's key associates was found dead, the list of potential suspects was dizzying. Was it a family dispute, a random murder, or a hit from a rival cartel? Had it been ordered by Pablo himself, after falling out with the victim (as with the brothers Moncada and Galeano)? Was it some faction of the Medellín cartel trying to take advantage of Pablo's vulnerable state? Was it a rogue squad of army or police? Might it be a hit by one of the paramilitary squads who specialized in terror and murder? The DEA? The CIA? Delta Force? Perhaps a squad of guerrillas, the *FARC* or *ELN,* demanding a tax on illegal earnings or avenging some slight, or perhaps just seeing an advantage in contributing to the nation's ongoing instability?

Given the timing and tactics, the most likely forces behind *Los Pepes* were the Moncada and Galeano families, against whom Pablo had declared open war, and the national police, which had lost hundreds of officers to Pablo's *sicarios* over the years. Pablo's executions of the Galeano and Moncada brothers had created civil war within the Medellín cartel. Having been in business with him for years, Dolly Moncada, Mireya Galeano, and Mireya's brother Raphael knew many of Pablo's secrets: where his money was invested, who his most trusted advisers were. They were certainly motivated. Within weeks after Pablo's escape, a DEA memo written by Murphy noted that the two families were trying to recruit *sicarios* "to battle Escobar," and were offering 20 million pesos ($29,000) to those willing to sign on. An October 16, 1992, memo by Murphy noted that Marta Moncada, a sister of the slain men, was cooperating with the hunt for Pablo. Writing in *The New Yorker* in 1993, journalist Alma Guillermoprieto reported that among the leaders of *Los Pepes* was a sister of the slain Galeanos and that their "troops" were drawn from the Search Bloc itself. Both the Galeano and Moncada families were angry, rich, and powerful, but they were not strong enough to go up against Pablo's organization on their own. Why not ally themselves with the big boys?

Daily DEA cable traffic from Bogotá to Washington, D.C., during the fall and winter of 1992–93 document how *Los Pepes* began coming together soon after Pablo's escape. In August, just two weeks later, the U.S. embassy flew an important new source to Washington; Dolly Moncada, the widow of William Moncada, the second of the two brothers Pablo had executed for allegedly withholding money from him. After William's disappearance, Pablo had sent word to Dolly demanding that she turn over to him all of her assets and threatening a war against her and her family.

Dolly was a dangerous woman. When she vanished in mid-August, Pablo came looking for her. Her former residence in Medellín was ransacked, and the caretakers were taken hostage. The kidnappers painted the word *Guerra* (War) on the walls. On August 4, a bomb exploded at a Medellín shopping center owned by the Moncada and Galeano families. Three weeks later Dolly's dead husband's business associate Norman Gonzales was kidnapped, held captive, and tortured over thirteen days. His tormentors tried drugs and electric shock in an effort to learn from him Dolly's whereabouts. Gonzales didn't know. Pablo then offered a $3 million reward for whoever could help him find her.

Instead of giving in to Pablo, an aggrieved and angry Dolly Moncada struck a deal with the Colombian government. In return for protection for herself and her family in the United States, Dolly handed over most of her family's assets and began cooperating in the pursuit. The Colombian government agreed to drop money-laundering charges against her sister.

The man who helped arrange Dolly's surrender and trip to the United States was Rodolpho Ospina, the grandson and great-great-grandson of Colombian presidents, who had himself gotten involved in drug trafficking back in the mid-1970s, and had quickly run afoul of Pablo. Ospina had survived two assassination attempts by the drug boss. Within days after Pablo's escape, Ospina was helping the authorities investigate the deaths of the Moncada and Galeano brothers. When word got out in Medellín that Ospina was cooperating, which it did quickly, he, too, was flown to the United States. Pablo put a $3 million price on his head.

Ospina was given the code name Juan Diego and the number SZE-92-0053. He proved to be a valuable ally. He explained how and why Gerardo Moncada and Fernando Galeano were killed. The drug boss's minions had discovered a secret cache where the Moncada and Galeano families had stashed $20 million in cash. The money had been sitting for so long it had grown moldy. Pablo had invited them to the prison for a meeting and then turned on them angrily. A DEA cable reported Ospina's account of what happened:

> Escobar argued that while he and his close associates were in jail and needed money for their expensive war with the Cali cartel, Galeano and Moncada preferred to store money until it became moldy rather than use it to help their friends. . . . Escobar convinced cartel members who genuinely liked Moncada and Galeano that if the two men were not killed, the Medellín cartel would be in a war with itself, and they would all perish. . . . Moncada and Galeano were killed by being hung upside down and burned. The informant says this is Escobar's favorite way of killing people. Their bodies were buried either in or just outside the prison. Afterwards, Escobar invited William Moncada along with Galeano's brother. Escobar invited them to the prison and then killed them.

Ospina's close relationship with the Moncadas and Galeanos made him a source of very current and useful information. He had plenty of reasons to cooperate. Apart from the price Pablo had placed on his head, his brother was about to be deported back to Colombia. Ospina's cooperation won his brother a year's stay on the deportation order. In late October Attorney General de Greiff called the U.S. embassy and asked authorities there to set up a meeting for him with their prize informant. De Greiff was flown to Washington, where Ospina's testimony helped build these four new murder charges against the drug boss.

Pablo hit back. On December 16, Lisandro Ospina, another of the informant's brothers, was kidnapped. Lisandro was a twenty-three-year-old student at MIT with no connection to his older brother's criminal activities. He had just finished a semester in Boston and was home for a holiday break. Thirty heavily armed men surrounded him as he shopped for clothes in Bogotá and took him away. He was later killed by his captors.

Ospina told agents in Washington that he wanted to return to Colombia and retaliate against Pablo personally. He was talked out of that, but he channeled his anger in another way.

For months now, in a series of debriefings with DEA agents, he had been outlining a broader campaign against Pablo. Impatient with what he saw as the polite legal tactics employed by official pursuers, he felt that the manhunt needed to go outside the law. He laid out an illegal vendetta that could have been a blueprint for the creation of *Los Pepes,* right down to the need to publicize their actions.

> SZE-92-0053 states that Pablo Escobar's apprehension should be planned by accomplishing five goals. First . . . key Escobar organization members . . . should be arrested or killed, if there are no charges pending against them in Colombia. [Second], SZE then named attorneys who handle Escobar's criminal problems and whose deaths would create havoc for Escobar. Third, the informant named properties and important assets belonging to Escobar which should be destroyed.

Ospina went on to list the key members of Pablo's current inner circle "essential to his survival" and five attorneys who, he said, "handle Escobar's criminal and financial problems and are worse than Escobar. These attorneys negotiate with the Colombian government on [his] behalf and are fully aware of the scope of [his] activities since [he] consults them before he carries out any action." These men should be killed, he said. Step four, according to Ospina, involved destroying Pablo's possessions. He enumerated Pablo's most prized properties and assets, his antique cars, his country homes, his apartment houses, his aircraft and airports:

> SZE claimed that in order to bring Escobar out of hiding, he needs to be provoked, or angered and made desperate so that he wants to strike back. The informant claimed that Escobar may then make mistakes. [He] recommended seizure and confiscation of Escobar's assets, or their literal destruction, as a means of angering Escobar.

Lastly, Ospina felt the pursuit needed to court the Colombian media. He noted that Pablo had bought tremendous influence during his campaign against extradition. "He controls the media through fear and payments, and has confused the Colombian public by having himself portrayed as a wronged Colombian citizen, not really as dangerous as he appears to be in the foreign press."

Ospina also suggested that the manhunt seek help from jailed Colombian drug traffickers who might be willing to trade useful information. Such an incentive was offered to Carlos Lehder, the former Medellín cartel leader who believed Pablo had turned him over to the authorities for extradition. The jailed cocaine boss described Pablo's methods of evading capture, how he moved from safe house to safe house and would never leave the immediate Medellín area. He gave the agents explicit insights into Pablo's habits and preferences:

> Escobar is strictly a ghetto person, not a farm or jungle person. He fears more the communist and nationalist guerrillas than the army, so he remains in the Magdalena Medio Valley, a non guerrilla region. Since the guerrillas remain in the high mountains one could disregard the mountains as Escobar's hiding place. . . . Escobar always tries to keep within distance range for his cellular phone to reach Medellín's phone base. That's approximately 100 miles, so he can call any time.
>
> Generally, P. Escobar occupies the main house with some of his hitmen, radio operator (Big High Frequency radio receiver), cooks, whores and messengers. For transportation they have jeeps, motorcycles and sometimes a boat. I have never seen him riding a horse. Escobar gets up at 1 or 2 P.M. and goes to sleep at 1 or 2 A.M.
>
> Fugitive Escobar uses from 15 to 30 security guards, with arms and WT (walkie-talkies). Two shifts of 12 hours each. Two at the main road entrance, some along the road, the rest around the perimeter of the main house (one mile) and one at his door. . . . The main house always has two or three gateway paths which run to the forest and thus toward a second hideout or near a river where a boat is located, or a tent with supplies and radios. Escobar is an obese man, certainly not a muscle man or athlete. He could not run 15 minutes without respiratory trouble. Unfortunately, the military-police has never used hunting dogs against him.

Anytime the lookouts on the far perimeter saw a vehicle approaching or a low-flying airplane or helicopter, they would "scream through those walkie-talkies," Lehder said, and Pablo would immediately flee. Until the Search Bloc got a lot smaller and a lot stealthier, Pablo would always know they were coming.

Lehder responded with his own suggestions for closing in on his former ally:

> The only realistic de facto solution, as I analyzed it, is a new military government or, at the very minimum, a freedom fighters brigade, controlled by the DEA, and independent of the Colombian politicians, police or army.... There is a great number of Colombian peoples from all walks of life that are genuinely willing to assist, support, finance and even participate in the effective forming of a civilian militia. . . . The rich, the poor, the peasant, the political left, center and right are willing to cooperate. Every day Escobar remains at large he becomes more powerful and dangerous.

When Lehder suggested a "civilian militia," it didn't require a stretch of the imagination. He was speaking a language well understood by the U.S. Special Operations Command. Organizing indigenous forces to combat insurgency was one of the founding doctrines of special warfare, exactly what President John F. Kennedy had had in mind when he'd created the Green Berets. In the ensuing thirty years, the John F. Kennedy Special Warfare Center and School at Fort Bragg, North Carolina, had compiled long experience in such work, from Vietnam to El Salvador. It was one of Garrison's specialties.

And if the Americans were looking for a "civilian militia" equipped to challenge Pablo Escobar on his own level, they did not have to look far. Colombia had a long history of death squads. One of the most notorious of its paramilitary leaders was Fidel Castaño, nicknamed "Rambo," a charismatic assassin and sometime drug exporter and diamond smuggler who had been close to the Moncada and Galeano families. Castaño was notorious for his brutality. He was rumored to have been responsible for the massacre of forty-five peasants in the Gulf of Urabá in 1988. After Pablo became a fugitive, Castaño contacted the Search Bloc to offer his help. In a cable to DEA headquarters written by Peña on February 22, 1993, the agent identified Castaño as "a cooperating individual":

> As a result of a disagreement with Escobar, Castaño contacted the CNP/Medellín task force [the Search Bloc] and offered his help in attempting to locate Escobar. Castaño advised the CNP that his disagreement with Escobar stemmed from his (Castaño) telling Escobar that he (Castaño) was not in agreement with his (Escobar) terrorist

campaign, i.e., bombs, police killings. Castaño was also concerned that Escobar could have him (Castaño) killed at any time as had been the case with the Galeano/Moncada brothers.

Castaño led the Search Bloc on an ill-fated raid in December, when a boat carrying three of Martinez's top officers capsized. Two of the officers were drowned as the raiding parties crossed the Cauca River. Castaño had reportedly made heroic efforts himself to rescue the men, and had pulled one of them from the water. In such ways he'd earned the trust and respect of the Search Bloc. The charismatic paramilitary leader brought dash and daring along with his valuable connections to the Colombian drug underworld. Few of Pablo's other former allies were evidently willing to take sides against him.

Peña wrote:

> Fidel Castaño had made telephonic contact with the incarcerated Ochoa clan (Jorge, Fabio and Juan David). Castaño asked the Ochoas to leave Escobar and join sides with him. Castaño explained that Escobar would have them killed just like the Moncadas and Galeanos. The Ochoas stated that they had recently given Escobar $500,000, however, they were thinking of abandoning him.... Castaño told the CNP/Medellín [the Search Bloc] that the Ochoas would never abandon Escobar for reasons of fear and that they "always lied in order to stay in neutral with everybody."

In Castaño, Lehder, Ospina, and the Moncada and Galleano families, the hunt for Pablo Escobar had gained allies who were eager to play by the bloody rules of Medellín criminal wars. Others were enticed to join the effort by a judicial decree sought by Attorney General de Greiff that granted amnesty to drug traffickers and other criminals who assisted the police in the manhunt.

One of those who took advantage of the decree was the pilot who called himself Rubin, who had fallen into cocaine smuggling through his friendship with the Ochoa brothers sixteen years earlier. Rubin's first impression of Pablo had never changed. He still saw him as a Medellín street thug, low class, who had bullied his way into the cocaine business. In the years that he and his friends the Ochoa brothers had worked for Pablo, he would occasionally remind his partners that "Pablo is nobody's friend." Indeed, when a close friend, married to one of the Ochoas' sisters, was kidnapped in 1985, Rubin immediately suspected Pablo. His partners refused to believe him, so Rubin began snooping on his own. When he'd collected evidence linking the kidnapping to Pablo, Rubin got a phone call from the drug boss, who asked, "How are you doing with your investigation?"

"We are very close," said Rubin.

"I want you to stop," said Pablo. "That guy is in the hands of very dangerous people, and you might find yourself in trouble."

Rubin understood perfectly. He stopped looking. He took the warning so seriously that he left Medellín and took his family with him. For months they moved from place to place and avoided telephones. Pablo tracked him down more than a year later—his kidnapped friend had been killed—and asked him for $1 million.

"I won't give you a dime," Rubin said.

"Do you know what you are doing?" Pablo asked.

"Yes. I know I'll have to hide for the rest of my life."

Not long after the escape, Rubin was approached by DEA agent Peña, who asked if he would be willing to help enlarge the search effort's pool of informants in Medellín. Rubin agreed. He joined the effort against Pablo, and his criminal past in Colombia was wiped clean.

By the end of that year, a notorious cast of characters had assembled to assist in the manhunt, some of them in the United States, most of them in the war zone of Medellín. In the States there were Ospina, Dolly Moncada, Lehder, and others. Among those in Medellín were Castaño and his brother Carlos, Marta Moncada, sister to the slain Moncada brothers, Mireya and her brother Raphael Galeano, the traffickers Eugenio García, Luis Angel, Oscar Alzate, Gustavo Tapias, Enrique Ramirez, and an assortment of others. Among the group was Leonidas Vargas, a drug dealer who was on the DEA's "kingpin" list, and a notorious former Galeano family *sicario*, Diego Murillo, an obese man with buck teeth and a face disfigured with scars who walked with a limp. He was known as Don Bernardo, or just Don Berna.

Originally enlisted as informants, the group had begun killing early in the hunt. Murillo and other members of the group stayed in a house just outside the Holguin base and utilized three vehicles. DEA agents and Delta Force operators saw them there often, huddling with Colonel Martinez's top officers. On some occasions, Don Berna's men acted as escorts for Peña and Murphy when they left the base (contrary to instructions) to meet with informants. The group used DEA-supplied money to entice people to give information, and threatened to return with guns if they did not.

Up until the end of 1992 the "civilian militia" worked quietly, but in January 1993 a decision was made, just as Ospina had advised, to take a more visible role. Someone suggested to this group of Colombian criminals that they give themselves a name, just as Pablo had created the Extraditables and, earlier, Death to Kidnappers. A name, the existence of an organized cell of Colombian citizens bent on destroying Pablo Escobar, would strike fear into those associated with or related to the fugitive, if not to Pablo himself. To amplify the menace they needed to advertise, use the media. Their initial appearance was electrifying and started a national guessing game about their identity. Ambassador Busby thought the group had the look of a classic military "psy-op," or psychological operation, but he didn't know whose it was. Others immediately concluded that *Los Pepes* were simply Pablo's rivals in Cali.

At least one person felt there was no mystery. The day after his properties were bombed, in a note that pointedly refused to acknowledge the name *Los Pepes,* Pablo sent a note to Colonel Martinez.

> ... Personnel under your supervision set car bombs at buildings in *El Poblado* where some of my relatives live. I want to tell you that your terrorist actions will not stop my struggle under any circumstances. And my views will not change. Your threats and your car bombs against my family have been added to the hundreds of young people that you have murdered in the city of Medellín in your headquarters of torture in the school Carlos Holguin. I hope that the Antioquian community becomes aware of what you do with the dynamite you seize, and of the criminal actions undertaken by men who cover their faces with ski masks. Knowing that you are part of the government, I wish to warn you that if another incident of this nature occurs, I will retaliate against relatives of government officials who tolerate and do not punish your crimes. Don't forget that you, too, have a family.

The colonel hardly needed to be reminded. His family had been living with the threat for years. Just four months earlier, three police officers assigned to protect his family had been gunned down in Medellín. The hit was a very personal message from Pablo. The officers had been on their way to pick up the colonel's youngest son to take him to school.

But the colonel was not going to back down. *Los Pepes* added new life to an effort that seemed to be going nowhere. A formidable array of enemies were now closing in around Pablo. The effort up until now had been devoted to finding Pablo himself and, in effect, to plucking him off the top of his mountain of financial, legal, and organizational supports. Now the tactics had shifted. Officially and unofficially, Pablo's enemies had begun to take down the mountain.

3

In February 1993, *Los Pepes* began killing in earnest. On the 3rd, the body of Luis Isaza, a low-level Medellín cartel manager, was discovered in Medellín with a sign around his neck that read, "For working for the *narco-terrorist* and baby-killer Pablo Escobar. For Colombia. *Los Pepes.*" Four other low-level cartel workers were found murdered in the city that day. The next day two more were found murdered, two men known to be Pablo's business associates. There were more bodies the next day, and the next, and the next, up to six people a day.

It was a controlled bloodbath, because all of the victims had one thing in common—Pablo Escobar. Among them was a former director of the *Policía Nacional de Colombia* who had been publicly linked to the Medellín cartel. On February 17, one of the dead was Carlos Ossa, the man thought to be financing Pablo's day-to-day operations. Ossa, who was shot several times in the head, had taken over the duties of a man who had disappeared after taking over for another who had also disappeared. On the same day Ossa's body was found, a government warehouse burned to the ground, destroying Pablo's collection of seventeen antique and luxury cars, valued at more than $4 million and including a Pontiac he had purchased in the mistaken belief that it had once been owned by Al Capone.

As the murders and fearful surrenders mounted, *Los Pepes* publicly offered cash rewards for information on Pablo and his key associates, and began broadcasting threats against the drug lord's family. Just a few weeks after surfacing, the vigilante group had spooked Pablo more than anything the government had been able to do.

On February 19, Peña learned from the prosecutor's office in Medellín that Pablo would try to fly his children to safety in Miami. Maria Victoria had purchased tickets for Juan Pablo, Manuela, and Juan Pablo's girlfriend, Doria Ochoa on an Avianca flight that was scheduled to leave Medellín at 9:30 AM.

Ambassador Busby moved fast. All along he had been looking for ways to put pressure on Pablo, methods that would make the fugitive drug boss stick his head up, so to speak. Now that *Los Pepes* were spreading fear throughout Pablo's world, the fugitive's family was his most vulnerable pressure point. It would not do to have them safely tucked away in the United States. Meeting with Colombian defense minister Pardo at his residence early that Saturday morning, Busby explained that he did not want the family to leave.

"Do they have visas?" Pardo asked.

They did. They were not criminals, Busby explained, so there had been no grounds for turning them down. The two men discussed options. If the Escobars had applied for simple tourist visas, perhaps they could be revoked with the argument that fleeing for their lives was not tourism. Busby had just about decided to simply cancel their visas on that basis when an aide suggested, "Why don't we poke fun at him?" Instead of declaring the Escobars ineligible for visas, they would reject them on the grounds that children under the age of eighteen could not travel to the United States without both parents.

Peña was at the airport when the children arrived, surrounded by bodyguards and their traveling companion, Doria Ochoa. Nine-year-old Manuela carried a small fluffy white dog. They were allowed to board the plane before police moved in. Three of the bodyguards were arrested; four others fled. Police shooed the children and their escort off the plane, creating tumult at the airport. A pack of reporters and cameramen arrived. Ochoa argued vehemently with Peña, who took their passports. Juan Pablo, a tall, chubby sixteen-year-old, joined in the commotion. In the midst of it all, the agent spied Manuela sitting on the terminal floor, quietly petting and cooing to her dog, shutting it all out. He felt sorry for her. She had a kerchief around her head, covering her ears, and he remembered the bomb blast some years before, which had reportedly damaged her hearing. He eventually handed back the passports, and the Colombian police informed Ochoa that they would not be allowed to fly.

The embassy took out newspaper ads the next day explaining that Juan Pablo and Manuela could obtain visas if both parents, Pablo and Maria Victoria, showed up in person to apply at the U.S. embassy.

By now Pablo knew how heavily invested the United States was in his pursuit. He was so thoroughly plugged in to the Colombian police that there was no way he could not know. Among the possessions found by the Search Bloc on another failed raid in March were detailed aerial maps of the area that the embassy had provided the Search Bloc soon after Pablo's escape. Such discoveries were deeply disheartening to the men up in the embassy vault. How could they trust any Colombian? There was a story in the Bogotá press just days after the maps were discovered that said Pablo had actually been found by the Search Bloc in January, but that they had accepted a $666,000 bribe to let him go. Attorney General de Greiff, reacting to the story, publicly accused Colonel Martinez's force of corruption. The story was false, but on some days it did seem as though *Los Pepes* were the only ones who shared the Americans' determination to get Pablo.

For his part, Pablo had always tried to avoid picking a fight with America, and the signs he was seeing clearly distressed him. Ambassador Busby received by mail a newspaper clipping in an envelope that looked to have been addressed in the fugitive's handwriting. The article clipped was a story about the decision to turn back the Escobar children, and in it a quote from one of Pablo's defenders, one line was circled: ". . . is it valid to cancel the visas of children because one is persecuting the father?"

On March 2, Busby received a handwritten letter from Pablo, with his signature and thumbprint at the bottom. It seemed some prosecutor in New York City had commented, in reference to the World Trade Center bombings, that no enemy of the United States could be ruled out in considering the source of the attack. Included on that list was the Medellín cartel.

> Señor Ambassador,
>
> After the terrorism that occurred in New York City, none of the United States law enforcement agencies have discarded the idea that the Medellín cartel is one of the possible suspects.
>
> I want to tell you that I didn't have anything to do with that attack, because in your country the government has not been participating in bombings, kidnappings, torture and massacre of my people and my allies.
>
> If all these sorts of things didn't happen when the extradition treaty was in place, then there is much less reason for it to happen now that it is not.
>
> You can take me off the list, because if I had done it I would be saying why I did it and what I want.
>
> With all consideration,
>
>   Pablo Escobar

The bloodbath continued. On February 28, the younger brother of a man who had handled real estate transactions for Pablo was kidnapped and killed, and the next day the realtor, Diego Londoño, turned himself in, claiming *Los Pepes* had also tried to kill him. That day Pablo's brother-in-law H.H., Hernan Henao, was killed by the Search Bloc when they raided his apartment in Medellín. H.H. had been arrested years earlier, but had been released from prison. Two weeks later the Search Bloc killed two of Pablo's top assassins in shoot-outs, and *Los Pepes* dispatched one of Pablo's top business associates. After another of Pablo's car bombs went off in Bogotá on April 15, killing eleven and injuring more than two hundred, *Los Pepes* exacted swift revenge, blowing up two *fincas* owned by Pablo's bankers.

Pablo's lawyers also became targets, for both the police and *Los Pepes*. The previous fall, the Search Bloc had raided a *finca* owned by attorney Santiago Uribe. The raiders were in the process of ransacking the place when Uribe himself drove up, saw what was happening, and tried to turn around to drive away. He was arrested, taken into the house, and questioned. Uribe denied knowing his fugitive client's whereabouts. Among his files they found letters from Pablo and tapes linking him to drug dealing, bribes, and murder—including the assassination just days before of Judge Myrian Velez, one of the "faceless" judges in Medellín, who had been appointed, supposedly in secret, to investigate the murder of *El Espectador* editor Guillermo Cano. Velez had been preparing to indict Pablo as the "intellectual author" of the murder.

In the letter about Velez's murder, Pablo denied responsibility but noted, "I think they did us a favor because she was aspiring to gain a higher position in the court system and she would have been very difficult to persuade to act in a righteous manner [i.e., accept a bribe]." All this evidence linking Pablo to murder and other crimes eventually would have been thrown out of court, having been obtained illegally. The DEA memo recounting this incident observed, "Upon completion of the search and as Uribe was departing the *finca*, the *PNC* supervising officer relayed a message that they [the national police] were continuing their search for Escobar and preferred that Escobar not surrender."

Another of Pablo's top lawyers, Roberto Uribe, had also been feeling the heat. Since that first meeting with the drug boss years ago at Nápoles, Roberto Uribe had grown fond of him, and had convinced him-

self that all the allegations against his infamous client were false—or that
Pablo had been forced to do certain things to protect himself. He hadn't
seen Pablo since the escape but had spoken to him on the phone several
times. Pablo had said his only options were to negotiate a new deal with
the government or remain a fugitive for the rest of his life. The lawyer felt
a professional obligation to work on a surrender deal, but so far had gotten nowhere with the Gaviria administration. He was convinced that the
government was no longer interested in surrender. The whole process was
now extralegal.

This assessment was based in part on his own experience with the
Search Bloc. After his office was raided, Roberto Uribe agreed to drive to
the Holguin school to answer questions.

"You're a criminal!" Colonel Martinez told him. "A terrorist!"

In the story Uribe later told a judge, the colonel's men then planted
a pistol and a stick of what looked like dynamite in his car and arrested
him. He was later released by a judge who dismissed the charges.

All of this was mild, and had occurred before *Los Pepes* had surfaced.
Now things were much worse. On March 4, one of Pablo's legal team, Raul
Zapata, was found murdered, and a note left with the body threatened four
other lawyers. Two of those on the list were killed weeks later as they were
leaving Modesto prison in Bogotá, one an attorney for Pablo's brother
Roberto. Any public outcry over these killings was far outweighed by anger over another huge blast in Bogotá, attributed to Pablo, on April 15. A
car bomb loaded with more than three hundred pounds of dynamite exploded at a busy intersection, killing eleven people and injuring more than
two hundred. The nightly news was filled with images of flaming vehicles,
victims trapped in the carnage crying for help, and bloody bodies.

Los Pepes answered immediately. They blew up three *fincas* owned
by members of the Escobar family. On April 16, police found the tortured
body of Pablo's most prominent lawyer, Guido Parra, along with that of
his eighteen-year-old son, Guido Andres Parra, stuffed in the trunk of a
taxi in a deserted area near an Envigado country club in Medellín. Parra
was the lawyer who had negotiated Pablo's surrender almost two years earlier, who had conferred with the families of the kidnapped journalists and
with the president, and who had confessed how much he feared his client.
He had been abducted from his apartment in Medellín by fifteen heavily
armed men who had arrived in three cars. Father and son were found with

hands bound in plastic tape and bullet wounds to the head, along with a chilling hand-lettered sign that read, "Through their profession, they initiated abductions for Pablo Escobar." It was signed, "*Los Pepes*," and had a postscript: "What do you think of the exchange for the bombs in Bogotá, Pablo?" The body of the taxi driver was found about a mile away, with a sign that accused him of working for the Medellín cartel.

Three of Pablo's best-known attorneys, Santiago Uribe, José Lozano, and Reynaldo Suarez, publicly resigned from his service. Lozano made the mistake of secretly continuing the work, for which he was shot twenty-five times in downtown Medellín as he walked with his brother, who was badly injured. In July seven other lawyers who had worked for Pablo or the cartel resigned (Uribe for the second time) after *Los Pepes* again publicly threatened "potential harm or murder." No one doubted that they meant it. Roberto Uribe, the lawyer whom Colonel Martinez had tried to lock up, sought protection from Attorney General de Greiff. He went into hiding, spending time in the United States and at a remote house on the Colombian Pacific coast. He couldn't work or contact his family or friends. He spent his time lying on the beach and watching television.

As lawlessness accelerated over the spring and summer, no one from Washington questioned it, or questioned America's commitment to the pursuit. Civilian overseers from the Clinton administration were new in office, and knew next to nothing about what the U.S. military was doing in Colombia. People were always getting killed by one faction or the other down there, so reports of bombings and murders did not seem out of the ordinary, and no one from Colombia or the U.S. embassy was complaining or explaining. No one except Pablo, that is. On April 29, he wrote a letter to de Greiff:

> *Los Pepes* have their headquarters and their torture chambers in Fidel Castaño's house [in Medellín], located on El Poblado Avenue near the country club.... There they torture trade unionists and lawyers. No one has searched the house or confiscated their assets.... The government offers rewards for the leaders of the Medellín cartel and for the leaders of the guerrillas, but doesn't offer rewards for the leaders of the paramilitary, nor for those of the Cali cartel, authors of various car bombs in the city of Medellín.
>
> The state security organizations have zero victories in the matter of the assassinations of the lawyers, zero victories in the *El Poblado* car bombs, zero victories in the investigation into the deaths of the trade

unionists and zero victories in the investigations into the massacres in which thousands of young Antioquians have died. I remain disposed to turn myself in if given written and public guarantees. . . .

Regards
Pablo Escobar

Up in the vault at the embassy, Centra Spike analysts weren't missing the distinct pattern in *Los Pepes*'s hits. The death squad was killing off the secret white-collar infrastructure of Pablo's organization, targeting his money launderers, bankers, lawyers, and extended family, as if using the very charts that Centra Spike and the CIA had painstakingly assembled over the previous six months. What's more, the hits often corresponded with fresh targeting information Centra Spike was turning over to CIA chief Wagner, who was passing it along to the Search Bloc. It was not just who *Los Pepes* killed but who they did not. There were certain key individuals in Pablo's inner circle who were monitored constantly by the Americans, often with video as well as audio surveillance. Not only were these people key to intelligence gathering, but anyone paying them a visit, threatening them, or killing them would likely show up in the American monitoring. These were the people *Los Pepes* left alone.

Supplying intelligence to abet murder, such as the street address of a target who was subsequently killed, certainly appeared to be in violation of Executive Order 12333. Not all of the men in Bogotá were eager to hazard their careers and freedom on the legal opinion authored in 1989 by the Defense Department's legal counsel. So they were careful. Major Steve Jacoby turned his Centra Spike intelligence over to Wagner, and what happened to it after that was officially, as far as he was concerned, none of his business. Wagner passed along to the Colombian government the information he thought would be most helpful, but there was also an unofficial channel. The complete daily intelligence reports were collected in a red book that was left in an area where any official visitors to the embassy could check them out. Colombian police officers paid regular visits. Everyone was pleased with the results *Los Pepes* produced. A DEA memo to Washington in April summed up the official attitude at the embassy:

The attacks by *Los Pepes* further demonstrate their resolve to violently retaliate against Escobar each and every time Escobar commits a terrorist attack against the GOC and/or the innocent citizens of Colombia. Although the actions are not condoned nor approved by the CNP nor the BCO [Bogotá country office, the U.S. embassy] they may persuade Escobar to curb such behavior for fear of losing members of his own family. Too, these types of attacks will seriously cut into those assets owned by Escobar and his associates.

No one in Washington was watching too closely. With every change of administration in Washington there came a window of opportunity for the covert ops community. It took President Clinton weeks to fill hundreds of staff positions, and it took the new appointees months to fully learn their jobs. Career military officers and bureaucrats were aware of this interruption in oversight and had been known to take advantage of it. So it might have been no coincidence that *Los Pepes* went public just days after Clinton moved into the White House.

After the bodies of Parra and his son were discovered, President Gaviria was moved to publicly denounce the vigilantes. He offered a $1.4 million reward for information leading to the arrest of its members. The announcement was promptly followed by a communiqué from the group, announcing that they were disbanding, having "made a contribution" to the effort against Pablo.

During the previous fall, Rodolpho Ospina, the DEA's SZE-92-0053, had listed six key members of Pablo's organization who needed to be taken out, one way or another. By summer three had surrendered and were in prison—Roberto Escobar, José Posada (whose replacement, Carlos Ossa, had been killed), and Carlos Alzate—and one, Mario Castaño, was dead. Of the five lawyers Ospina had named, all were either dead or had publicly resigned. And despite *Los Pepes*'s announced disbanding, the killings continued. There were twenty more murders of Pablo's associates over the next three months, including his brother-in-law Carlos Henao and his cousin Gonzalo Marin. A nephew was kidnapped and never found.

By the end of June many of Pablo's relatives had fled the country or were trying to. The United States used all its influence to deny them safe havens. In early July the president of neighboring Peru announced that his country would not allow Pablo's relatives to enter, even as tourists. Meanwhile, Pablo's brother Argemiro and his son, as well as his sister Luz Maria and her husband and three children, were discovered in Costa Rica, where they were officially deported and flown back to Medellín. When Nicholas Escobar, a nephew, and his family were traced to Chile, the embassy prevailed on the government there to evict them. They appealed through Chile's courts, which bought them a few weeks. The effort to expel Nicholas, who was the son of Pablo's incarcerated brother Roberto, spilled into the Colombian press, and the embassy found itself criticized for "harassing" Colombian citizens. After losing their appeals in Chile, Nicholas and his family flew to Frankfurt, Germany, where, to the consternation of U.S. officials, the government refused to cooperate with continued tracking and electronic surveillance. Few other relatives slipped the net. In mid-July, Pablo's wife, Maria Victoria, filed a legal petition demanding that the Colombian government allow her children to leave the country. It was denied.

Pablo made another offer to surrender in March, just before the Search Bloc killed Mario Castaño, "El Chopo," the man who had succeeded Tyson Muñoz as chief of all the cartel's *sicarios*. The new surrender offer was delivered to the Roman Catholic bishop of the city of Bucaramanga. All Pablo asked now was that his family be given government protection, that he be given a private cell with his own kitchen (to prepare his own food in order to prevent poisoning), and permission to phone his family three times a week. President Gaviria reiterated the government's refusal to accept any conditions for Pablo's surrender, but Attorney General de Greiff sounded a dissenting view.

"I do not see any difficulty in abiding by these requests, not as a concession but as a solution."

De Greiff was increasingly at odds with the president. The pipe-smoking prosecutor believed he might be able to orchestrate an end to the country's *narco* plague on his own. *Los Pepes*, whom he had helped create through the amnesty program, were the stick. His ability to provide protection and legal forgiveness was the carrot. As the search for Pablo degenerated into a killing mission, de Greiff used his influence to push for Pablo's capture or surrender, not death. He became the good cop to Colonel Martinez's bad cop. His office assumed responsibility for protecting the drug boss's immediate family and offering bodyguards (paid for and fed by the Escobars) for the apartment building where they lived in Medellín. And he began to push, at least publicly, for the investigation and prosecution of *Los Pepes*.

By early August the new Clinton administration overseers had noticed how neatly the dirty work of *Los Pepes* dovetailed with the U.S. mission, and representatives from the Justice Department and the Pentagon made trips to Bogotá seeking answers. Busby was asked directly about the death squad in August, when Brian Sheridan, the deputy assistant secretary of defense for drug enforcement policy and support, visited Bogotá. The ambassador told Sheridan that there was no reason for concern and no evidence linking the group to Delta, Centra Spike, the Search Bloc, or the Colombian government.

But there were plenty of reasons for concern. The DEA had reported since the first appearance of *Los Pepes* that "[evidence] suggested that the police were cooperating with the group at some level, including sharing information," according to a memo written by Agent Murphy. High-level DEA officials knew that their source Rudolpho Ospina had helped form the group, and they knew of its connection to the Search Bloc because Ospina had told them about it. The informant's account of how and by whom *Los Pepes* was formed was outlined in great detail in a secret memo to Joe Toft, written more than a month before Sheridan's visit by Gregory Passic, DEA chief of financial investigations. Identifying Ospina only by his DEA source code, SZE-92-0053, Passic related Ospina's account of meeting with two officers in Colonel Martinez's Search Bloc (Majors Gonzales and Rieno [Martinez's chief operations officer, who subsequently drowned]) in the months after Pablo's escape. "SZE did in fact introduce remnants of the Moncada and Galeano trafficking groups to the *PNC* in Medellín who agreed to assist in locating Escobar," Passic wrote. "SZE states that some of the survivors of the Galeano/Moncada families had evolved into *Los Pepes*. Because he had introduced some of these people to the *Policía Nacional de Colombia* (*PNC*) last year [before *Los Pepes* went public] that connection with him exists. He described *Los Pepes* as Fidel Castaño, Carlos Castaño, Mireya Galeano, Raphael Galeano, Freddy Paredes, and Eugenio Ramirez, with the Cali cartel being financial backers. He is unaware of how involved the Medellín *PNC* group [the Search Bloc] is in the actions of *Los Pepes*, but states there is definitely a Cali, *PNC*, *Pepes* alliance of shared information on Escobar and his associates."

Busby hadn't seen this information, but he had seen enough to express his own concerns at length in a secret cable entitled "Unraveling the Pepes Tangled Web," dated August 1, just days before the meeting with Sheridan. The ambassador referred to himself throughout in the third person:

The GOC [Government of Colombia] has long been worried that police officials may have been cooperating with *Los Pepes,* and that the attorney general, Gustavo de Greiff, has now told Ambassador Busby that he has new, "very good" evidence linking key members of the police task force in Medellín charged with capturing Pablo Escobar to criminal activities and human rights abuses committed by *Los Pepes.* Our own reporting since early February has also suggested that the police were cooperating with the group at some level, including sharing information.

The cable was sent to the State Department, rather than the Pentagon, and carried instructions that it not be shared with other agencies. Sheridan would not see it until months later. In it, Busby discussed the circumstantial links between the Search Bloc and *Los Pepes.* The ambassador noted that he had met with President Gaviria on April 13 to "express his strongest reservations about the group." The ambassador requested that all police contact with Fidel Castaño cease, and he was assured that it would. The cable went on to note that when President Gaviria decided to crack down on *Los Pepes,* he had summoned a top police commander and told him to "pass the word." Busby noted:

> Gaviria's effort to send such an important message to *Los Pepes* via one of his key police commanders, however, indicated that the president believed police officials were in contact with *Los Pepes.*

The message clearly got through. The day after Gaviria sent it was the day *Los Pepes* announced they were disbanding. But the death squad continued its savage work, and evidence of a link to Colonel Martinez and the Search Bloc mounted. Busby wrote:

> On July 29, [Attorney] General de Greiff told the ambassador that the Fiscalia [attorney general's office] had enough evidence to issue warrants against the Medellín task force commander, Colonel Hugo Martinez, a "major," and four or five lower ranking police officials. The charges include accepting bribes, trafficking, and a series of human rights abuses, including kidnapping, torture and very possibly murder. According to De Greiff, he had "very good" witnesses.... De Greiff states that while some in the government had long assumed that *Los Pepes* may have been formed with the tacit support of the police in Medellín, and that the *Bloque de Búsqueda* [Search Bloc] was cooperat-

ing with the group on information sharing, "they went too far." He recalled that after early "harmless" attacks on *fincas* and apartments, in March the *Pepes* began targeting killing specific associates of Escobar. At this point, according to de Greiff, police officials were probably already too deeply involved with *Los Pepes* to withdraw. The witnesses' testimony indicates that not only were some members of the bloque and *Los Pepes* running joint operations, some of which resulted in kidnappings and possibly killings, but that the leadership of *Los Pepes* was calling the shots, rather than the police.

Gaviria had intervened to prevent the arrest of Martinez and the others for fear "the police might not obey" the order, the cable explained. The president was concerned that a public scandal involving the colonel and the Search Bloc would effectively end the hunt for Pablo, conceding another huge victory to the drug boss. "It would be terrible, if after all the deaths and upheaval in the country, Escobar was victorious," the cable noted. Gaviria had promised, however, that charges would be brought against Martinez and the others eventually, "even if they are national heroes."

Busby wrote that he had encouraged de Greiff to take immediate action against Martinez "if there was good evidence. . . . The investigation could then proceed at its own pace and the GOC would maintain the integrity of the unit." If "tainted officers" were kept in place, he wrote, "we would have no choice but to withdraw our support for the unit." The cable concluded:

> The ambassador's thinly veiled threats to withdraw our support unless immediate action was taken seem to have been heeded. . . . The Escobar *sicarios* have every reason to hate Martinez and the Bloque, and would not hesitate to lie if they thought they could gain revenge. We know Escobar has tried to link the Bloque and the *Pepes* in the past, and this could be part of that campaign. On the other hand, it is not hard to believe that policemen who have been hunting Escobar for years without success, who have seen the bloodshed firsthand, could not have been attracted to an "easy solution." Like the *Pepes*— with a push from Cali. The key points are for us to distance ourselves from the accused—by having them transferred—until the matter is clarified, and to continue to pursue the investigation.

The ambassador didn't know it, but the Colombian government was getting different advice from the DEA. One day after Busby wrote his

cable, DEA chief Toft and agent Bill Ledwith met with de Greiff. According to a DEA cable about that session, both Americans urged the attorney
general to leave Martinez in place:

> Obviously, the impending implications and repercussions which would
> be experienced by the GOC should this information become public
> would almost certainly overwhelm the Gaviria administration. Also,
> this type of information could potentially elevate Escobar once again
> to the status of being a hero in Colombia. . . . As information, the BCO
> [Bogotá country office/ the U.S. embassy] has enjoyed a long and suc-
> cessful working relationship with Colonel Martinez.

The DEA men noted Colonel Martinez's long service in the effort
against Pablo, how he had run the first war and had been called back from
Spain to resume the effort. They told de Greiff of the hardships he had
endured, the attempts on his life and his family. But mostly they argued
that the colonel was getting results.

> Of interest is the fact that the Medellín cartel has been decimated and
> practically brought to its knees, all under the leadership of Colonel
> Martinez. To date, the BCO continues to support Colonel Martinez
> and his subordinates.

That was apparently the message that got through. Martinez was not
transferred, there were no charges against him or any members of his Search
Bloc for involvement with *Los Pepes* nor would there ever be, and regardless of the concerns outlined in the memo, American support for the unit
continued. Toft never told Busby about his meeting with the attorney
general.

In the summer of 1993, despite their pledge to disband, *Los Pepes*
continued their bloody work, sometimes with evil panache. On July 14, a
prize stallion owned by Roberto Escobar was stolen, its rider and trainer
shot dead. The stud, named Terremoto, or Earthquake, was worth millions. The horse was found three weeks later, tied to a tree just south of
Medellín, healthy but neutered.

THE KILL

October 1993–December 2, 1993

1

Colonel Martinez did not protest when he learned that his superiors in Bogotá were planning to replace him and had even picked his successor. He offered to step aside. As the first anniversary of Pablo Escobar's escape passed, there seemed to be better reasons to leave than to stay. Colonel José Perez, his supposed replacement, was a respected officer who had been working on a poppy-eradication program, which meant he probably had a comfortable relationship with the U.S. embassy, so maybe this time they would finally accept the colonel's resignation and he could get on with his life. He requested a transfer to Bogotá, citing stresses caused by his long separations from his family, who had been sent back to the capital for their own protection.

Stress wasn't just an excuse. The hunt had created great strains in families, the colonel's perhaps most of all. His children had been forced out of school for long periods when they were in hiding, and he hardly saw them or his wife, who understandably blamed him for the problems in their marriage and with their children. As much as he wanted to finish the job, and as much as he felt that to step down would be an admission of failure, he was ready to do it gladly.

But his request was again rejected. Perez never came, and the war went on. The colonel and his men were locked in a battle to the death with Pablo and his *sicarios*. One day when his men whooped in celebration after receiving word that a raid had killed yet another of Pablo's henchmen, one of Pablo's *sicarios,* recently captured, witnessed the celebration and was clearly saddened by the news. Ever polite, Martinez apologized for the display, and the captive told him, "No need to apologize; it is how we react when one of your men is killed."

The toll of the hunt was terrible, but the police could afford to lose more men than Pablo could. By the summer of 1993 the once powerful Medellín cartel was in shambles. Pablo's old *fincas* stood empty, looted and burned. His old palatial estate, Nápoles, was now a police headquarters. Many of his former allies had abandoned him, offering to trade information about his whereabouts in return for government acquiescence in their own drug trafficking. But the man himself was still at large, moving from hideout to hideout, trying to hold together his crumbling empire, still setting off bombs, still sowing terror.

There were those who refused to believe that with all his resources and support Martinez could not have found Pablo if he was really trying. An article in *Semana* polled officials in Bogotá for opinions about the Search Bloc's failure, and reported that "corruption" was believed to be the primary reason. The second reason most frequently cited was "inefficiency." Some of the colonel's top officers complained that the effort was ruining their careers.

The Americans provided money, guidance, and information, and their support kept him in command, but Martinez knew that he still lacked their complete trust. One day late in the summer of 1993, Colonel Santos, the Delta commander at the Holguin base, and DEA agent Peña brought him a tape Centra Spike had recorded of a radio conversation between Pablo and his son. Martinez was excited. It was the first time he had actually heard Pablo's voice in more than a year. He wanted his men to study it, analyze it. The gringos allowed him to listen to the tape but refused to give him a copy.

Martinez was furious. Peña and Santos were apologetic, but they had their orders.

"Look, Colonel," Peña said. "I feel bad about it myself. You want to kick us all out of here, shit, kick us out. We'll leave right now."

He secretly allowed the colonel to copy the tape, but Martinez stayed angry about the official snub. He had long since embraced American technology and had even allowed the covert American role in his command to grow. On July 14 he had met at the Holguin school with U.S. Army colonel John Alexander, down from Joint Special Operations Command headquarters at Fort Bragg, and agreed to allow Centra Spike to establish a ground-based listening post in the Medellín suburbs to supplement its Beechcraft flights. Martinez had also proved agreeable to Alexander's suggestion that Delta begin playing a more active role in "development of targets and subsequent operational planning." The ambassador himself had met with Martinez at the Holguin base on July 22, the first anniversary of Pablo's escape, to tour the facility and underscore America's continuing urgency and commitment.

Martinez was willing to try anything. If his superiors would not let him off the hook, finding Pablo and finishing this was the only way out. When he learned that a special unit of Colombian police had been achieving success in tests with a new portable direction-finding kit, he asked for that, too.

There was only one problem. The special unit included his son Hugo.

"Send the team, but I don't want you to come here," the colonel told his son. Martinez had known about his son's work for a long time, and without telling Hugo had twice intervened to keep his unit from coming to Medellín. The task was simply too dangerous. Coming and going from the protected base would blow their cover, so the team would have to live and work undercover in the city. Given the bounty Pablo had placed on the head of every police officer in Medellín, and the even higher reward for killing a member of the Search Bloc, he feared putting his son in such a position.

"It's my unit, Dad," Hugo pleaded.

"Send someone else," the colonel said.

"No, I'm ready to go," Hugo said. "This gives me and my team and our equipment an excellent chance to prove ourselves."

"I really don't want you to come. You're too much of a target for him."

"No, Dad, I really want to be involved. I really want to come." Hugo explained that he and his mother, brother, and sister had been living with the threat of Pablo now for years. Once, knowing that his conversation was being recorded and would eventually reach Colonel Martinez's ears, Pablo had said, "Colonel, I'm going to kill you. I'm going to kill all of your family up to the third generation, and then I will dig up your grandparents and shoot them and bury them again."

"I'm already involved," pleaded Hugo. This way he would at least have the chance to fight back. As a family, he told his father, they needed to resolve this, "so that it is not always going to be hanging over our heads. We can do it together." Hugo told his father that he was an important part of the surveillance team. "It won't work as well without me."

Young Hugo looked nothing like his father. He was short, stocky, and dark where his father was tall, fair, and slender. He shared his father's keen intellect, but was also a visionary, an infectious leader, the kind of man who could convince other people to follow him even when only he understood where they were going. Certainly the colonel had some of that. He had managed to keep the Search Bloc together through years of great difficulty, and keep them focused on a task that seemed impossible. But the father was aloof. He led by stern discipline and example. Hugo led with enthusiasm. When he got talking about technical matters that often only he understood, Hugo flushed with pleasure. He would grab sheets of paper and a pencil and begin making scratchy diagrams of his ideas, leap to his feet, gesture, explain, exhort. His belief in technology was evangelic.

During his father's first war against Pablo, Hugo had been a student at the national police academy in Bogotá, and as a cadet he had escaped much of the change Pablo's threats had imposed on his mother, brothers, and sister. He worried about his family, and their predicament angered him. When he graduated, Second Lieutenant Hugo Martinez was sent to the *DIJIN*, which was primarily an investigative arm of the Colombian judiciary.

He was placed with an electronic-surveillance unit that had been given a new portable eavesdropping and direction-finder by the CIA. It looked like a prop from an early science-fiction movie, a gray metal box about one square foot in size, with cables snaking out the sides to supply electricity and data, and a spray of antennae on the top, one at each corner and six more in the center. It had a screen no bigger than the palm of his hand that displayed a green line, which indicated both the strength and the direction of a signal. The whole contraption fit inside a bulky suitcase and was used in concert with the much larger French and German equipment, which was housed in three big gray vans. The vans would park on the hills just outside Bogotá and raise their antennae. To the uninitiated they looked like electric-company repair vehicles. The three vans would triangulate the target signal, placing it within a proscribed area of the city. Hugo would then cruise through the streets of the hot neighborhood with another officer in an unmarked car, wearing headphones connected to the box that picked up the radio signal and indicated its strength by varying the pitch of a homing tone. In theory, Hugo's team would pinpoint the signal to the correct building, even the correct floor and apartment.

It never worked. The equipment functioned somewhat in flat, unobstructed terrain, but in the city, where they needed it most, the jumble of electrical wires, walls, and competing signals made it hopeless. They tried other systems. One, from France, was promptly dubbed "the Rooster." It had to be lugged around by the operator outside of a vehicle, with a box that hung on straps over his shoulders, attached by cable to a handheld antenna that looked like a Buck Rogers ray gun. The gun was held head-high as the operator moved, which made him comically conspicuous walking down a city street. Trying to use it on a real undercover mission in a dangerous neighborhood would have been like wearing a neon bull's-eye on his back. Hugo went back to working with the CIA kit.

Their progress in direction finding was delayed because the team's simple eavesdropping capability was in demand. When President Gaviria learned that the national police could pull a van up to the curb outside a building and listen to conversations inside, Hugo's team was assigned to eavesdrop on guerrilla leaders who were in Bogotá for another of their endless rounds of peace negotiations. The snoop squad was able to supply government negotiators with inside information about the guerrillas' negotiating strategies, and alert them to new proposals before they were made. This service, of course, had nothing to do with the task of radio location. But Hugo found that his superiors were not especially interested in the technical details of his work, no matter how hard he tried to explain. They understood only that his unit could monitor more frequencies than any other equipment in Colombia, that they were portable and reliable, and that was enough. So the team developed a reputation for surveillance wizardry that overstated the actual case. In time, they got so good at analyzing the conversations they overheard that they were able to steer assault teams to the right places without having actually used any of their equipment.

They were not really getting better at radio direction finding; for that purpose the equipment was still useless. But they didn't let on. Each small victory brought them a better assignment. In 1991 and 1992 they were used against guerrillas in the southern part of the country. It was only after these missions that Hugo's commander was able to return to Bogotá and resume testing. They worked there for eight months.

And they got better. They combined the various components, American, French, and German, and developed techniques through trial and error. Hugo himself had fallen in love with the funny boxes. The more he worked with the kits, the more attuned he became to subtle nuances in the images they displayed and the sounds they emitted in his headphones, and what they meant. It was like learning a new language, or learning to navigate a terrain with an unfamiliar sixth sense. Hugo felt the box was telling him what he needed to know, but he had not yet learned to hear it.

In the first three or four months after Pablo's escape, Colonel Martinez had banned all cell-phone use in Medellín and closed down all repeater stations for transmitting signals, which forced people to use standard phone lines and limited radio communications to point-to-point—that is, the radio operators could not use repeaters to amplify and relay signals over long distances, so the only effective way to communicate between two radios was for there to be a clear line of sight between the transmitter and receiver. The idea was to isolate Pablo. He was too smart to use normal phone lines, but if he tried to communicate through the uncluttered airwaves he would be much easier to find. Pablo responded by using messengers. He resumed regular radio communication only in the spring of 1993, as he grew increasingly concerned about *Los Pepes* and began scheming to get his family out of the country. Pablo found places where he could see the top of the apartment building, *Altos del Campestre,* where his family was living under heavy guard, and he spoke most often to his son, Juan Pablo.

This was the weak link that the colonel wanted to exploit with the new, highly touted portable surveillance unit. They arrived in Medellín with Hugo, who had worn down his father's resistance. They found apartments in the city and were delivered six new CIA direction-finders, each with a Mercedes van. Three teams were created. Their arrival stirred high hopes in the Search Bloc. A CIA direction-finding crew had been working in the city since the previous November, with poor results. But the false reputation Hugo's unit had earned preceded it, and they had arrived in time to take advantage of an important new piece of information.

Medellín prosecutor Fernando Correa, who had taken to meeting frequently with Pablo's family, had noticed some things. The family was virtually imprisoned in *Altos del Campestre,* and lived in terror of *Los Pepes.* Increasingly their energies were spent looking for a way out. They were despondent. Maria Victoria wrote in a letter to her husband at about this time:

> I miss you so very much I feel weak. Sometimes I feel an immense loneliness takes over my heart. Why does life have to separate us like this? My heart is aching. How are you? How do you feel? I don't want to leave you my love. I need you so much, I want to cry with you. . . .
> I don't want to pressure you. Nor do I want to make you commit

mistakes, but if our leaving is not possible, I would feel more secure with you. We'll close ourselves in, suspend the mail, whatever we have to. This is getting too tense.

Chubby Juan Pablo, a hulking, imperious sixteen-year-old who stood six feet tall and weighed more than two hundred pounds, acted as the man of the house, at least in Correa's presence, and appeared to be making all the decisions for his family, even his mother. He spent hours with binoculars observing the neighborhood from his high perch, locked in the apartment, keeping a nervous eye out for those who appeared to be keeping an eye on them. He was watching when three men stepped out of a car and fired a rocket-propelled grenade at their apartment building. No one was hurt in the blast. Juan Pablo calmly noted their appearance and the make and model of their car. He also wrote down the license numbers of cars driven by those he suspected of working for Colonel Martinez, photographed men outside the building he found suspicious, and indignantly pushed the prosecutors who visited the family to pursue and arrest those he described. Unlike his mother, who was clearly overcome by the situation, Juan Pablo seemed to relish it. He seemed to enjoy his dealings with Correa and other representatives from the attorney general's office and used their fear of his father to bully them and build himself up in their eyes. He received coded written messages from his father and wrote him sprawling, cocky, even jaunty letters, conspiring happily in the cat-and-mouse game. In an undated letter written that fall, Juan Pablo bragged about standing up to a representative from the attorney general's office:

Remembered Father,
     I send you a big hug and warm wishes.
     I see that Corrales [Roberto Corrales, a liaison from the attorney general's office] is in high spirits, fighting *Los Pepes*. He doesn't have another choice anyway.... The prosecutor [de Greiff] played the fool about us leaving the country, ... to test us, to check what we were going to say and how we were going to react. I have been firm about your conditions and I have persuaded them. I even told them that you had planned to deal with the Cali people after turning yourself in, because you were willing to have peace back in the country.
     Corrales was very rude to me. We were talking and he started to tell me, "I have to look for your father because that is my mission.

I am not from here or there [I am not allied with one side or the other], I am a righteous person and he (you) knows that I am serious about that." So I told him that there was no need for him to tell me that to my face every time he came around here because he has been here three times and all three times he has said the same thing—that I knew that was his job but that he had to respect me, because it was my father he was talking about, and I told him he should calm down because my father was also after all those who were looking for him, and that destiny will say who finds whom.

He answered: "I'm afraid because it's my job and no one has told me to stop looking for your father, because there are forty arrest warrants against him." I answered: "This is not for you to be afraid, but for you to show me some respect because I am with him [Pablo] and I support him," so he'd better cut it out or else. Then I told him that the prosecutor was the most fake guy in this country, that how did he expect us to believe him regarding you turning yourself in if he wasn't a man who kept his word, and that he had protected us so far only to trick us with false promises. And he answered: "I don't allow anyone to speak about my boss at my table," and I told him: "I, like a member of this family, cannot allow you either to say bad things about my boss, who is my father."

Juan Pablo then passed along some information about where he thought Colonel Martinez sometimes stayed overnight in Medellín, and wrote out two pages of description of the men and cars he had been cataloging outside the apartment building. He concluded by suggesting that his father send a scare into a local TV station that had aired pictures of *Altos del Campestre:* "It would be good to tease the TV people so they won't make the building stand out so obviously, because when they came here they told me they were going to erase the tape and they didn't do it. Take care of yourself. I love and remember you. Your son."

On one official visit, Correa noted that Juan Pablo carried a beeper, and when it went off (at regular times during the day), he would abruptly leave the apartment. Correa presumed it was to speak on a phone or radio with his father. The prosecutor had seen cellular phones in the apartment, and on one of his trips he'd found a radio transmitter/receiver hidden behind the trapdoor on the ceiling of the building elevator. Colonel Martinez instructed Correa, on his next visit, to note the make, model number, and frequency range of the radio. He also asked Correa to do what he could to encourage Juan Pablo to speak for longer periods of time with his father.

Armed with the knowledge that Juan Pablo's radio had a frequency range of 120 to 140 MHz, and with a rough idea of when the Escobar father and son spoke, Hugo and his teams set about intercepting these calls and locating Pablo. They at first tried working with the CIA team. Hugo told his father, "With me there, you know you will get everything."

One of the first problems faced by the new unit, when they got out into the streets of Medellín, was deciphering the deceptive lingo Juan Pablo and his father had constructed to confuse their pursuers. They used code words and phrases as a signal to switch frequency, which they did quickly and often. At first it prevented the surveillance teams from getting even a general fix on Pablo's location, because every time father and son switched frequency, the signal would temporarily be lost. The direction-finding cars drove in random fits and starts throughout the city, racing a few blocks in the direction of a signal and then pulling over to the curb when they lost it. After a few days of this it became clear that with so many walls, overhead wires, high-rises, and other obstructions, central Medellín was the worst kind of environment for direction finding. They would fix on a signal coming from one direction, then lose it, and when it returned, it would send them in an entirely new direction.

In the first few weeks, the excited Search Bloc followed the efforts of Hugo and his teams with great interest. Once or twice they launched raids, breaking into the houses of frightened Medellínos who had no connection to Pablo Escobar. Very quickly, enthusiasm for this new tool dried up. The new little vans and CIA equipment were just another disappointment. The colonel told them to keep at it, but in time everyone assumed the only reason the teams were still around was because Martinez's son was working with them. This was humiliating for Hugo, because he knew it was true. But it wasn't true in the way everyone suspected.

Without a doubt, the rapid series of complete failures they produced would have sent any other unit packing, their antennae and weird little boxes heaped with scorn. But Hugo had his father's ear. They would sit together until late at night with the son working his evangelical spell, selling his father on the amazing potential of the machine, how clever its theory, how close they were to actually making it work. When it failed again and again he would explain to his father exactly why, his crew-cut head hunched over paper as he sketched out his diagrams with arrows and filled the margins with math. "It isn't something simple and straightforward," Hugo explained. His father listened and listened and asked questions and, in time, was converted. The rest of the Search Bloc may have considered the technology a useless whim, a father's indulgence, but the colonel had become a believer.

He believed it in part because of Hugo, but also because he needed to believe it. There had to be a way out of this endless struggle. The chase had boiled down to this contest between two men and their sons. Pablo's son was his weakness. The colonel's son might yet prove to be his strength.

2

In July 1993, Eduardo Mendoza, the idealistic young vice minister of justice whom Pablo had taken prisoner the night of his escape, was living a new life in America. He had sat through four months of stinging, humiliating, televised investigation before the Colombian Senate. He was lectured, insulted, and scoffed at as he tried to explain the mountain of circumstances that had made him look so guilty. He lost everything. When the Senate finished, retreating to prepare its report, Mendoza left the country. Giving his stereo to his brother and his law books to a friend, the lawyer who had sat beside him during those long months, trying to defend him, Mendoza flew to New York City.

In debt, disgraced, and with his future still clouded, he spent three months looking for work, applying at law firms that handled work from Colombia, hoping his experience there would be considered valuable. But there was no demand for a disgraced former vice minister of justice from Colombia. No one would hire him. His legal education was useless to him. In the winter of 1993, he found a job as foreman in a Miami warehouse, for a company that manufactured airplane parts, and one day that summer on his way to work, driving a battered used car and listening to a Spanish news station, he learned that he had been officially summoned for *indagatoria* in Bogotá.

Having helped draft the country's criminal statutes, Mendoza knew well what *indagatoria* meant. It was roughly equivalent to being summoned to appear before a grand jury in the United States, except in Colombia the questioning was done by a prosecuting judge, and even more than under the American system, such a summons was a prelude to indictment and imprisonment.

His friends urged him not to return. He had started a new life in America. In those lonely New York months he had met Adriana Echavarria, a young woman whose father was Colombian but whose mother was American, and they were in love. Adriana had grown up in the United States with her mother, and while she had maintained ties with her Bogotá family, she saw the country as most Americans did, a violent, corrupt, dangerous place. Having survived such an experience there, what kind of crazy man would go back, knowing he was going to be indicted and jailed?

But Mendoza knew he had to go back. He was innocent of the charges against him. His only hope of regaining the life he had lost was to prove it. The Senate had not yet issued its report. The investigation of the comptroller's office into the prison contracts had found nothing illegal in Mendoza's work. Ironically, the one misstep they found he had made was in ordering the luxury items removed from *La Catedral* in the months before Pablo's escape. Technically, as he had determined himself, Pablo's big-screen TVs, stereo equipment, waterbeds, and other amenities had all been legal. Mendoza was censured, and the seized goods were given to Pablo's family. The *procuradoria* investigation had found Mendoza, along with a lineup of others in the Justice Ministry and the army, negligent but not complicit in the chain of events that enabled Pablo's escape. It was recommended that he be fired, which, since he had already resigned, was moot.

The *indagatoria* pertained to the most serious of the probes, the attorney general's. It was the only one that carried the threat of criminal charges and prison. If Mendoza stayed in the United States, he knew Colombia would attempt to have him arrested in Miami and fight to extradite him. That would just make him look more guilty. He saw only two alternatives. He could break completely with his past and live as a fugitive in the United States, or he could go back and face the judges.

Adriana and his friends thought the first alternative was best. Colombia was a mad place, they argued with him. An honest man could not survive there. There was no moral imperative to answer charges brought by such a corrupt, misguided country. But Mendoza would not agree with them. He could not so completely renounce his country or his past. On the July day he flew back to Bogotá, almost a year to the day since he had flown up to Medellín and confronted Pablo, Adriana drove him to the airport in Miami and they both sat for a long time clinging to each other in the car. Mendoza was convinced he was throwing away his future. He would lose her, his reputation, everything. He was going to jail. But he felt he had no choice.

On the first day of *indagatoria* in Bogotá he brought along a small tube of toothpaste and toothbrush. The judges grilled him from 8:00 A.M. until midnight. They accused him of masterminding the whole thing, of building Pablo's fake prison, of covering up evidence of his supposed tunnel, of plotting and facilitating his escape—why else would he have flown up to *La Catedral* that evening? Why was a vice minister of justice needed to move a prisoner? They asked Mendoza how much money he had been paid and where he had hidden it. He held his ground as best he could. "Why would I have had to fly up to the prison to help him escape if I had been orchestrating the whole thing all along? Why wouldn't I have just let him out whenever he wished?" he asked. At the end of the session, much to Mendoza's surprise, the chief judge simply told him, "Okay, Señor Mendoza, we'll see you tomorrow morning at eight A.M."

He had so completely expected to be locked up that he had no place to stay. He slept that night on the sofa at his lawyer's house. His only consolation was that Adriana showed up. As afraid of Colombia as she was, as set against his going as she had been, she had defied her mother and flown to Bogotá to be with him. She was not allowed in the chamber when he was being questioned. She stayed at her aunt's house, sent word to him, and waited for him to call. He went to see her briefly after the first day's grilling. When he saw her for the first time there in Bogotá he was overcome by her courage, love, and loyalty. Her being there was both good and bad. He decided that if he somehow escaped this, he would ask her to marry him. But the prospect of marrying this smart, beautiful, and loyal woman was so sweet that it made the likelihood of his indictment and imprisonment all the more bitter. Look what a future was being taken from him!

The next morning the questioning resumed, and after another long day, he was again curtly instructed to return the following morning. He visited Adriana and told her about the day, then went back to his friend's couch. On the third day he noticed a shift in the tone used by his questioners. They were no longer as accusatory. Now the questions they asked seemed to be seeking insight and information. Mendoza told them everything he could remember about his year in the Justice Ministry, and about that night. They sent him home again and asked him to return a fourth time, and at the end of the fourth day the chief judge told him, "Okay, Señor, we suggest you get on a plane and leave and just forget about all this."

It was the happiest day of his life.

3

It was during the summer of 1993, as Mendoza was undergoing this ordeal, that most of the Centra Spike unit departed Colombia for two months. The unit joined the hunt for Somali warlord Mohamed Farrah Aidid.

The Somalia adventure lasted until October 3, when the task force's mission erupted into a fierce, fifteen-hour-long gun battle in the streets of Mogadishu that left eighteen American soldiers dead and scores more wounded. The battle had caught the Clinton White House by surprise, and in the weeks afterward, the administration began taking a harder look at covert operations worldwide.

It was in this climate that journalist Alma Guillermoprieto wrote a prescient article for *The New Yorker,* published on October 25, called "Exit El Patrón," that detailed the rapidly declining fortunes of the fugitive Pablo Escobar. It was a surprising look at the recent events in Colombia, far more insightful than anything previously published in the United States and certainly a far cry from the translated, summarized accounts from the Colombian press delivered by the embassy to the State Department. Guillermoprieto named the most likely individuals behind *Los Pepes,* the Moncadas, Galeanos, and Fidel Castaño, but also linked the illicit terror campaign against Escobar directly to Colonel Martinez's Search Bloc in Medellín. Describing her source as "a recently lapsed member of *Los Pepes,*" a man she called "Candido," she explained, "At the time the *Pepes* began their operations, Medellín was so crisscrossed with Search Bloc patrols and checkpoints that it would have been impossible for any group of Escobar's former associates—most of whom are wanted by the government, of course—to operate against him undetected. The logical solution was to ask for police and army volunteers to moonlight against their common enemy. . . . Candido, who seemed as boyishly enthusiastic about *Los*

Pepes as if he were still in their ranks, explained that both the Search Bloc and the regular police were frustrated by the legal and logistical restrictions on their operations against Escobar and were eager to join an effective organization like *Los Pepes,* who operate in small patrols, with sure targets and with trial- and paperwork-free executions to show for their efforts."

Guillermoprieto's story failed to draw a link between the murderous exploits of *Los Pepes* and the American units assisting the Search Bloc, but the connection leaped out at Lieutenant General Jack Sheehan, who as J-3 in the Pentagon was director of all current operations overseas, including special operations activity. Sheehan already strongly suspected that Delta and Centra Spike were overstepping the strict limits of their deployment order, which confined them to the Holguin base—the "forward staging base"—and restricted their role to training, intelligence gathering, and analysis. Sheehan was not a big fan of special operators anyway, and he regarded the men in charge, Generals Downing and Garrison and Ambassador Busby, as aggressive. He called such men "forward leaners," by which he meant that in their eagerness to succeed they sometimes tended to stray beyond the strict parameters of their missions. He had heard backchannel talk about Delta operators going out on raids with the Search Bloc, and he worried about a possible U.S. relationship, direct or indirect, with *Los Pepes.*

There wasn't just the fear that Delta operators were running around Colombia killing people. Sheehan doubted that was going on, although there was no telling. Delta's snipers were the best in the world. They would not have to actually be with raiding parties to play a lethal role, and if they were willing to let the Colombians take credit and the Colombians were happy to accept responsibility, who would ever know? What was more likely, even evident, was that information being gathered and analyzed by Centra Spike and Delta was being used to guide *Los Pepes.* That fell into the category of supplying "lethal information," something allowed only with authorization from the president and notification of Congress. The Clinton administration had just gotten badly burned by Garrison and his special operators in Somalia. The deployment order for sending the special ops units to Colombia in 1992 had been very clear. They were there to provide training. If they were going out on missions, even legitimate ones, they were exceeding their authority. What would happen if one of

Colonel Santos's men got hurt or killed out on one of the raids? It would raise an unholy stink in Congress, which had not been consulted. Beyond these concerns, Sheehan felt that what was at issue was civilian control of the military, something both he and his boss, General Colin Powell, chairman of the Joint Chiefs of Staff, took very seriously.

While the hunt for Pablo went on in Colombia, the American involvement had created a string of issues inside the Pentagon. When it was decided that chopper pilots for Colonel Martinez's Search Bloc needed training to fly at night with night-vision goggles, American pilots were sent to Medellín. The pace of the hunt was demanding, so any training would have to be given on the job. This provoked a big fight over whether sending pilots along to conduct training violated the prohibition against sending American soldiers along on raids. The pilots got permission to go.

So now there were American pilots going out on raids, which opened the door slightly for Garrison. After the repeated frustrations in the fall of 1992, Garrison wanted to send Centra Spike's skilled operators with their portable direction-finding equipment out with the American pilots on the Search Bloc choppers. Steering a raid to a specific spot required smooth coordination between the technician and the pilot, something the Americans had perfected. Here Garrison saw an opportunity to get official permission to send Delta operators out on raids (which they had been doing unofficially for many months with winks up and down the chain of command). The joint special operations commander argued that with an American pilot and technician accompanying the Search Bloc, Delta needed to go along, too, to provide protection.

The Joint Chiefs of Staff approved the request, but an under secretary of defense, Keith Hall, refused to concur without approval from the White House. Officers on Hall's staff were waiting at the White House for a meeting with President Clinton's staff when a colonel with the Joint Chiefs of Staff called to say they had decided to withdraw the request.

As time went by, Sheehan's misgivings about Colombia grew. He took his concerns to Powell, and the chairman, shortly before leaving the job in late September, asked him to look into it. Sheehan also discussed his concerns with Brian Sheridan, the deputy assistant secretary of defense who had met with Busby in Bogotá in August. Sheridan told Sheehan about that conversation, about how the ambassador had assured him there was no connection between *Los Pepes* and the legitimate forces pursuing Pablo. But acting on Sheehan's concerns, Sheridan started shaking the tree at the State Department and discovered the Busby cable about the vigilante group.

That cable and the *New Yorker* article seemed to confirm their worst suspicions. Then, in November, two CIA analysts met with Sheehan, Sheridan, and other top brass to report that *Los Pepes* were, in fact, Colonel Martinez's Search Bloc. The death squad's tactics matched those taught by Delta, which suggested that members of the Search Bloc were actually comitting the *Los Pepes* murders and bombings, which meant that the United States had bought, trained, and, in part, led the group. "These guys have gone renegade, and we're behind it," the analyst told Sheehan.

Others at the meeting criticized the report.

"Bullshit," one of them said, explaining that Ambassador Busby had been monitoring the situation and was convinced American forces hadn't been involved.

Sheehan believed the CIA report. He said he was taking the matter to the chairman and that all American special forces engaged in this hunt for Pablo were going to be pulled out of Colombia. Sheridan concurred. He expressed concern about how the revelation, or even suspicion, of an American military link to Colombian death squads would harm President Clinton.

It was late on a Friday afternoon, and the only hope of stalling the immediate withdrawal was to find someone on the Defense Department staff to countermand Sheehan. A young female staffer at the meeting, an aide to a two-star admiral on the defense secretary's staff, took off her shoes and sprinted down the hallway to quickly deliver the news.

Busby was furious when he learned of Sheehan's decision. As he understood it, the analysts who had briefed the Joint Chiefs were from the CIA's Directorate of Intelligence, not its Directorate of Operations. The two factions were often at odds, and the ops side usually prevailed. Whatever suspicions the ambassador had about *Los Pepes*, they were not sufficient to pull the plug on the manhunt. An American pullout at this point would almost certainly end the effort. Pablo would win. The ambassador was angry about not having been consulted. President Gaviria had stuck his neck out a long way politically for this operation, and Busby knew that his friend's administration probably wouldn't recover if the Americans backed out on him now. If Sheehan got his way, in Busby's view, it would amount to an unforgivable American betrayal. What allies would believe promises of American support in the future?

Busby had plenty of clout in Washington. He started making phone calls. As Sheehan would later remember it, the ambassador called Dick Clark, an assistant on the National Security Council in the White House. Clark intervened with Deputy Defense Secretary Walter B. Slocumbe, and a compromise was worked out with Sheehan. The lieutenant general still wanted Delta and Centra Spike out of Colombia, but he agreed to back off for a few weeks. Sheehan noted the irony. The general concerned about upholding civilian control of the military had been temporarily outflanked by civilians.

Sheehan was convinced that the mission in Colombia had strayed beyond its legal bounds. It was shaping into a first-rate blowup in Washington, but the issue would never come to a head. It was about to be overtaken by events in Colombia.

4

After the initial failures of the portable direction-finding kits in Medellín, the unit's leaders were sent packing, and Colonel Martinez placed his son Hugo in command. The Search Bloc continued to provide security for them, although the team was now considered a joke. Hugo himself was regarded with amused contempt.

Determined to redeem themselves, he and the other men began working round-the-clock shifts with the CIA agents, monitoring the known frequencies on the radio used by Juan Pablo. With Centra Spike gone, the Colombians placed an antenna on a hilltop just outside the city that helped the mobile units fix on the signal from Juan Pablo's radio. This effort showed that Pablo was now talking one hour each evening, roughly between 7:15 and 8:15. Hugo assigned one scanner to monitor the frequencies most often used, and another to scan the entire 120 to 140 MHz range. They listened night after night.

Through trial and error, they were able to break the code employed by father and son. If Pablo said, "Let's go up to the next floor" or "The evening has ended," it was a signal to shift to a specific frequency. Once the police units knew the code, they were able to follow the signal as it shifted. It was clear to Hugo that Pablo and his son believed their clever precautions made it impossible for their conversations to be tracked for more than a few moments at a time.

Still, in early October they had more setbacks. Working with the CIA agents, Hugo's team tracked Pablo's location to San José Seminary in Medellín. The CIA plane had tracked the fugitive's radio signal to that neighborhood, and the mobile units had placed him inside the large seminary complex. Pablo had a long-standing cordial relationship with the Catholic church in Medellín, and his son had attended San José's elementary school years before, which meant that his father likely knew people there. It was considered a promising target, and the colonel planned a big raid.

The next day, when Pablo's voice came up on the radio at the appointed time to talk with his son, the tracking equipment again pointed to the seminary. The signal on the screen and in his headphones told Hugo that Pablo was speaking from inside the complex's main building. The raid was launched while Pablo was still talking. Doors were blown off, flash-bang grenades exploded, assaulters loudly descended . . . and Pablo kept talking, as though nothing were happening. Apparently, wherever he was, nothing was. When the leaders of the assault teams came to Hugo with the news that they had found nothing, Pablo was still talking on the radio.

"He's in there!" Hugo insisted, trusting his equipment and his ability to read the signals.

"He's not in there," the major in charge of the raid said. "*We're* in there. We've done our search."

Pablo was still talking. There was no background noise, nor had he been startled. By the evidence in his ears, Hugo had to conclude that the raid had not even come close. Yet his equipment pointed him straight to the seminary! The assault teams, more convinced than ever that they were wasting their time, and with deepening scorn for the teams' worthless gizmos, continued searching on the chance that Pablo had a secure hiding place somewhere on the grounds. Over the next three days five hundred men proceeded to take the seminary and the attached school apart. They poked holes in walls and ceilings, probed the buildings next door, looked for secret rooms, tunnels. They found nothing and left behind a furious archdiocese.

Hugo remained convinced that Pablo had been close. He had listened to the drug boss talk until he'd ended his conversation that evening and quietly hung up, and that was it. The next day, Juan Pablo came on the air at the appointed time and Pablo did not. This convinced Hugo that the raid had spooked him. But why hadn't they found him?

It was not possible to fail more spectacularly. Hugo was a laughing-stock at the Holguin base. Disappointment overcame his usual enthusiasm. He grew demoralized. He gave up his command over the surveillance teams, turning the main effort back over to the CIA men, and prevailed on his father to let him keep just his small Mercedes van and two men to work on the equipment alone. Working with the kits had always been Hugo's favorite part of the job anyway.

Now there were competing groups in the city trying to track Pablo, Hugo's vehicle and the ones coordinated by the CIA. Over the next few weeks they picked up Pablo's signal several times, and even though the force itself had no faith in the equipment, again and again they were ordered to conduct raids. The colonel protested that they needed to marshal their intelligence and men, to wait until the fix was certain and the opportunity was right. But his superiors in Bogotá had grown suspicious and impatient. Even the U.S. embassy wanted more raids.

The most spectacular of these came on October 11, after Centra Spike found Pablo in a *finca* on a high hill near the village of Aguas Frías, an affluent suburb. The hilltop *finca* had a clear line of sight to the high-rise apartment building where Pablo's family was staying, which would explain why he would have chosen it. It had taken a few days for his voice to come back up on the radio after the ill-fated seminary raid. The Search Bloc feared that the raid might have scared him off the airwaves. But he had made another call days later, coming on again at one of the regular times with his son. He gave no indication that anything untoward had happened.

Actually, Pablo was in bad shape. Just as Guillermoprieto had written, his fabulously wealthy and powerful organization had been dismantled and continued to be terrorized by *Los Pepes*. Just in the past two weeks, five members of his extended family had been killed, presumably by the vigilante group, and several of his remaining key business associates had been kidnapped and killed. Whoever was not dead was in prison, or running and hiding. In an effort to raise money for his war against the state and to continue his flight, Pablo's bankers were selling off his assets around the world. A DEA cable in October noted that an Escobar family physician was traveling and selling off the family's properties, a seventy-thousand-acre timber farm in Panama, estates in the Dominican Republic, and two twenty-acre lots in southern Florida. Efforts were also under way to sell his art collection, jewelry, and precious stones, including a collection of uncut emeralds valued in excess of $200,000. Pablo's primary link with the rest of the world was now his loyal teenage son. Just as the colonel hunted Pablo with his son at his side, the drug boss and his son conspired daily to evade them. They were now talking by radiophone four times daily. So long as the Search Bloc knew where the son was and could monitor his communications lines, the colonel felt he would never completely lose track of the father.

For two days running, both Centra Spike and Colombian telemetry teams traced Pablo's radio to the top of the hill in Aguas Frías. It was a spectacular locale, a small, heavily wooded mountain in the vast range of the Occidental Cordillera—rugged, lush green country. There was only one road up the mountain to the *finca*, which was actually a collection of small cottages around a main house. The colonel ordered a surveillance team to load a radiotelemetry kit on a helicopter and fly over the area. As it happened, they were passing directly overhead at the moment Pablo made another call. The kit indicated that the radio call had come from directly below. Alarmed, the major in charge of the exercise immediately ordered the chopper back to Holguin base. When he returned, he told the colonel good and bad news. Pablo had definitely been there, but he might not be there any longer. The colonel decided to launch a raid on the *finca* immediately if Pablo made another call that afternoon.

Martinez could sense the ring closing around Pablo. When Delta sergeant Vega had left Medellín in November for his regular rotation out, the colonel had warned him.

"You will miss it," he said. "We are going to find him soon."

He consulted daily his stones and other ritual objects and saw omens of a resolution. It was a gut feeling, but also a calculation. The colonel knew Pablo couldn't hold out much longer. His ability to run was now very limited, and their ability to find him was improving every day. Now, at Aguas Frías, it felt like the whole effort was coming together. The electronic surveillance had tracked Pablo to a likely hideout and monitored his presence there. All of the direction-finding equipment agreed. This was the day they would get him.

The usual time for Pablo's call was four o'clock, so with choppers circling near the hilltop just out of earshot, and with forces poised to move quickly up the hill, the colonel and his top officers gathered in his operations center around a radio receiver, waiting for Pablo's voice to crackle on the air. There was no call at four. The men waited breathlessly. Five minutes later there still was no call. It was beginning to look like the fugitive had slipped the noose again. But at seven minutes after the hour, Pablo's voice came up, and the assault force hit the *finca*.

He wasn't there.

The colonel cordoned off the mountain for four days, establishing an outer perimeter, an inner perimeter, roadblocks, and search teams. Late on the day of the raid, Search Bloc helicopters dropped tear gas and raked the forests around the *finca* with machine-gun fire. More than seven hundred police officers and soldiers searched the mountain with dogs, but did not find Pablo. He had managed another miraculous escape. The assault teams had assumed that Pablo would be in the main house. It turned out— they learned this listening to Pablo's phone calls in the coming days—that in order to improve the signal, every time he called his son he would hike away from the *finca* into the woods farther up the hill. So he'd had a ringside seat as the choppers descended. He'd hidden in the woods and then fled down in darkness, evading the men looking for him. He later sent his wife a battery from the flashlight he'd used to light his way down, telling her to keep it "because it saved my life."

Despite its failure, the Aguas Frías raid gave a boost to the electronic-surveillance teams, because there was ample evidence that Pablo had been where they'd said he was. In the primary house, the base for a radiophone was found, turned on, with the portable handset missing. The radio was preset to the frequency Pablo had been using for the last four weeks in his talks with Juan Pablo. The house was run-down except for the usual gleaming, newly installed bathroom. The assaulters found two women at the house; they said Pablo had been staying there for several days. They explained, quaintly, that Pablo had been "dating" the youngest, who was eighteen. The other had been his cook. Both women confirmed that Pablo had been nearby when the choppers came down, and they gave the Search Bloc a description. He had been wearing a red flannel shirt, black pants, and tennis shoes. His hair, they said, was clipped short, but he wore a long black beard with no mustache. In the house the police found eight joints, a large quantity of aspirin ("suggesting a great deal of stress," speculated the DEA memo describing the raid), a wig, a videocassette of the apartment building housing his wife and children, several music cassettes, two automatic rifles (an AK-47 and a CAR-15), just over $7,000 in cash, and photos of Juan Pablo and Manuela. They also found false ID documents and a list of license plate numbers Juan Pablo had evidently compiled of vehicles driven by officers assigned to the Search Bloc.

The documents they found confirmed that Pablo was struggling and was very worried about his family. One letter said Maria Victoria needed money to continue supporting the attorney general's forces and bodyguards hired to protect her and the children. She complained that it was very expensive to feed sixty people and that she'd had to purchase beds for them. The letter blamed Colonel Martinez for the recent grenade attack on the apartment building, for which *Los Pepes* had taken credit. There were unsent letters Pablo was preparing for former associates in Medellín demanding money, threatening, "We know where your families are." There was one from a friend indicating that the government of Israel had agreed to accept and shelter Pablo's family. (The Israeli government later denied it.) DEA agent Murphy wrote:

> On a positive note, intelligence obtained at the search site and recent Title III intercepts [electronic surveillance] indicates that Escobar no longer enjoys the financial freedom he once had. While he may continue to be a Colombian land baron, Escobar and his organization are extremely short of cash. This is supported by some of the extortion letters seized at the search site and the fact that Roberto Escobar is firing some of his workers.

The day after the raid, the surveillance teams waited for Pablo to come back on the radio. He did not. Juan Pablo was heard frantically trying to make contact with his father at the appointed hours. He urged his father to simply key the microphone once to indicate he was alive if it was too dangerous to speak. Receiving no response, Juan Pablo began cursing and threatening the Search Bloc, which he correctly assumed was listening.

Whenever the teams returned empty-handed from a raid, the colonel would lead them into his operations room and ask them all to name the coordinates they had pinpointed for Pablo beforehand. In late October Centra Spike had returned, so the Search Bloc was now getting a confusing array of data. Martinez would pull from his stack of aerial photographs the appropriate portion of the city, pin the photo to the wall, and ask each group to mark their coordinates with a grease pen. All of the marks on the photo were close together, but they were never exactly the same. The coordinates given by Centra Spike and Hugo were usually significantly at odds with the CIA's. The agency men were convinced their reading had been correct, and Hugo and Freddie Ayuso, the Centra Spike representative, defended their own. Because of bad blood between the agency and Centra Spike, Ayuso had begun sharing information directly with Hugo, an arrangement that eventually prompted the agency team to complain and then to leave Medellín in anger. Their departure mattered little at the time. Ever since the Aguas Frías raid, Pablo's voice had vanished from the airwaves.

After fifteen months of futile searching, Martinez and his men were under increasing attack in the press. How could they not have found him by now? Attorney General de Greiff was their loudest public scourge, calling them inept and privately still urging that Martinez be removed and prosecuted along with the rest of *Los Pepes*. In mid-November there were new allegations that Colonel Martinez and others on the Search Bloc were corrupt. In a tape-recorded conversation with Gilberto Rodríguez Orejuela, one of the leaders of the Cali cocaine cartel, a Colombian senator working as a DEA source was told that the southern trafficking group had a good "working relationship" with Martinez, and with General Octavio Vargas, second in command of the national police.

"Rodríguez Orejuela told [the informant] they had bandits working within the Search Bloc and identified two of these individuals as 'Alberto' and 'Bernardo,'" wrote Agent Murphy. "Rodríguez Orejuela described Bernardo as a very ugly looking person with no tact or conscience. The informant advised that Rodríguez Orejuela states they had made an arrangement with *PNC* General Vargas and Colonel Martinez regarding a reward for Escobar's capture. According to Rodríguez Orejuela, the Cali cartel will pay a total of $10 million immediately following Pablo's capture and/or death. Of this, $8 million has been promised to the Search Bloc and $2 million for the informants who provide the information that leads to a successful operation."

This information particularly disturbed DEA chief Toft, who saw that the great concentration of effort on Pablo might actually be strengthening the cocaine industry in Colombia.

In Medellín, Hugo was ready to give up. He had failed, let his father down, even exposed him to ridicule and accusation. All the lieutenant's naive enthusiasm and confidence had worn away. The damned equipment didn't work. He felt that it never would.

But Hugo hadn't counted on what a strong convert he had made.

"The only way we will ever find Pablo is with your equipment," his father insisted. "The technology! It is our advantage over him. Technology!"

The colonel set about bucking up his son's spirits by sending him after an easier target. Martinez had a friend in Bogotá who was a shortwave-radio nut, and for months he had been listening in on the conversations of a man named Juan Camilo Zapata, a flamboyant Bogotá cocaine dealer who had built himself a replica of a castle on the eastern outskirts of the city. Zapata was a middleman in the Medellín operation, and even though he was now living there, he was far enough removed from the inner circle of Pablo's empire to have escaped the dragnet of the Search Bloc and *Los Pepes*. He was a relatively small operator. But because the colonel's friend had a fix on him, knowing what frequencies he used and when he normally talked on the radio, it gave Hugo a real-world target to work with while they waited for Pablo to break his silence.

Hugo went to work first on tape recordings his father's friend had made, familiarizing himself with Zapata's voice and the code words he used when talking business. Tracking Pablo was especially hard because the drug boss, understandably, was so wary that he spoke only very briefly on the radio, varied his frequencies, and moved often from place to place. Zapata was, by comparison, a sitting duck.

One of the drawbacks to taking this detour, however, was that the colonel could not afford to give his son the usual backup support. Since nobody expected the Search Bloc to be looking for Zapata and, indeed, no one in the police department cared a great deal about catching him just then, Hugo and his two-man team spent days cruising alone in their white Mercedes van, far more exposed than they normally would have dared to be. They drove and parked in high-risk neighborhoods, places where Pablo remained a popular figure and where policemen were routinely gunned down. At one point, Hugo stayed for too long in one spot listening to one of Zapata's calls. A child on skates rolled up to the car and handed him a piece of paper. "We know what you're doing," it read. "We know you are looking for Pablo. Either you leave or we're going to kill you."

Hugo was more careful after that, but he tinkered daily with his equipment, playing with Zapata's signals in order to fine-tune his antennae and dials. He got to where he could discern subtle shifts in the line displayed on the monitor. He could tell if the signal was being reflected off a wall, and he learned to distinguish the interference patterns caused by electrical wires or nearby water. He could detect different reasons why a signal was weak, whether it was farther away or just emanating from a smaller power source. These were all things he had worked on in the past, but as he practiced on Zapata's signals, Hugo felt his months of learning coming together. He knew that no one else could read the monitor as well as he could at that point, and day by day his confidence was restored.

Zapata made it easy. He was a very superstitious man, and every day he spoke at length to a witch, a fortune-teller, in whose judgment he placed great weight. With others, his conversations were usually brief, like someone who suspected his calls might be monitored. His brevity was calculated to protect information about his dealings. Zapata clearly never suspected that something other than the content of his calls would betray him. So when he spoke to his witch, he believed that nothing of interest or importance could be given away, and he stayed on the line for so long that Hugo could take his time perfecting his direction-finding technique. Eventually, he and his father planned an operation to arrest Zapata, positioning squads throughout the neighborhood and then waiting for him to make another call to his witch. He made the call but, coincidentally, this time from a different place. The witch told him to be very careful because she suspected something bad was going to happen, a message that spooked Hugo. The raid was called off, and Hugo once again endured the silent scorn of his father's men.

"It was just bad luck," the colonel told his son. "The important thing is that you found him. When he comes back on the radio, we'll prove it."

Less than a week later, Hugo had traced his location once more. An assault team raided the house and killed Zapata.

Hugo was ebullient. He had done it. There had been a lot of hype about his unit and its equipment, but he knew this was the first time he had actually pinpointed a target with it. At the Holguin base he walked once more with his head held high. It was November 26.

5

That night the U.S. embassy learned that Pablo's wife and children were planning once more to flee Colombia. They were going to fly to either London or Frankfurt. The family had become increasingly desperate. They had been under around-the-clock protection by agents from Attorney General de Grieff's office ever since the failed effort to fly Juan Pablo and Manuela to Miami in March. In the intervening months, *Los Pepes* had killed members of their extended family and burned most of the family's properties. The vigilante group seemed to be toying with the Escobars, picking off cousins, in-laws, and friends, including some who had been living in *Altos del Campestre*, demonstrating that they could hurt Maria Victoria, Juan Pablo, or Manuela whenever they chose to. The rocket-propelled grenade that had been fired at the building in October and another grenade that went off outside the front doors in early November were more like warnings than actual attempts on their lives. It felt like the threat was closing in. The Colombian government was officially protecting Pablo's family, but they were also effectively holding them in place. So long as Pablo was worried about them, his voice would keep popping up on the radio.

The pressure had notched tighter in late October, when de Grieff threatened to withdraw his protection. Increasingly at odds with the Gaviria administration, the crafty, pipe-smoking attorney general was playing a complicated game. He was still trying to engineer Pablo's surrender before he could be found by Colonel Martinez's men, and he was not above playing hardball with the drug lord, who had just engineered the kidnapping of two teenage boys from wealthy families in Medellín and extorted $5 million in ransom. De Grieff informed Juan Pablo that unless his father turned himself in by November 26, the guards would be withdrawn. Maria Victoria, Juan Pablo, and Manuela would "only be entitled to the same security as any other Colombian citizen," he said. Everyone knew how unsafe it was to be an average Colombian citizen.

Maria Victoria was terrified. In a letter she wrote to de Greiff on the 16th, she asked the attorney general to come in person to *Altos del Campestre,* pleading with him to give her husband more time to surrender. She wrote that the family was "anguished" and "worried," and argued that they were not responsible if her husband refused to give up and should not be punished for it. She reminded de Greiff that she and her children were not criminals, and said that they were trying to get Pablo to turn himself in.

The same day, de Greiff received a note from Juan Pablo that began, "Worry, desperation, anguish and anger are what we feel in these confusing moments." He urged the attorney general to investigate the kidnappings and killings of several close family associates, who he said were victims of the Search Bloc and *Los Pepes.* He wrote that on November 5, his longtime childhood friend Juan Herrera, who was living with the Escobars at *Altos del Campestre,* was kidnapped and was probably dead, although his body had not been found. On November 8, the administrator of their apartment building, a close friend, was kidnapped and killed. On the same date, the family's maid was kidnapped and killed. On November 10, he said, masked men kidnapped their personal tutor, who was presumed dead. On November 15, Juan Pablo argued, the police attempted to kidnap one of their chauffeurs. Ten armed men surprised and tried to take him, but the chauffeur exchanged shots with them and escaped. He urged de Greiff to investigate and prosecute these crimes as vigorously as the state was pursuing his father.

Juan Pablo had grown increasingly imperious. He comported himself as his father's protector, spokesman, and heir. He was suspected of having been personally involved, along with his father, in a bombing that had killed a top Search Bloc officer a year ago, in December. In negotiations with the attorney general's office, Juan Pablo vigorously defended his father's honor. By early November the son (speaking several times a day with his father) was hammering out a secret deal with the attorney general for the long-awaited surrender, a compact so secret that de Greiff did not share the plan with President Gaviria or the U.S. embassy. In it, the attorney general agreed to several of Pablo's terms: to transfer Roberto Escobar from isolation to a part of the Itagui prison where other Medellín cartel members were housed, to place Pablo in the same section upon his surrender, and to allow him twenty-one family visits each year. The deal hung up over a disagreement on getting Pablo's family out of Colombia. Pablo was insisting that he would not turn himself in until Maria Victoria and the children were flown to a safe haven. De Greiff was promising to help the family flee, but only after the surrender.

Word of these manuevers leaked in early November, and was received with alarm at the U.S. embassy. In a November 7 memo, DEA agent Murphy wrote:

> Obviously, if the above is true, and the BCO [Bogotá country office] has no doubts about its accuracy, then the GOC [government of Colombia] and particularly the [attorney general's] office has not been straightforward with the BCO or other American embassy personnel. Should Escobar agree to the one remaining condition regarding his family's departure from Colombia, his immediate surrender may be imminent.

Surrender, of course, was what the Americans, the national police, and Pablo's other enemies hoped to prevent. With his wife and children baiting the trap, and *Los Pepes* waiting in the wings, Pablo was isolated and desperate. If he managed to get the family away to safety, there was no telling what would happen. Free of his worst fears, Pablo could go underground, disappear completely from Centra Spike's screens. The Colombian government feared a renewed bombing campaign in Bogotá and an even bloodier phase of the struggle.

Pablo and de Greiff did finally agree. The attorney general decided to accept Juan Pablo's solemn promise that his father would surrender on or before the November 26 deadline, either at de Greiff's office in Medellín or at the apartment building. De Greiff began laying plans to get the family out of the country.

When he learned of the family's pending flight, Ambassador Busby went to work. He was assured by Defense Minister Rafael Pardo that the Colombian government was opposed to letting the Escobars go, but there was no legal reason to prevent them from leaving. So the government concentrated on slamming doors of entry to all the family's known destinations. Maria Victoria had purchased tickets to both London and Frankfurt. Since the London flight, if they took it, stopped over in Madrid, Pardo contacted the Spanish, British, and German ambassadors, formally asking that they refuse entry and return the family directly to Colombia if possible.

The attorney general was now working in open defiance of the president. He had told Gaviria that he disagreed with effectively holding the Escobars hostage, and because he was officially an "independent entity," he was going to help the family leave Colombia in order to complete the deal for Pablo's surrender. When word spread that the family was looking for a haven in Canada, Pardo contacted the Canadian ambassador, only to learn that de Greiff had called to request that the Canadian government allow the family to enter. The Colombian government was now split on the matter, so Busby threw his support behind Gaviria, contacting the various governments himself and winning assurances that the Escobars would be turned away.

At the same time all this was going on, de Greiff informed the U.S. embassy that Pablo was in Haiti. News reports leaked out that Pablo had managed to escape Colombia. The embassy traced de Greiff's sources to Miami, and dispatched Agent Peña to investigate. In the light of what happened over the next two days, the story appears to have been a ruse, an effort to distract the authorities and create enough confusion to help slip the Escobar family out of Colombia. But if Pablo had been planning to lie low in order for the Haiti ploy to work, events soon conspired to flush him back out on the airwaves in Medellín.

6

DEA special agent Kenny Magee was friendly with the security chief for American Airlines at the El Dorado Airport in Bogotá, so he was picked to follow the Escobar family. A blue-eyed former Jackson, Michigan, cop who had come to Bogotá four years earlier, Magee had flunked Spanish in his senior year of high school; he had told his teacher, "I'm never going to need Spanish," and she had said, "You never know." He showed up at the airport on Saturday, November 27, with two plainclothes *PNC* colonels, and with Agents Murphy and Peña. Magee had purchased tickets on both of the early evening flights booked by the Escobars. The planes were leaving within ten minutes of each other, and they didn't know which one the family would take, so they pocketed their boarding passes and waited for the Escobars to show up.

It wasn't hard spotting them. The family's plans had evidently been leaked to more than just the national police and the U.S. embassy, because when their plane from Medellín landed in Bogotá early in the afternoon, they found about three dozen reporters waiting inside the terminal. The small plane, a regular commercial flight, stayed out on the tarmac and all of its passengers except the Escobars were let off. Members of the attorney general's bodyguard detail carried the Escobars' luggage to a waiting Avianca Airlines bus followed by a force of more than twenty heavily armed men escorting the family—Maria Victoria, Manuela, Juan Pablo, and his chubby twenty-one-year-old Mexican girlfriend. The family members held jackets over their heads to avoid being photographed, boarded the bus, and were driven to a remote entrance to the airport where they could wait out in private the six hours until their overseas flight.

Five minutes before the Lufthansa flight to Frankfurt was scheduled to depart, the family emerged from the room surrounded by their bodyguards and were hustled through the main terminal. All but Juan Pablo held jackets over their heads. Pablo's son shouted threats at the mob of reporters pushing around them and then disappeared down the jetway. Magee and the Colombian policemen followed, taking seats in business class. It was the first time Magee had seen the family. Maria Victoria was a short, fat woman with glasses, very conservatively and stylishly dressed. Nine-year-old Manuela was tiny and cute, and clung to her mother. Juan Pablo and his older girlfriend stayed with each other, apart from his mother and sister. Magee was wearing blue jeans and a long-sleeved shirt and carried a shoulder bag with a camera built into the bottom. He began snapping pictures of the family surreptitiously. An enterprising journalist had the seat next to Juan Pablo, trying to interview him, with what appeared to be little success.

When the plane landed in Caracas for a brief stopover, there was so much security out on the runway that Magee thought it looked as if a head of state was arriving. It was a nine-hour flight from there to Frankfurt, through Saturday night and into Sunday morning, and the family slept through much of it. Juan Pablo slumped deep into his seat and put his head back, alternately dozing and staring at the ceiling. His girlfriend had her head on his shoulder, and, in two other seats, Manuela slept curled against her mother. Maria Victoria spoke only with her daughter, and always in whispers.

Unknown to the family, just an hour after their flight had left Bogotá, a spokesman for the German Interior ministry had released a statement to the press announcing that the Escobars would not be allowed to enter Germany. Soon afterward, an angry Pablo was on the phone, blowing his Haiti cover story. He called the Presidential Palace in Bogotá.

"This is Pablo Escobar. I need to talk to the president," he told the operator at the palace.

"Okay, hold on, let me locate him," said the operator, and immediately patched the call through to the national police. After a delay, a police officer posing as a palace operator came on the line and said, "We can't get in touch with the president right now. Please call back at another time."

The police officer had sized it up as a joke and hung up. The phone rang again.

"This is Pablo Escobar. It is necessary that I talk to the president. My family is flying to Germany at this time. I need to talk to him right now."

"We get a lot of crank calls here," the officer said. "We need to somehow verify that it is really you. It's going to take me a few minutes to track down the president, so please wait a few more minutes and then call back."

With that, he informed his superiors that Pablo was making calls to the palace. President Gaviria was notified, and he said he would not speak with Escobar on the phone. When Pablo called back a third time, his hunters were waiting, and the call surfaced on the electronic web.

"I'm sorry, Mr. Escobar, we have been unable to locate the president."

Pablo went berserk. He swore at the officer on the phone and said he would detonate a bus filled with dynamite in front of the palace and set off bombs all over Bogotá. He would bomb the German embassy and begin killing Germans if his family was not allowed to enter that country. Minutes later he made similar threats on the phone to the German embassy and the Lufthansa office in Bogotá.

No one had been able to get a precise fix on his location, but he was without a doubt still in Medellín.

When the Lufthansa plane finally landed in Frankfurt Sunday afternoon, it was forced to taxi to a remote spot on an alternate runway, out of the view of press members waiting in the terminal. President Gaviria had been on the phone to officials in Spain and Germany, urging them to refuse the Escobars. He explained that if the family was safely removed from Colombia he expected another vicious bombing campaign. It was not the kind of request from a head of state that other nations would be likely to ignore. There was nothing to be gained by Spain, Germany, or any other country in allowing entry to the family of such a notorious outlaw. Interior Ministry officials drove out to the plane to process the other passengers' passports and immigration documents, including Magee's and the Colombian colonels', and a bus took them to the terminal. The Escobars were taken by bus to an office in the international section. Maria Victoria, who was carrying $80,000 and large amounts of gold and jewelry, asked for a lawyer and was provided one. They immediately petitioned for political asylum, then waited through another long night for a ruling.

Magee was met in the main terminal by two DEA colleagues based in Germany, and they waited together to see what would happen next. Early Monday morning the Escobars' petition was denied. The family was escorted by a heavily armed contingent of German police back out to a plane bound for Bogotá that had been kept waiting for two hours. Also placed back on the plane were three men the German authorities determined were personal family bodyguards, men the authorities described as "thugs." Magee jumped into another car and followed them out, boarding the plane with four German immigration officers assigned to escort the family back to Colombia. He sat two rows in front of the family and across the aisle. At some point during this long flight home, the DEA agent sat down with the German immigration officers in the smoking section of the plane. They had seized the Escobars' passports and they agreed to allow Magee to photograph them. He took the passports into one of the plane's lavatories, laid them out on the narrow counter, and snapped a photo of each. As he pulled the door open, sticking the passports in his back pocket, he encountered Juan Pablo in the doorway. It gave Magee a start, but the boy was just waiting to use the toilet.

He and the rest of the family looked exhausted. They had been on planes or in airports since Saturday afternoon, and they had gotten nowhere. When the Lufthansa flight landed again at El Dorado Airport, the weary Escobars were escorted off the plane and turned over once again to Colombian authorities.

Magee inspected the seats where the family had been sitting. He found several large empty envelopes with large dollar amounts written on them, two credit cards, and a discarded note that read in English, "We have a friend in Frankfurt. He says he will be looking for us so he can help us. . . . Tell him to call Gustavo de Greiff." Magee assumed it was a note they had hoped to pass to someone at the airport in Frankfurt, but they had never reached the terminal.

After the family was taken into custody at the airport, Defense Minister Pardo ordered de Greiff to drop his office's protection of them. The Escobars were escorted by the national police to Hotel Tequendama in Bogotá, a large modern complex that besides the hotel includes retail shops and an apartment tower. Fed up and exhausted and frightened, Maria Victoria told government officials that she did not wish to return to Medellín, and pleaded to be sent anywhere in the world outside Colombia. She said she was tired of living with her husband's problems and just wanted to live in peace with her children.

Pablo phoned the hotel not long after the family arrived, conveying a brief message to Juan Pablo.

"Stay put there," he said. "Put pressure on the authorities to leave for another country, call Human Rights, the United Nations."

As if to tighten the screws on Pablo, *Los Pepes* chose the day of his family's return to Colombia to issue another public pronouncement. In a communiqué to the press, the group said that they had respected the government's wish that they desist long enough. They were going to resume actions against Pablo Escobar.

Pablo responded bitterly. On November 30, he handwrote a letter to the men he suspected of leading the vigilante group. Among those he listed were Colonel Martinez and the "*DIJIN* Members in Antioquia" (the Search Bloc), Miguel and Gilberto Rodríguez Orejuela, purported leaders of the Cali cartel, and Fidel and Carlos Castaño. He accused the government of hypocrisy and of targeting his family for persecution, and he complained that his rights were not being respected. "I have been raided 10,000 times," he wrote. "You haven't been at all. Everything is confiscated from me. Nothing is taken away from you. The government will never offer a warrant for you. The government will never apply faceless justice to criminal and terrorist policemen." He sealed the letter with his thumbprint and forwarded it to his few remaining frontmen for public release.

By now Pablo's lamentations were music to his pursuers' ears. They finally had his family right where they wanted them. Out from under Attorney General de Greiff's protection, Pablo's wife and children were in the hands of *Los Pepes*, at least as far as he was concerned. They knew he would be frantic. Police at the hotel reported hearing Manuela singing a Christmas carol to herself as she wandered the empty hotel—which cleared out quickly when word spread of the Escobars' presence. She had substituted the traditional chorus with one of her own that went, in part, "*Los Pepes* want to kill my father, my family, and me."

7

After his success tracking down Zapata, Hugo's father gave him a few days off to visit with his wife and children in Bogotá. But on his first night back, Saturday night, came the Escobar family's ill-fated flight to Frankfurt. With Maria Victoria and the children camped at the Hotel Tequendama, the colonel knew Pablo would be calling there. He summoned Hugo and the other men back to the base. Hugo was disappointed at having to cut short his vacation, but he was also excited. His success had restored his confidence, and he knew Pablo would most likely be back on the airwaves often over the next few days.

Colonel Martinez took steps of his own to make sure they were making the most of this moment. Unsure of his own colleagues in Bogotá, the colonel had someone he trusted assigned to the hotel-complex switchboard. The officer had been a friend of his son's in the intelligence branch and had lived for a time at Tequendama. They devised a system to tip off Hugo immediately every time Escobar phoned. All calls to the hotel came through the switchboard, so if a call sounded like Pablo, they would delay making the connection to the family's apartment upstairs or divert the call to the wrong apartment—anything to hold off until Hugo had been alerted. That way, the monitors in the air and on the ground could start tracing the call before the conversation even started.

Pablo gave them plenty of chances. Over the next four days he would call six times. Even though the first few conversations were very short, Pablo checking to see how the family was holding up and urging his son to continue doing everything possible to get out of Colombia, Centra Spike was able to get a precise fix on his location, a middle-class neighborhood in Medellín called *Los Olivos* near that city's football stadium, a sector that included blocks of two-story row houses and some office buildings. For his part, Pablo tried to confuse his pursuers, who he knew were listening, by speaking from the backseat of a moving taxi, using a high-powered radiophone that was linked to a larger transmitter that his men constantly moved from place to place.

Pablo himself had moved into a row house on Street 79A, building number 45D-94, in the third week of November, more than a month after his rapid flight from the *finca* at Aguas Frías. It was a simple two-story brick row house with a squat palm tree planted in front. It was one of many houses he owned in the city. Pablo carried dozens of real estate ads with his notebooks and was always buying and selling hideouts. He had the places furnished and renovated (with a new bathroom) in advance of his arrival. That way he was always home, even though he had no home. He moved with his collection of wireless phones. It didn't trouble him to know that the authorities listened whenever he spoke on the phone, both the Colombian government and the gringos, with their spy planes and fancy listening devices. It had been that way for years. He used the knowledge to feed disinformation, to keep the fools running in every direction but the right one. The game wasn't to avoid being overheard—that was impossible—but to avoid being targeted. The taxi he used as a mobile phone booth was driven by his sole bodyguard and companion, "Limón," Alvero de Jesús. He had the yellow taxi parked downstairs.

It was evident from Pablo's phone conversations and the letters he had written over the last few months how infuriated he was with his reduced circumstances, but clearly he also felt some pride. The same man who had posed dressed up as Pancho Villa and Al Capone had been the most wanted fugitive in the world for nearly sixteen months—for more than three years if you counted the first war. After so much carnage, so many millions spent to hunt him down, he was still alive, and still at large. Many people wanted him dead: the Americans, his rivals in the Cali cocaine cartel and their government lackeys, the Search Bloc and its alter ego *Los Pepes.* As he moved from place to place in Medellín he took comfort in all the simple people of his home city who still believed in him, who still called him *El Doctor* and *El Patrón,* who remembered the housing projects he had bankrolled, the soccer fields, the donations to church and charity, and had little affection for the government forces closing in on him. And even though his organization had been taken apart, so many of his friends killed or in jail, he believed he could still right things. There would be many, many scores to settle once he did that. As Juan Pablo had sneered to a representative from the attorney general a few months before, "My dad is also searching for everyone who is after him and destiny will say who finds who first." The enemies of Pablo Escobar would rue the day they set themselves against him, and he would return, with his family, to live the life he so relentlessly and ruthlessly sought, nothing less or more than to be a wealthy respected Medellín don, patron of the poor, defender of the faith, and scourge of the streets.

But Maria Victoria and the children had to be gotten out of the way. How was it that when he, Pablo Escobar, kidnapped and killed his enemies it was called a crime, but when the government kidnapped and killed his friends and family it was called justice? They were in terrible danger, and they were his responsibility. Any harm that came to them would cause him great pain, but would also be the greatest insult. If he could not protect his own family, his enemies and friends would know he was finished. He hadn't seen his wife and children in more than a year and a half.

Pablo clearly admired the way Juan Pablo had stepped forward in this crisis, and he was relying on him more and more to protect Maria Victoria and Manuela. The fugitive drug boss had to get his family out of Colombia, not just for their protection but in order to free his hands.

With Maria Victoria and the children safe, he could turn on his enemies full force, unleash a bombing and assassination campaign that would bring the government to its knees and send his would-be rivals in the Cali cartel scurrying for cover. He had done it before. He knew how to hurt the elite in Bogotá, how to give them a war they would have no stomach for. He had done it three years earlier, when he'd had them begging him to stop, offering him anything he wanted if he would only stop. That was the road back.

Hugo got an incorrect fix on the first call Pablo made to Hotel Tequendama on Monday, but by Tuesday Centra Spike and the Search Bloc's own fixed-surveillance teams in the hills over Medellín had placed Pablo in *Los Olivos*. Colonel Martinez knew they were very close. At first he asked permission to cordon off the entire fifteen-block neighborhood and begin going door-to-door, but that was rejected—in part because Santos and others at the embassy advised against it. Pablo was expert at escaping dragnets like that. Closing down the neighborhood would just let him know they were on to him. Instead, the colonel began quietly infiltrating hundreds of his men into *Los Olivos*.

Hugo stayed with a group of thirty-five in a parking lot enclosed by high walls, where the men and vehicles could not be seen from the street. Similar squads of men were sequestered at other lots in the neighborhood. They stayed through Tuesday night, until Wednesday. Food was brought in. There was only one portable toilet for all the men. Hugo spent virtually all this time in his car, waiting for Pablo's voice to come up. He ate and slept in the car. On Wednesday, December 1, Pablo spoke for longer on the phone with his son, wife, and daughter as they wished him a happy birthday. He was forty-four years old that day. He celebrated with marijuana, a birthday cake, and some wine.

Hugo raced out of the lot in pursuit of this signal and traced it to a spot in the middle of the street near a traffic circle. There was no one there. The conversation had just ended. Hugo was convinced that his scanner was right. Pablo had evidently been speaking from a car. He returned to the parking lot discouraged, and the men camped out there were again disappointed. Hugo waited until about eight on Thursday morning before his father gave the men permission to come back to base, clean up, and rest. Hugo drove back to his apartment in Medellín, took a shower, and then lay down and fell asleep.

On this day, Thursday, December 2, 1993, Pablo awoke shortly before noon, as was his habit, and ate a plate of spaghetti before easing his widening bulk back into bed with his wireless phone. Always a heavy man, he had put on about twenty pounds living on the run, most of it in his belly.

On the run didn't accurately describe it. He spent most of his time lying low, eating, sleeping, talking on the radio. He hired prostitutes, mostly teenage girls, to help him while away the hours. It wasn't the same as the lavish orgies he had arranged in years past, but his money and notoriety still allowed some indulgences. He had trouble finding jeans that would fit him. To get a waist size to accommodate his girth he had to wear pants that were a good six inches too long in the leg. The light blue pair he wore today were turned up twice in a wide cuff. He wore flip-flop sandals and had pulled on a loose blue polo shirt.

Prone to stomach disorders, he might have been feeling the effects of his birthday revelry the night before. On this afternoon the only other person in the house was Limón. The two others staying with them, his courier, Jaime Rua, and his aunt and cook, Luz Mila, had gone out after fixing breakfast. At one o'clock Pablo tried several times to phone his family, posing as a radio journalist, but the switchboard operator at the Tequendama, per his instructions from Colonel Martinez, told him they had been instructed to block all calls from journalists. He was put on hold, then asked to call back, but finally he got through on the third attempt, speaking briefly to Manuela and then to Maria Victoria and his son.

Maria Victoria sobbed on the phone. She was depressed and fatalistic.

"Honey, what a hangover," said Pablo sympathetically. She continued crying. "These things are a drag. So, what are you going to do?"

"I don't know."

"What does your mother say?"

"It was as if my mother fainted," she said, explaining that they had last seen her as they left the airport Friday in Medellín. "I did not call her. She told me bye, and then—"

"And you have not spoken to her?"

"No. My mother is so nervous," said Maria Victoria, explaining how all the deaths in the previous year had just about killed her mother with sorrow.

Hugo was awakened by a phone call from his father.

"Pablo's talking!" the colonel said. The weary lieutenant dressed quickly and hurried back out to the parking lot, where the other men were assembling.

"So, what are you going to do?" Pablo asked his wife gently.

"I don't know, I mean, wait and see where they take us and I believe that will be the end of us."

"No!"

"So?" Maria Victoria asked flatly.

"Don't you give me this coldness! Holy Mary!"

"And you?"

"Ahhh."

"And you?"

"What about me?"

"What are you going to do?"

"Nothing. . . . What do you need?" Pablo asked. He did not want to talk about himself.

"Nothing," said his wife.

"What do you want?"

"What would I want?" she said glumly.

"If you need something, call me, okay?"

"Okay."

"You call me now, quickly. There is nothing more I can tell you. What else can I say? I have remained right on track, right?"

"But how are you? Oh, my God, I don't know!"

"We must go on. Think about it. Now that I am so close, right?" Pablo said, in what appeared to be a suggestion that he was about to surrender.

"Yes," said his wife, with no enthusiasm.

"Think about your boy, too, and everything else, and don't make any decisions too quickly. Okay?"

"Yes."

"Call your mother again and ask her if she wants you to go there or what."

"Okay."

"Remember that you can reach me by beeper."

"Okay."

"Okay."

"Chao," said Maria Victoria.

"So long," said her husband.

Then Juan Pablo got back on the line. He had been given a list of questions from a journalist. Often, when Pablo was in trouble, he used the Colombian media to broadcast his messages and demands, and to try to whip up public sentiment in his favor. Other times, when he was displeased with the media, he would have reporters and editors killed. Juan Pablo wanted his father's advice on how to answer the questions.

"Look, this is very important in Bogotá," said Pablo.

"Yes, yes."

Pablo suggested that they might also be able to sell his answers to publications overseas, an opportunity to lobby publicly for his family to be given refuge. For now he just wanted to hear what the questions were. He would call back later to help his son answer them.

"This is also publicity," Pablo said. "Explaining the reasons and other matters to them. Do you understand? Well done and well organized."

"Yes, yes," said Juan Pablo. Then he read the first question: "'Whatever the country, refuge is conditioned on the immediate surrender of your father. Would your father be willing to turn himself in if you are settled somewhere?'"

"... Go on."

"The next one is, 'Would he be willing to turn himself in before you take refuge abroad?'"

"Go on."

"I spoke with the man, and he told me that if there were some questions I did not want to answer, there was no problem, and if I wanted to add some questions, he would include them."

"Okay. The next one?"

"'Why do you think that several countries have refused to receive your family?' Okay?"

"Yes."

"'From which embassies have you requested help for them to take you in ...?'"

"Okay."

"'Don't you think your father's situation, accused of X number of crimes, assassination of public figures, considered one of the most powerful drug traffickers in the world ...?'" Juan Pablo stopped reading.

"Go on."

"But there are many. Around forty questions."

Pablo told his son he would call back later in the day. "I may find a way to communicate by fax," he said.

"No," said Juan Pablo, apparently concerned that use of a fax would somehow be too dangerous.

"No, huh? Okay. Okay. So, good luck."

Pablo hung up.

*   *   *

Hugo and the rest of the men had not been able to assemble in time to chase this signal, but Centra Spike and the Search Bloc's own fixed listening posts had triangulated it to the same *Los Olivos* neighborhood where the calls had originated earlier. They hunkered down and waited for the promised next call. If Pablo was going to try to answer forty questions, he was going to be on the phone a long time.

"How many are there?" Pablo asked, evidently concerned now about the duration of his call. He had called back precisely at three o'clock.

"A lot," said Juan Pablo. "There's about forty questions."

Juan Pablo began relaying the journalist's questions. The first asked the son to explain what it would take for his father to surrender.

Pablo instructed, "Tell him, my father cannot turn himself in unless he has guarantees for his security."

"Okay," said Juan Pablo.

"And we totally support him in that."

"Okay."

"Above any considerations."

"Yep."

"My father is not gonna turn himself in before we are placed in a foreign country, and while the police in Antioquia—"

"The police and *DAS* is better," interjected Juan Pablo. "Because the *DAS* are also searching."

"It's only the police."

"Oh, okay."

Pablo, resuming: "While the police in Antioquia—"

"Yeah."

"Okay, let's change it to 'While the security organizations in Antioquia—'"

"Yeah."

"—continue to kidnap—"

"Yeah."

"—torture—"

"Yeah."

"—and commit massacres in Medellín."

"Yes, all right."

"Okay," Pablo said. "The next one."

Hugo had driven out of the parking lot in pursuit as soon as his friend on the switchboard at the Hotel Tequendama had alerted him that Pablo was on the line. They had recognized his voice right away when he'd called, even though he was still pretending to be a journalist. Per instructions, they had delayed, then finally put the call through.

All of the men at Hugo's parking lot followed him out. The rest of the Search Bloc were converging from their positions. Hugo felt terribly excited and nervous. He could feel all of his father's men, hardened veteran assaulters, close on his heels. Ever since they had nailed Zapata, his stock with the men in the Search Bloc had risen some, but they remained very skeptical. He knew that if he failed now, again, with all of these men awaiting his direction, he would never live it down.

The tone in his earphones and the line on his scanner directed Hugo to an office building just a few blocks from the parking lot. He was certain that was where Pablo was speaking. No sooner had he named it than the assault force descended, crashing through the front doors and moving loudly through the building.

Pablo continued to speak calmly, as though nothing was happening.

Hugo was amazed. How could his equipment be wrong? Clearly he was not in the office building where the men had just launched the raid. Hugo felt panicked. He took two long, deep breaths, forcing himself to calm down. So long as Pablo was talking, he could still be found. In the passenger seat of the white Mercedes van, he closed his eyes for a moment and then looked again more carefully at the screen. This time he noticed a slight wiggle in the white line that stretched from side to side. The line spanned the entire screen, which meant the signal was being transmitted close by, but the wiggle suggested something else. From his experience he knew that this vibration meant he was picking up a reflection. It was very slight, which was why he hadn't noticed it before. When the reflection was off water, the line usually had a slight squiggle in it, but this line had no squiggle.

"This is not it! This is not it!" he shouted into his radio. "Let's go!"

To his left was a drainage ditch with a gently moving stream in a deep concrete gully. To cross over to the other side, where Hugo was now convinced the signal originated, his driver had to go up a block or two and turn left over a bridge. When the van had crossed the bridge and arrived on the other side of the ditch, Hugo realized that only one car had followed him. Either the others hadn't heard or were ignoring him.

Pablo's conversation with his son continued.

Juan Pablo repeated the journalist's question about why so many other countries had refused to allow him and his mother and sister entry.

"The countries have denied entry because they don't know the real truth," said Pablo.

"Yes," answered Juan Pablo, taking notes as his father spoke.

"We're gonna knock on the doors of every embassy from all around the world because we're willing to fight incessantly," Pablo continued, "because we want to live and study in another country without bodyguards and hopefully with a new name."

"Just so you know," said Juan Pablo. "I got a phone call from a reporter who told me that President Alfredo Christiani from Ecuador, no, I think it is El Salvador—"

"Yes?" Pablo got up and moved to the window, mindful that this conversation had gone on for several minutes. Twenty seconds was usually the rule. Pablo looked down at cars moving on the street below as he listened.

"Well, he has offered to receive us. I heard the statement—well, he gave it to me by phone."

"Yes?"

"And he said if this contributed in some way to the peace of the country, he would be willing to receive us, because the world receives dictators and bad people, why wouldn't he receive us?"

"Well, let's wait and see, because that country is a bit hidden away."

"Well, but at least there's a possibility, and it's come from a president."

"Look, with respect to El Salvador."

"Yeah?"

"In case they ask anything, tell them the family is very grateful and obliged to the words of the president, that it is known he is the president of peace in El Salvador."

"Yeah."

Pablo stayed at the window looking out. When Juan Pablo related a question about the family's experiences under government protection, his father answered, "You respond to that one."

"Who paid for maintenance and accommodation? You or the attorney general?"

"Who did pay this?" Pablo asked.

"Us," said Juan Pablo. "Well, there were some people from Bogotá who got their expenses paid by [de Greiff], but they never spent all of it, because we supplied the groceries, mattresses, deodorants, toothbrushes, and pretty much everything." Juan Pablo rattled off two more of the questions, but his father abruptly ended the conversation.

"Okay, let's leave it at that," Pablo said.

"Yeah, okay," said Juan Pablo. "Good luck."

"Good luck."

The signal pointed Hugo straight ahead. The line of the screen lengthened and the tone in his earphones grew stronger as they proceeded up the street. They drove until the signal peaked and then began to diminish, the line pinching in at the edges of the screen and the tone slightly falling off. So they turned around and crept back the other way more slowly. The line stretched gradually until it once again filled the screen.

They were in front of a block of two-story row houses. There was no telling which was the one that housed Pablo. They cruised up and down the street several more times. Hugo stopped staring at his screen and instead stared intently at the houses, one by one.

Until he saw him.

A fat man in the second-floor window. He had long, curly black hair and a full beard. The image hit Hugo like an electric shock. He had only seen Pablo in pictures, and he had always been clean shaven except for the mustache, but they knew Pablo had grown a beard, and there was something about the man in the window that just clicked. He was talking on a cell phone and peering down at traffic. The man stepped back from the window. Hugo thought he had seen a look of surprise.

The face of Pablo Escobar assembled slowly in Hugo's brain. For a split second he was confused, disbelieving. Him! He had found him! Years of effort, hundreds of lives, thousands of futile police raids, untold millions of dollars, countless false leads and man-hours, all of the false steps, false alarms, blunders . . . and here he was at last, one man in a nation of 35 million people, one man in a rich, ruthless, and regimented underworld he had virtually owned for nearly two decades, one man in a city of millions where he was revered as a legend, a task literally more difficult than finding a needle in a haystack.

Hugo leaned out of his van and called to the car behind him, "This is the house!"

It was in the middle of the block. Hugo suspected Pablo had been spooked by their white van cruising slowly down the street, so he had told his driver to keep on going down to the end. Shouting into the radio, Hugo asked to be connected to his father.

"I've got him located," Hugo told his father.

The colonel knew this was it. Those were words he had never heard before. He knew Hugo would not be saying it unless he had seen Pablo with his own eyes.

"He's in this house," said Hugo.

Hugo explained excitedly that only he and one other car were there. He thought Pablo had seen him and that his gunmen were probably on their way. He wanted to clear out, fast.

"Stay exactly where you are!" Colonel Martinez ordered his son, shouting into the radio. "Station yourself in front and in back of the house and don't let him come out."

Then the colonel got word to all his units in the area, including those still thrashing through the office building blocks away, and told them to converge on the house immediately.

Hugo's two men got out of the car and positioned themselves against the wall on either side of Pablo's front door. Hugo drove the van around the block to the alley, counting the houses until he could see the back end of Pablo's. Terrified, with weapons ready, they waited.

It took about ten minutes.

* * *

There was a heavy metal front door. Martin, one of the lieutenants assigned to the Search Bloc assault team, stood ready as his men applied a heavy steel sledgehammer to it. Martin had not worn his bullet-proof vest today, and he had a moment of anxious regret, just as the hammer crashed into the door. It took several blows before it went down.

Martin sprinted into the house with the five men on his team, and the shooting started. In the din and confusion, he quickly sized up the first floor. It was empty, like a garage. There was a yellow taxi parked toward the rear, and a flight of stairs leading up to the second floor. One of Martin's men stumbled on his way up the stairs, and everyone stopped momentarily. They thought the man had been hit.

Limón leaped out a back window to the orange tile roof as soon as the team burst through the front door. The way the house was constructed, there was a back roof surrounded by walls on three sides that could be reached by dropping about ten feet from a second-story window. Limón hit the tiles and began running, and as he did the Search Bloc members arrayed in the street behind the house opened fire. There were dozens of men up and down the block with automatic weapons, some of them standing on the tops of their cars. One Search Bloc shooter had climbed to the second-floor roof of the house next door.

Limón was hit several times as he ran. His momentum carried him right off the roof. He fell to the grass below.

Then came Pablo. He stopped to kick off his flip-flops, then jumped down to the roof. Having seen what had happened to Limón, he stayed close to one wall, where there was some protection. The shooter on the roof overhead could not get a clear shot directly down at him, so there was a break in the firing momentarily as Pablo quickly moved along the wall toward the back street. No one on the street had a clear shot at him yet. At the corner, Pablo made his break.

He went for the crest of the gently sloping roof, trying to make it to the other side. There was a thundering cascade of fire and Pablo fell near the crest. He sprawled forward, dislodging orange tiles.

The shooting continued. Martin's team inside the house had found the second floor empty. When he stuck his head in the open window to look out on the roof, he saw a body and then heard an eruption of more gunfire. He and his men fell prone on the floor and waited as rounds from the street below crashed through the window and into the walls and ceiling of the room. Martin believed he and his men were taking fire from Pablo's bodyguards. He shouted into his radio, "Help! Help us! We need support!"

Everyone was shooting on automatic from below. Rounds chewed up the brick walls around the enclosed rooftop. It felt as if it took minutes for the shooting to die down, for the Search Bloc to realize they were the only ones shooting. Finally, it stopped.

The shooter on the second-floor roof shouted, "It's Pablo! It's Pablo!"

Men were now scaling the roof to see. Someone found a ladder and placed it under the second-floor window, and others climbed down to the roof from the window. Major Aguilar grabbed the body and turned it over. The wide bearded face was swollen, bloody, and wreathed in long, blood-soaked black curls. The major grabbed a radio and spoke directly to Colonel Martinez, loudly enough for even the men on the street below to hear.

"Vivá Colombia! We have just killed Pablo Escobar!"

AFTERMATH

Police on the scene said that Pablo was hit as he ran across the roof by men shooting from the alley behind the house and by one, Major Hugo Aguilar, who had climbed to the next-door rooftop. Lieutenant Hugo Martinez, who watched from the street, said that Pablo came running out from the wall with guns in both hands, shooting and shouting, "Police motherfuckers!"

It makes for a theatrical ending, and it might be true. But throughout his years as a fugitive, Pablo Escobar was a runner, not a fighter. His response whenever the police descended was to disappear as fast as he could out a back door or, as in this case, a window. He had never tried to shoot it out and he would have known how futile—indeed, how fatal—this had been for scores of his *sicarios*. It is possible that he realized he was surrounded and, seeing Limón shot down, decided on an attempt to blast his way clear. But for him to have emerged with guns blazing, like the bad guy in an old Western, would have been strongly out of character.

Autopsy reports showed that Pablo was hit three times. One round entered the back of his right leg just above the knee joint and exited the front of the leg about two inches below the kneecap. Another round struck him in the back, just below the right shoulder blade, and did not exit his body. The third entered at the center of his right ear and exited just in front of the left ear, passing straight through his brain.

The shots to his leg and back most likely would have knocked him down, but probably would not have killed him. The shot to his head killed him instantly. So either all three shots hit Pablo roughly simultaneously or the killing shot was administered after Pablo was down. The exact placement of a round in the right ear of a running man from a distance demonstrates either extraordinary marksmanship or luck—a similar amazing shot felled Limón, who died of a bullet wound to the center of his forehead. It is more likely, given the placement of these death wounds, that both men were shot in the head after they fell.

Colonel Martinez has pointed out that a shot fired from within three feet would have left telltale gunpowder marks on Pablo's skin, which are not evident in autopsy photographs. But a shot fired from three to four feet away is consistent with a shooter administering a coup de grâce while standing over a downed man. One telltale sign of a shot fired from such close range would be a spray of blood. Hours after the shooting, DEA agent Steve Murphy recalled a member of the Search Bloc offering to sell his shirt and pants for $200 as souvenirs because both had been sprayed with Pablo's blood.

Killing Pablo had been the goal of the mission from the beginning. No one wanted to see him taken prisoner again. Seven years after the shooting, Colonel Oscar Naranjo, who was chief of intelligence for the *Policía Nacional de Colombia* at the time, said that Pablo was executed at close range after he went down.

"You have to understand, the anxiety of that team was so high," he said. "Escobar was like a trophy at the end of a long hunt. For him to have been taken alive . . . no one wanted to attend that disaster."

As for Pablo exiting with two guns blazing, photos of the death scene on the rooftop do show two weapons near the body. But his pursuers acknowledge altering the crime scene in at least one significant way: they carefully shaved off the corners of their victim's whiskers to give him that peculiar Hitler-style mustache that would be featured in all the news reports of his death. It was one final indignity for the man who had embarrassed them for so long.

The colonel had been feeling especially low that morning. When he had told his son and the other men to go home and get some sleep, it was because he believed that Pablo had escaped again. Only this time it was his fault. On many, even most, of the failed raids, which now numbered in the thousands, Martinez had felt pressured to launch his men prematurely. It ran counter to his nature. The colonel was a careful man. He would have preferred conducting fewer, more selective operations, but his superiors in Bogotá and the Americans were never happy unless the Search Bloc was banging down doors, as though exertion alone meant progress. The Americans in particular were always pushing for him and his men to move faster, even though the target information they gave him was generally imprecise. The colonel had reason to believe that the Americans could pinpoint

Pablo with more accuracy than they let on, because they did not want to reveal the precision of their instruments. The data they gave him usually placed Pablo within an area of a few hundred meters, which in Medellín could mean an entire city block. With his son and the portable equipment in the field, the colonel was certain that his men could improve on that information on their own, so he had refused to launch an all-out raid on any of Pablo's previous calls to the Hotel Tequendama until Hugo had obtained a precise fix. He believed that this delay had allowed Pablo to slip away.

Four times that week the colonel had defied orders from Bogotá to launch. In the halls of power, of course, they had their own interpretation of this reluctance. The colonel knew they would be whispering about him, saying that he had sold out to Pablo. But this time, he told his men, he had wanted "zero error."

So he had waited. When Pablo came back up on the radiophone he was elated. He phoned Hugo, who had fallen asleep back at his apartment, and summoned all the other men to return to their hiding places. The colonel's wife was visiting. They had planned to fly back to Bogotá together that day, but now that trip was on hold. Pablo had promised to call his son back.

When he did, the colonel listened on the radio as the men hit the office building, then as Hugo, off on his own, actually spotted Pablo in the window. Over the din of the office-building raid, it was the colonel who picked out his son's voice calling for help. He ordered the bulk of the assault force to move quickly to his son's aid. Then he sweated out the ten minutes it took for them to get there. He listened as the shooting started, and then received Major Aguilar's jubilant confirmation of success.

In the background, the colonel could hear men firing their weapons into the air in celebration. He got on the phone and notified his superiors. After that, word spread quickly around the world.

Defense Minister Rafael Pardo was returning from a late lunch when he entered his office in Bogotá and found all the lights on his phone blinking at once. Most of the lines were dedicated links to his top generals, so obviously something big was up. He picked up the line from the top army commander, who was in Medellín that day to give a lecture.

"Minister, Escobar is dead," said the general.

"What happened?"

"He was killed in a [Search Bloc] operation."

"Is it confirmed?" asked Pardo. He had heard similar premature reports in the past. "Get the fingerprints."

"But Minister, it is him. I am in front of him."

"Get the fingerprints anyway."

Pardo called President Gaviria.

"Señor President, we think we've killed Escobar."

"Do you have confirmation?"

"Not yet. It will be twenty minutes before we can be certain."

But the defense minister knew they had gotten him. When he hung up, he called his secretary into his office.

"Bring me the press release for Escobar's death," he said.

"Death in an operation or death by natural causes?" she asked.

"By operation!" Pardo announced triumphantly. Then he opened a box on his desk and withdrew a big Cuban cigar, lit it, leaned back, swung his feet up, and savored a few private moments of victory.

Ambassador Morris Busby called Washington, asking to speak with Richard Canas, the National Security Council's drug enforcement chief at the Old Executive Office Building, across the street from the White House. Canas was on the phone with a reporter when his secretary interrupted.

"It's Buz," she said.

"We got Escobar," Busby told him when Canas took the call.

"Are you sure?" Canas asked.

"Ninety-nine percent," said Busby.

"Not good enough. Has one of our people seen it?"

"Give me a few minutes," said Busby.

Days before Pablo was shot, Javier Peña had left for Miami to check out the sources who claimed the fugitive drug boss had fled to Haiti, so Steve Murphy was dispatched to Medellín. The trips north to the Holguin base had become a drag for the two DEA agents. Steve had to leave his wife back in Bogotá whenever he made the trip, and as much as he admired the Delta guys and, lately, the SEALs who rotated in and out of the base, he didn't enjoy sharing the privations of their life there, sleeping on air mattresses or cots, living in a tiny suite of rooms in the barracks. They passed hours reading books and playing cards or video games, eating pizza, and watching movies on the VCR. Sometimes the Delta guys would take a case of hand grenades out to a range and throw them. Murphy had been doing law enforcement work for almost twenty years and he had never lost his enthusiasm for it, but those days in late 1993 were the closest he ever came to feeling burned out.

The base was small enough that everyone knew immediately when something unusual had happened. Murphy and a SEAL were sitting on a bench outside their rooms that Thursday morning when they noticed increased traffic in and out of the colonel's office. Murphy walked over to poke his head in. The colonel had a phone in one hand and a radio handset in the other.

"What's up?" Murphy asked one of the Colombian officers in the room.

"It's the colonel's son. He thinks he's found Pablo."

Then the colonel was shouting into the radio, "Stay exactly where you are!"

As soon as Major Aguilar shouted "Vivá Colombia!" over the radio, Murphy made a dash back to the American quarters to call his boss, Joe Toft.

Toft had already heard.

"You better get your ass out there and bring pictures back," Toft told him.

Murphy managed to flag down Colonel Martinez's vehicle as it was leaving the base.

When they arrived in the neighborhood, the colonel's men were setting up barricades in the street. Crowds had begun to form as word spread that Pablo had been killed. Murphy went into the house, climbed to the second floor, and was directed to look out the window to the rooftop. There he saw Pablo's barefoot body stretched on the tiles, with men from the raiding party standing around him, sharing swigs from a bottle of Johnnie Walker Scotch whiskey. The Search Bloc was celebrating hard already. They had fired off so many rounds into the air after Pablo was killed that neighbors had come to their windows to wave white handkerchiefs. Hugo thought at first that this was their way of applauding the Search Bloc's success. It didn't occur to him until later that they had been offering to surrender.

Murphy shouted to the men around the body and they posed glee-fully, raising their rifles like big-game hunters around their trophy buck. The DEA agent snapped their picture. He then climbed out to the roof and took more pictures of Pablo's bloated body and bloody face, and more shots of the men posing around him.

Then Murphy gave the camera to one of the shooters and posed alongside Pablo's body himself.

Before he left, a Colombian officer confiscated his film. When he got it back, the roll was developed, but several of the negatives had been re-moved. The picture of Murphy, in a bright red shirt, posing beside the dead body would eventually cause a sensation in Colombia, suggesting that Americans were the ones who had tracked down and killed Pablo. That one and others on the roll, all of them grotesque, would eventually end up gracing the office walls of many in Washington and in the U.S. military who had taken part in the successful mission.

Moments before Murphy's call, Toft had gotten the news from his friend *PNC* general Octavio Vargas.

"Joe-ay!" Vargas shouted happily into the phone. "We just got him!"

Toft immediately stepped out into the hall on the embassy's fourth floor and shouted, "Escobar is dead!"

Then he ran upstairs to give the ambassador full confirmation of the kill. Busby was ecstatic.

Busby called Canas back.

"Got him," he said. "Dead. Gone forever."

Canas left his office jumping up and down. He walked across the street to the White House to deliver the good news, and no one was free to hear it. He did eventually meet with NSC assistant chief Dick Clark, and they sent a message in writing to their boss, Anthony Lake.

Busby felt a deep sense of satisfaction. After nearly twenty years of doing this kind of work, he felt that this was the most impressive feat he had ever been involved with. To have stuck with the chase for so long, sixteen hard, frustrating, bloody months, an effort involving military, dip-lomatic, and law enforcement agencies spanning two administrations, two countries! All the money and men and time devoted to this chase, most of which would never be widely known. It had been ugly. Hundreds of people had been killed, police, cartel members, and the innocent victims of Pablo's bombs. Busby thought about all the different agencies that had cooperated in an unprecedented way, the thousands of people who had worked on it, the hundreds who had been killed, and now . . . *the son of a bitch was gone!*

He left that afternoon to visit the Presidential Palace to congratulate Gaviria in person. The president was all smiles. Extra editions of the Bogotá newspapers were already on the street. *El Espectador* had a giant headline that read FINALMENTE SI CAYO (FINALLY, HE'S DOWN). Gaviria signed a copy for the ambassador.

The yellowed front page is now in a pillowcase with other memorabilia at Busby's home in Virginia. He is retired from the State Department but still does consulting work with various government agencies.

"I know it's unseemly to celebrate someone's death, but the effort to get Pablo Escobar was an amazing accomplishment," Busby said. "When I think of all the different forces involved, all of them dedicated to finding this one man . . . well, all I can say is, I wouldn't have wanted to be Pablo Escobar."

The former ambassador said he was unaware of some of the connections between *Los Pepes* and the Search Bloc, as noted by the DEA cable traffic from the period, and he still insists that the evidence is sketchy at best. "If I had believed such a connection existed," he said, "it would have been a showstopper."

Colombian TV stations recorded the excited scene as Pablo's body, with his swollen, bloody face and the peculiar Hitler mustache, was strapped on a stretcher, handed down off the roof, and loaded into a police ambulance. It was driven to the Medellín coroner's office. Cameramen were allowed in the morgue to videotape and photograph his body stripped and stretched out on a slab. To the amusement of Pablo's killers, much was made of the mustache.

Within the special ops community in the United States, Pablo's death was regarded as a successful mission for Delta, and legend has it that its operators were in on the kill. If so, and perhaps by design, there is no evidence of it. Some of the Search Bloc members I interviewed said there were Americans among the assault force that day; others said there were not. It is possible they were there, and even might have killed Pablo, without being seen. The Search Bloc and the U.S. embassy had known for days the neighborhood where Pablo was staying. They may have known which house. If they knew exactly where Pablo was hiding, Delta could have positioned snipers for a shot at the fugitive when he came out of the house. The unit's snipers are among the best in the world. It would explain the precision of the killing shot.

Looking over autopsy photos showing the entrance wound, one Delta Force member told me, "Pretty good shootin', huh?"

Colonel Santos says he was in the United States when Pablo was killed. Over the duration of the manhunt, dozens of operators and SEALs had spent time in Medellín. A member of SEAL Team Six who was based in Medellín on the day Pablo was killed said that he had spent the entire day at the base "reading, studying Spanish, and playing video games; it was like being in a compartment on a ship." Once word got back to the base that Pablo had been killed, he said, "We were locked down tight for a couple of days. They were real paranoid about anyone discovering that we were there. Then we flew back to Bogotá and home."

Analyzing the hit, Centra Spike was convinced that, in the end, Lieutenant Hugo Martinez had found Pablo not because he had mastered the portable direction finder but out of pure dumb luck. The unit had told Colonel Martinez days before in what neighborhood they would find Pablo. The way the American experts saw it, the Search Bloc had blundered around the area long enough, following the imprecise readings on Hugo's equipment, until at last he had simply seen Pablo in the window.

The surveillance tapes showed that Hugo had been wrong about Pablo spotting him from the window. In the ten minutes while he and his men had waited for reinforcements, expecting to shoot it out with Pablo's *sicarios* at any moment, Pablo had made several other short calls, none of which betrayed any knowledge that there were police waiting for him outside.

No matter how the final one hundred yards finally had been closed, Centra Spike's commanders were delighted. Justice had been exacted against terrible odds. Killing Pablo would not end cocaine exports to the United States or even slow them down—everybody knew that—but the Americans had signed on for this job believing that it was about something bigger. It was about democracy, the rule of law, standing up for justice and civilization. Pablo was simply too rich, too powerful, and too violent. He was a would-be tyrant who had been faced down by an imperfect but nevertheless democratic, free society. And America had helped. Centra Spike had learned a lot in the last sixteen months, and they weren't finished in Colombia. There was still the Cali cartel and the guerrillas.

But this day was for celebration. There were parties in Medellín, Bogotá, and Washington. Banners reading PEG DEAD! were draped and champagne corks were popped.

Major Jacoby told his men later, with satisfaction, that he had driven home and pulled off a shelf the dusty $300 bottle of Rémy Martin cognac he had bought in January 1990 when Centra Spike had first put Pablo in its crosshairs. He drank half of it all by himself.

Hermilda Escobar forecast doom after her son was killed.

"God forbid what's going to happen," she said. "A lot of horrible things are going to happen with the guerrillas and the one who sold him out. What's going to happen . . . it's not like I want it to happen. . . . I forgive them. I forgive them with all my heart the ones who did me wrong by taking my son away. I forgive them."

A reporter asked her if there would be retaliations for Pablo's death.

"There will be," she said, "but I pray to God a lot for God to help them [Pablo's killers] and for them not to go through what we went through."

After Pablo was killed, Hugo ran into the house and found the drug boss's portable phone. That was his trophy. He used it to phone his commanding officer, Major Luis Estupinan, and congratulate him.

That evening, the men of the Search Bloc in Medellín partied late, but Hugo and his father did not join them. Such overt displays were not the colonel's style. When the men started shooting their weapons into the air, the colonel put an end to the party.

The next morning, the colonel and Hugo and some of the other top men in the Search Bloc were honored in Bogotá. That evening, back at their home, the colonel's youngest son, Gustavo, who was ten, was looking through a sack of Pablo's personal items that the colonel had collected and brought home with him. In the bag was a small loaded handgun, and as Gustavo examined it, the gun went off.

Gustavo wasn't hurt badly, but the bullet passed close enough to scratch the skin of his belly. It was as though Pablo had fired one more shot from the grave. The colonel gathered all the items and put them back in the sack and delivered them that night to police headquarters, as though they were a curse.

He still feels haunted by the dead drug boss. Martinez got a great deal of personal satisfaction from killing Pablo, and he was finally promoted to general, but he paid a heavy price. The years he spent in pursuit of the drug boss were years he lost with his wife and children.

"When I think about Pablo Escobar, I think of him as an episode in my life that completely altered the way I was living," Martinez said in his home in the village of Mosquera. "What I wanted to do with my children and my family was considerably altered. I don't blame him as a person or anything like that. However, being involved in those operations, I abandoned my family and my sons, who needed me in what was a crucial time in their lives. The challenge reminds me of something negative about my life as a policeman, negative in terms of personal satisfactions. We had very few professional satisfactions resulting from those operations, because I was the victim of what happens to any person whose name becomes public."

Martinez was accused of accepting money from the Cali cartel and of being involved with the illegal activities of *Los Pepes,* accusations he denies.

"The saddest part was that there were even some chiefs of police who thought we were sold out, and they let us know what was on their minds," said Martinez, who argues that the allegations against him originated with Pablo. "[He] accused us of running *Los Pepes.* Pablo Escobar made the accusations against me in writing, against General Vargas and members of the Cali cartel, saying we were *Los Pepes.* Those accusations were published by the press, almost everybody heard about them, and perhaps those accusations sparked the rumor about us having some kind of link with them."

There is strong evidence from a variety of sources that the Search Bloc cooperated with *Los Pepes.* Fidel Castaño, before he was killed in 1994, acknowledged that he was one of the leaders of the death squad, and Martinez admits that Castaño collaborated with his men. Americans at the Holguin base remember Don Berna, Diego Murillo, another of the *Los Pepes* leaders, working closely with the Search Bloc officers on a regular basis. Murillo got to know DEA agent Javier Peña so well that he once presented him with a gold watch. Perhaps Martinez knew nothing about the extracurricular efforts of the men under his command, but it seems unlikely. What is more likely is that today, years later, the general would like to be remembered as the man who led the lawful forces that pursued Pablo, as the man who won a battle to the death with the world's greatest outlaw. He would prefer that the work of *Los Pepes* stay in the shadow, and he says their contribution was unimportant. "They were a nuisance, a distraction," the general says. He is the only one who makes this argument.

"*Los Pepes* were key," said one American soldier involved in the hunt. "But you aren't ever going to get to the full truth about them, because nobody is going to tell you. You have to *surmise*."

No one has been prosecuted for the murders committed by *Los Pepes*. In the official *DAS* total of "Medellín cartel members" killed during the second war, the deaths attributed to the death squad are (perhaps tellingly) lumped together with those laid to the Search Bloc: one hundred and twenty-nine. Members of the vigilante group boast that they alone killed as many as three hundred. One hundred and twenty-seven people were killed by Pablo's bombs. One hundred and forty-seven police officers were killed in the manhunt, and one hundred and thirty-two cartel members were arrested—many of whom are already out of jail.

Both Colonel Martinez and his son were decorated by the police for their efforts. Hugo was offered a commission abroad and spent two years in Washington working with the Colombian embassy. When I interviewed him he was a captain and was station commander for the city of Manizales. He has since been transferred back to his old electronic-surveillance unit and lives in Bogotá.

After the colonel was made a general in 1994, he went on to serve for a year as director of *DIJIN*. He served for a time as head of instruction for the *PNC*, and as its inspector general, and in 1997 he followed his son to Washington, where he spent a year as military attaché to the Colombian embassy. He left the police force the following year, when General José Serrano was appointed to the top post. General Martinez did not see eye to eye with the new *PNC* chief, the man whose new uniform had inspired him to join the police so many years before, so he retired. He now maintains a small farm and spends time there and in Bogotá.

For a while, for safety reasons, Martinez considered moving with his wife and family to another country. They toured South America together, visiting Brazil, Uruguay, Argentina, and Chile, and decided that Uruguay and Argentina were the places where they would feel most comfortable. Just as he began to inquire about emigrating in 2000, there were news reports that Pablo Escobar's wife and son had been arrested in Argentina. So the one place he thought safest turned out to be the very place where the Escobar family was hiding!

Oddly, Martinez said he felt sorry for them.

"Just as I was trying to go someplace else for security, so were they," he said. "I hurt to see they are still suffering for something that happened so long ago. They are also trying to escape from all that."

In the days after Pablo's death, his wife and children were interviewed up in their suite at the Hotel Tequendama by a Bogotá TV crew. Looking haggard but composed, Maria Victoria portrayed herself as just another victim of the country's violence.

"There's no positive response to any of this," she said. "I don't know if you notice, but we are also a family who feel we've gone through the same despair the country has. And psychologically, I'm very concerned whether my children will be able to survive this complex situation."

Little Manuela, perched on a windowsill, defended her father.

"You can't say anything about my dad . . . absolutely nothing, because no one knows him, just God and himself. . . . I see my dad as an innocent person. It seems to me very painful that the president of Colombia has congratulated those who [killed my father] . . . because they got the most wanted man in the world. And I don't think it is fair that my father had to be killed."

A subdued-looking Juan Pablo told the reporter that he wanted to get on with a normal life.

"I don't want to die violently," he said. "I want to give a gift of peace to my country. . . . The truth is that we've been here a lot of days. We can't take it. We're desperate. What people want most at Christmastime is freedom and so many marvelous things that the world can offer you. Unfortunately, because of fate, we're confined to this place. We're getting to desperate limits. My little sister cannot take it anymore because this is a jail. . . . We don't have much hope."

Not long after Pablo's death, his teenage son paid an unexpected visit to the embassy in Bogotá. He asked to see Busby, who refused to meet with him. The ambassador called downstairs to Toft.

"Hey, Joe, Pablo Escobar's son is downstairs. I'm not going to see him, okay?"

Toft agreed to meet with Juan Pablo, who was suspected of having been involved in murders and in plotting against the Search Bloc. He had heard Juan Pablo's rants on the surveillance tapes. He stepped into the room to encounter a worried, fat, soft-looking young man. Toft was impressed with the boy's poise under the circumstances.

"He told me that he and his family were in great danger, and they were appealing for visas to save their lives," Toft remembered later.

"What will it take for me to get a visa?" Juan Pablo asked.

"All of the cocaine and cocaine money in the world would not get you a visa," Toft told him.

Juan Pablo did not appear surprised by the answer.

"Are you sure we can do nothing?" he asked again. "Is there anything, *anything* we could do to earn a visa?"

"Even if you helped put the whole Cali cartel in jail, we would not give you a visa," Toft told him.

And Juan Pablo left.

The family eventually fled to Buenos Aires, where they lived quietly until their arrest in 2000. An accountant who had been linked romantically with Maria Victoria and had been rejected by her went to the authorities and alleged that the family had been illegally laundering money. Maria Victoria and Juan Pablo were charged with conspiracy, and now face the possibility of jail in Argentina or deportation.

Centra Spike suffered in the bureaucratic wars following its success in Colombia. Its former commanders believe that the unit's ability to get better results than the CIA with smaller, cheaper equipment led to harassment, internal investigations (into expense-account fraud and accusations of fraternization), and trumped-up charges. Whether the charges were trumped up or not, the unit was effectively disbanded. Careers ended, and many of the men involved in the manhunt for Pablo Escobar are now out of the army. Some are still doing the same kind of work for the Pentagon as contract employees.

The army still has the unit that was then called Centra Spike. Its former leaders feel that its effectiveness has been much reduced.

The death of Pablo Escobar may have been cause for celebration in official circles in Washington and Bogotá, but for many Colombians, especially in Medellín, it was an occasion for grief. Thousands of people attended the funeral and followed his casket through the streets. They swarmed to get closer, and sometimes mourners opened the lid to stroke his face.

There were chants of "We love you, Pablo!" and "Long live Pablo Escobar!" and shouts of anger directed toward the government, promises of revenge. The mob followed the casket to the cemetery, where Pablo's sister told a TV reporter that her brother had not been a criminal and that any violence attributed to him was necessary to "defend" himself from government persecution.

Pablo's grave in Medellín is still carefully tended. On the simple stone there is a photograph of a mustachioed Pablo in a business suit. There are flowering bushes framing the grave, and ornate iron bars that stretch over it supporting three flowerpots.

Eduardo Mendoza again works for César Gaviria, who is general secretary of the Organization of American States. The former Colombian president had lost touch with his old friend but tracked him down when I asked for help finding him.

Just as the judges at his *indagatoria* recommended, the disillusioned former vice minister of justice left Colombia. His innocence before the law did not clear his name in public. People would come up to him in restaurants in Bogotá and tell him, "Get out. They are going to kill you." Some would say, "You are a crook." The army still blamed him for Pablo's escape. They claimed that the only reason Pablo got away was because they had to storm the prison to rescue Mendoza. No one would hire him. Many of his old friends would no longer speak to him. He was an outcast.

So he flew back to New York, stayed at the New York Athletic Club for several weeks, and then enrolled as a graduate student at Yale University, studying Latin American literature. He ran out of money after four months. When he met with the dean to tell him why he was leaving, the school offered Mendoza a scholarship, and he spent three years earning a master's degree.

It was there, on a cold December afternoon, that he learned of Pablo's death. He returned to his apartment—he called it his "monk's cell"—after classes and checked his voice mail. Usually there was just a message from Adriana, but on this day the recorded voice said he had twenty-five messages.

The first was from his brother.

"They've killed Escobar!" he said. Every other recording carried the same message. In some, he could hear partying going on in the background.

He reflected on how much his life had changed since that day he'd agreed to go to Envigado to "formalize" the transfer of a prisoner. Over the years, Mendoza had worked up a greater sense of anger at the officials who had scapegoated and persecuted him than for Pablo himself. His friends had hurt him worse than Pablo ever had. In the end, it all just made him sad. He couldn't feel any sense of satisfaction about Pablo's death. It was just a footnote for him now, a final detail from a story that for him had already ended badly—but not as badly as it might have.

After finding Mendoza, Gaviria hired him. Eduardo married Adriana and they have twins, a boy and a girl. He now works as a lawyer for the Organization of American States.

About the way his administration treated his old friend, Gaviria says, "It was a difficult time for us all."

Roberto Uribe, the Medellín lawyer whose work for Pablo had made him a target of *Los Pepes,* was still in hiding when his former client was killed. Uribe had long since realized how much Pablo had pulled the wool over his eyes. He saw him now as a vicious criminal. When he heard the news on a car radio, he felt not sadness but relief. It meant he had made it.

* * *

After his initial elation, Joe Toft felt a knot in his stomach. He felt it the entire time he was smiling, embracing colleagues, talking to the Colombian press. He hurried over to PNC headquarters in Bogotá, where a party was in full swing. He sipped champagne and exchanged hearty rounds of thanks and congratulations, embraced drunken colleagues, slapped each other on the back. But even as he went through these motions of victory, Toft was haunted by the feeling that somehow they had lost. Pablo was dead, but the good guys had lost.

It was an awful feeling, but Toft couldn't shake it. In the weeks after Pablo's death, Agent Kenny Magee had official certificates printed up for all of those directly involved in the manhunt. "Because of your selfless dedication and willing sacrifices, the world's most sought-after criminal was located and killed. . . ." the proclamation began. It had a space at the lower right to be signed by Toft, and to the left, a touch of wit: the signature and thumbprint of Pablo Escobar. Someone in the Colombian press obtained a copy and felt it was in bad taste, particularly the thumbprint, but Toft and many of the others had their copies framed.

The DEA station chief's pride was mixed with regret. He felt that to get Pablo they had sold their souls. For months now the information had piled up in his office, evidence that his friends in the Colombian government had been taking payoffs from the Cali cocaine cartel—even his friend General Vargas was suspected of taking bribes—and that they all had been behind the murderous campaign of *Los Pepes*. Toft admired the solid detective work that had finally found Pablo, the technological wizardry of Centra Spike and Delta Force, the patience, courage, and tenacity of Colonel Martinez and the Search Bloc. In retrospect, now, he wished they had just relied on all that legitimate effort to get the job done. It might have taken them longer, Toft believed, but it would have been better. It would have been the right way, and they would have gotten him in the end just the same. Instead, they had taken this terrible shortcut.

Toft felt guilty himself. He believed DEA information hadn't been shared directly with *Los Pepes,* but he also knew that the death squad had collaborated with the Colombian Search Bloc. His agents Peña and Murphy had seen Don Berna and the other *Los Pepes* contacts at the Holguin school. He knew that the death squad hits matched the intelligence reports gathered at the embassy and passed along to the Search Bloc. He knew that some of the DEA's own sources were founding members of the group. Still, Toft was torn. On the one hand, *Los Pepes* were effectively dismantling the Medellín cartel and stripping away the layers of protection around Pablo. But on the other hand, he couldn't in good conscience support the group's violent, illegal methods. So he had morally held his breath. He had done nothing and had kept the worst of his misgivings and evidence to himself. Inside the embassy, he had been the most gung ho all along. When Busby had raised doubts about the colonel and *Los Pepes,* it had been Toft who, behind the ambassador's back, had pushed to keep the colonel in place, and who had reassured the Colombian government of continued American support. Now, with Pablo dead, Toft worried that they had created a monster. They had opened a bridge between the Colombian government, its top politicians and generals, and the Cali cartel that would be difficult, if not impossible, to shut down.

Agent Murphy had spelled it out in a memo to headquarters three months earlier, after meeting with a high-ranking Colombian police official he did not name:

> As stated by the CNP [*PNC*] source, sometimes it is necessary to talk with the worst sections of society in order to catch a criminal. [He] continued by saying that they feel they have spoken with "the devil himself" in this investigation. . . . Fidel and Carlos Castaño, who are the alleged leaders of the illegal anti-Escobar group known as *Los Pepes,* as well as some of the world's foremost cocaine traffickers and money launderers. . . . While this kind of activity may be extremely revolting for the CNP, at the same time, it is necessary.

Murphy went on to write that the Cali cartel had also gotten involved in the manhunt, noting, "This only makes good business sense." Murphy predicted that the alliance between Cali and the government, forged during this manhunt, might combine to create "a super cartel."

> Should this ever happen, the GOC and CNP would be virtually helpless in their attempts to corner such an organization. This, too, would be devastating for the U.S.

Others at DEA headquarters had the same concerns. Four months earlier, in the same cable he had received from Gregory Passic, chief of financial investigations for the DEA, relating Rodolpho Ospina's description of how *Los Pepes* were formed, Passic had written, "Luis Grajales [one of the cartel leaders] told [Ospina] that Cali basically controls everyone in the government outside of [Attorney General] de Greiff." Another of the cartel bosses told Ospina that they had "an impressive library of audio and video recordings, mostly recordings of bribes paid to police and politicians," the memo said. At one meeting the leaders had discussed advancing $200,000 to a Colombian police general. The advance would cover four months, it was explained, because, Passic wrote, "they pay the police generals $50,000 each per month to 1) ensure they continue their hunt for Escobar and 2) provide Cali with information on DEA's efforts against Cali."

Toft had received information of his own, of course, just a month ago, when one of his trusted sources, the Colombian senator (who was later assassinated), had held that meeting with Gilberto Rodríguez Orejuela. The Cali boss had outlined exactly how much money was being paid to various Colombian police officials as a reward for targeting Escobar. The connections with *Los Pepes* were all obvious to Toft.

But what good would it have done for him to object? If someone like Passic knew, why should Joe Toft be the one to harp on it? He suspected that if he had made more of an issue out of it, spelled out for everyone that they were all in bed with the Cali cocaine cartel and a ring of vigilante murderers, then the DEA and the army surely would have withdrawn from the pursuit, and Pablo would have remained at large. So he had gone along. He had stressed to his men, Murphy, Peña, Magee, and the others, that under no circumstances were they to provide assistance directly to *Los Pepes,* but at the same time he knew that everything they gave Colonel Martinez was shared with the vigilante group. It was an ugly business, killing Pablo, and the DEA was certainly no stranger to cooperating with ugly people to get a good job done.

But Toft was convinced that Cali was the big winner in all this. In the years they had focused on Pablo, the southern cartel had consolidated its operations, cemented its relationship with the Colombian government, and become a cocaine monopoly. So the victory was bittersweet. Toft hated what drugs were doing to America. He had always thought that he and the others in the DEA were fighting a war for America's future. He believed strongly in the cause, and felt as if he had become a point man in the fight.

He had gone from busting petty drug users in San Diego to tracking down the most notorious cocaine kingpin of them all. Yet somehow, Toft felt, he had managed to make things worse.

When he had first come to Colombia, to the front lines of the war, Toft had been mesmerized by statistics. The amounts of cocaine they seized were mind-blowing. It took him a full year to realize that even those huge seized amounts were a tiny fraction of what was being shipped north, and that the Colombian officials he had trusted were, in fact, playing a game. They were pleasing Uncle Sam and the DEA by grabbing shipments here and there, but they were into the cocaine business up to their eyeballs. It was then he had realized that Pablo Escobar was the real power in Colombia, and how pervasive and insidious was his influence. He had known it would be difficult to get him, but only now, after Pablo was dead, did he realize how difficult the larger task would be. Killing Pablo had not ended the cocaine industry; it had merely handed it off to new leaders, who had presumably learned from Pablo's mistakes. To prevail now would take . . . how many men? How many lives? How much money? How much compromise? Those were the questions balled in his gut that afternoon and evening, as they all toasted the death of Pablo.

In the coming months, as the Colombian police refocused their efforts on the Cali cartel, Toft became convinced that it was all a sham. He believed that no one with real power was going to jail unless they chose to do so. They were agreeing to have their hands slapped in order to preserve their multibillion-dollar business. Colombian cocaine shipments hadn't slowed during the hunt for Pablo. The best estimate for 1993 would be between 243 and 340 tons of cocaine available for sale in the United States, with 70 to 80 percent of it shipped from Colombia. An estimated $30.8 billion would be spent by Americans for the white powder by the end of that year. Prices were down for the drug. All in all, there was more cocaine available for sale in the United States at cheaper prices that year than ever before in history. Indeed, throughout the remainder of the decade, cocaine prices in the United States gradually declined. The bottom line was that regardless of the billions spent in the war on drugs, there was more than enough cocaine for everybody in America who wanted to buy it.

Of course, killing Pablo had not primarily been about drugs. His violence was his death sentence. His violence and his ambition. But Toft was a drug man, a cop. He had never lost sight of why he was in Colombia, and as he watched the rounds of congratulations in the days, weeks, and months after Pablo's death, he grew more and more cynical about the whole effort.

Six months after Pablo's death, Toft retired and left Colombia, dropping a small bomb in his wake. Angered by the praise being heaped on Colombia by Washington, embittered by the silent betrayals among his circle of Colombian friends, Toft went on television in Bogotá to accuse the president-elect, Ernesto Samper, of being in the pocket of the Cali cocaine cartel. Toft handed reporters copies of secret tape recordings in which Miguel Rodríguez Orejuela, one of the world's most notorious drug traffickers, talked about transferring $3.5 million to Samper's campaign chest. The new president denied the allegations, even though the tapes were authenticated. He claimed that the money had never been accepted by his campaign. Toft didn't believe him, and neither did Busby or other Americans at the embassy. The "*narco*-cassettes" tainted Samper's entire four-year term, and strained relations between the two nations.

It also led to a real crackdown on the Cali cartel. Embarrassed by the revelations in Toft's tapes, the United States pressured Colombia for more action. The tainted General Vargas was replaced by General Serrano, who led a rapid crackdown on corruption in the *PNC* and on the Cali leaders, arresting Gilberto and Miguel Rodríguez Orejuela and six of its other leaders in just two months.

Toft today lives in Reno, Nevada, and plays a lot of tennis. His daughter, Jennifer, is now a DEA agent.

"I don't know what the lesson of the story is," he says. "I hope it's not that the end justifies the means."

SOURCES

I started working on *Killing Pablo* in 1997 after seeing a framed photograph of a dead fat man surrounded by cheerfully posing soldiers on the office wall of a U.S. military man.

"What's that?" I asked.

"That, my friend, is Pablo Escobar," my source said. "I keep that on my wall to remind me that no matter how rich you get in this life, you can still be too big for your britches."

Until then, I was unaware of the extent of U.S. military involvement in the hunt for Escobar. The bulk of this book rests upon interviews I conducted with Americans and Colombians involved in the pursuit from 1989 until his death on December 2, 1993. There are many important sources missing from my list of interviewees, primarily those of military personnel. I don't like relying on anonymous sources, but in this case I was lucky to obtain detailed corroboration of their stories from more than a thousand pages of mostly secret cables from the U.S. embassy in Bogotá to Washington. The cables are from a variety of embassy personnel, but mostly from DEA agents. The whole amounts to a daily record of the manhunt through the eyes of the Americans who took part, and much of the second half of this narrative is drawn from it. I received the DEA's permission to interview its agents early on in this process. Joe Toft, Steve Murphy, Javier Peña, and Kenny Magee spent a lot of time helping me sort out this very complicated story. Former U.S. ambassador Morris D. Busby was also extremely helpful, and kindly reviewed an early draft of the story prior to its being published as a newspaper series in *The Philadelphia Inquirer.* Former Colombian president César Gaviria, now general secretary of the Organization of American States, sat for several interviews and allowed me to poke through his archives, and Eduardo Mendoza, in addition to telling me his own story, served as a patient adviser, chief consultant on Colombian history and politics, translator, intermediary, and friend.

To help me through the mountain of material on this subject generated by Colombia's very courageous journalists, I employed a series of translators and researchers: Julie Lopez, in the United States, and Ricky Ortiz, Maria Carrizosa, and Steve Ambrus in Bogotá. Colombian journalist Gerardo Reyes, of *El Herald,* was extremely helpful to me on my second trip to Colombia in 2000. In the course of preparing a documentary film on this subject with KR Video Inc., I worked closely with Chris Mills and Wendy Doughenbaugh, and learned a great deal from them as they compiled videotape from a rich variety of Colombian sources. I was also fortunate to have the chance to work with the globe-trotting reporter Mike Boettcher of CNN, an extraordinary raconteur whose wealth of background information and sources was both invaluable and astonishing. I am grateful to them all.

INTERVIEWS

Joe Toft, Steve Murphy, Javier Peña, Kenny Magee, César Gaviria, Eduardo Mendoza, J. J. Ballesteros, Roberto Uribe, General Hugo Martinez, Captain Hugo Martinez, Lieutenant Colonel Luis Estupinan, Morris D. Busby, Judy Busby, Raphael Pardo, "Rubin," Octavio Vargas, General José Serrano, Mike White, Poncho Renteria, Robert Wagner, Gustavo de Greiff, Colonel Oscar Naranjo, General Ismael Trujillo, Major Luis Cepeda, Sergeant José Fernandez, Ambassador Richard Gillespie, Diego Londono, General Jack Sheehan, Brian Sheridan, Walter B. Slocombe, Randy Beers, General George Joulwon, Anthony Lake, Ambassador Robert Gelbard, Mike Sheehan, Richard Canas, General Colin Powell, Jim Smith, Janet Christ, W. Hays Parks, L. H. "Bucky" Burruss.

BOOKS

The Andean Cocaine Industry, by Patrick L. Clawson and Rensselaer W. Lee III, St. Martin's Press, 1996. An excellent overview with lots of statistics detailing the growth of cocaine trafficking and efforts to fight it.

Bandeleros, Gamonales, y Campesinos, by Gonzalo Sanchez and Donny Meertens, El Ancora Editores, 1983. Passages translated for me by Eduardo Mendoza.

Che Guevara: A Revolutionary Life, by Jon Lee Anderson, Grove Press, 1997. A classic. The definitive life of Che, and a rich and sweeping portrait of South and Central America during the 1940s, 1950s, and 1960s.

Clear and Present Dangers: The U.S. Military and the War on Drugs in the Andes, Washington Office on Latin America, 1991.

Cocaine Politics: Drugs, Armies and the CIA in Central America, by Peter Dale Scott and Jonathan Marshall, University of California Press, 1998.

Colombia: A Lonely Planet Survival Kit, by Krzysztof Dydyuski, Lonely Planet Publications, 1995. An extremely useful travel guide with concise abstracts on Colombian history, geography, flora, fauna, climate, etc.

Colombia and the United States: Hegemony and Interdependence, by Stephen J. Randall, University of Georgia Press, 1992. A straightforward history of U.S.-Colombian relations over three centuries.

Colombia: Democracy Under Assault, by Harvey F. Kline, Westview Press, 1995. A scholarly summary of Colombian history from prehistory to the 1990s.

Colombia: The Genocidal Democracy, by Javier Giraldo, S. J., Common Courage Press, 1996. A left-wing polemic against the tradition of violence in Colombia and its ties to wealthy capitalist interests and the United States. Passionate but one-sided.

Death Beat: A Colombian Journalist's Life Inside the Cocaine Wars, by Maria Jimena Duzon, HarperCollins, 1994. Captures the excitement and despair of a working journalist in Colombia during this period.

El Patrón, Vida y Muerte de Pablo Escobar, by Luis Canon, Planeta Colombiana Editorial S.A., 1994. One of the best accounts of Pablo's life, although it is melodramatic and tends to repeat information of questionable authenticity. An artful clip-job.

Gaitán of Colombia: A Political Biography, by Richard E. Sharpless, University of Pittsburgh Press, 1978. An excellent biography of the Colombian political leader gunned down in 1948; affords a detailed look at the country at midcentury.

Kings of Cocaine: Inside the Medellín Cartel—An Astonishing True Story of Murder, Money, and International Corruption, by Guy Gugliotta and Jeff Leen, Simon & Schuster, 1989. A fun, solidly researched portrait of the drug war's early days, with colorful portraits of all the main characters, including Pablo.

Mi Hermano Pablo, by Roberto Escobar, Quintero Editores, 2000. A curiosity. More a collection of random, brotherly memories than a comprehensive biography.

News of a Kidnapping, by Gabriel García Márquez (translated by Edith Grossman), Penguin Books, 1998. A compelling, eloquent, and painful miniature of the tortuous series of kidnappings, murders, and negotiations that led up to Pablo's surrender in 1991.

The Palace of Justice: A Colombian Tragedy, by Ana Carrigan, Four Walls Eight Windows, 1993. An angry journalist's account of the debacle that followed M-19's seizure of the Palace of Justice in 1985. Carrigan doubts all of the official versions of the event, including government claims that Escobar was behind it.

Panama, by Kevin Buckley, Touchstone, 1992. A terrific story of America's tangled relationship with Manuel Antonio Noriega, which touches here and there on the dictator's dealings with the Medellín cartel.

The White Labyrinth: Cocaine and Political Power, by Rensselaer W. Lee III., Transaction Publishers, 1998.

Whitewash: Pablo Escobar and the Cocaine Wars, by Simon Strong, Pan Books, 1996. This is the best book I found about Pablo Escobar and the entire period of the drug wars in Colombia, up until the year of Pablo's surrender in 1991. This edition includes a chapter updating the story with Pablo's death, but it lacks the detail of the rest of the account. Strong did an amazing research job.

ARTICLES

"The Bogotazo," by Jack Davis, CIA Historical Review Program, declassified in 1997.

"*Escobar: 17 Años de Historia del Criminal,*" *El Tiempo,* December 3, 1993.

"Exit El Patrón," by Alma Guillermoprieto, *The New Yorker,* October 25, 1993. An extremely prescient, insightful, and well-reported piece, amazingly timely.

"I Won't Study Law Because the Law Changes Every Day Here," *El Colombiano,* July 9, 1991. Translated by Ricky Ortiz.

"Implications for the United States of the Colombian Drug Trade." A Special National Intelligence Estimate, CIA. Volume II–Annex E, June 28, 1983.

"Inside America's Troubled Wars Against the Cocaine Cartels," by Douglas Fish, *The Washington Post Magazine,* July 21, 1996.

"On the Trail of Medellín's Drug Lord," by Andrew and Leslie Cockburn, *Vanity Fair,* December 1992.

"This Is How We Killed Galán." An interview with Jhon "Popeye" Velasquez. *Semana,* October 1, 1996. Translated by Maria Carrizosa.

"An Unforgettable Day," by Poncho Renteria, *Semana,* April 6, 1993. Translated by Stephen Ambrus.

DOCUMENTS

"The Andean Strategy: Its Development and Implementation—Where We Are Now and Where We Should Be Going," T. K. Custer, Dept. of Defense, September 15, 1991. Unpublished.

"Chronology of Significant Drug-Related Events in Colombia, 1989–1993," DEA (compiled by DEA agents at the U.S. embassy in Bogotá).

"Colombia and the United States Chronology," Michael Evans, National Security Archive. (The Archive Chronology).

Memorandum of Law, Dept. of the Army, "Executive Order 12333 and Assassination," November 2, 1989, by W. Hays Parks.

National Security Decision Directive 221, April 8, 1986. The White House. Declassified 3/26/98.

National Security Decision Directive 18, August 21, 1989. The White House. Declassified 5/5/94.

PROLOGUE: DECEMBER 2, 1993

Colombians often use two given names, the paternal family name, which is the primary last name, followed by the maternal family name. Pablo Escobar's full name was Pablo Emilio Escobar Gaviria. For simplicity's sake, for English readers, I have used throughout the paternal family name. Pablo was not related to Colombian president César Gaviria. Hermilda Escobar and her daughter were videotaped by Colombian TV as they arrived at the scene on foot. Most of this description is drawn from that footage. **She had been ill . . . fainted.** Hermilda's interview with a TV reporter that day. **There were those who said . . . feared him.** TV and newspaper reports and interviews with Medellínos. **"We are family . . . like Hitler's.** Capt. Hugo Martinez, Maj. Luis Estupinan, videotape. **It was hard to tell . . . at rest."** Hermilda's TV interview.

THE RISE OF *EL DOCTOR*: 1948–1989

1

There was no more . . . urban disorders." *Gaitán of Colombia,* 29–34, 170–182; *Che Guevara,* 90–91. The CIA description of Gaitán is from "The Bogotazo," 76, and the comment on Castro, 78. **El Bogotazo was . . . troubled past.** "The Bogotazo,"

78–80; *Gaitán,* 178–180. *Colombia: Democracy Under Assault,* 40–45. **Colombia is a land . . . race of men.** *Colombia: Democracy Under Assault,* 26–39. *Colombia: A Lonely Planet Guide,* 10–30; *Colombia: The Genocidal Democracy,* from the introduction by Noam Chomsky, 7–16. *Colombia and the United States,* 90–120. Information about bandits is from *Bandeleros.* The story about God and the Colombian people was told to me by Eduardo Cabal, a Bogotá businessman. **It was here . . . to be loved.** Pablo's birthdate is from *Whitewash,* 17. Most accounts of Pablo's death on December 2, 1993, point out that he died on the day after his forty-fourth birthday. *King of Cocaine,* 24–25. *El Patrón.* The Forbes estimate of Pablo's wealth was reported in the Cockburns' "On the Trail," 96. *Kings of Cocaine,* 337. **When he was . . . that chapel.** 75. **Pablo did not . . . they smoked dope.** *Whitewash,* 17–25. My interview with "Rubin," the Medellín pilot who was one of Pablo's contemporaries. **Colombian dope . . . boredom as ambition.** Pablo's smoking habits and physical description are from my interviews with Rubin, Roberto Uribe, and Centra Spike analysts. **With his cousin . . . with that fantasy.** *Whitewash,* 18–29. *Kings of Cocaine,* 24–27. *Mi Hermano Pablo,* 13–35. The tradition of *contrabandistas* from *The White Labyrinth,* 34. Also various Bogotá newspaper features about Pablo, particularly from *El Espectador* and *El Tiempo.*

2

Pablo Escobar . . . afraid of him." My interview with Rubin. *The Andean Cocaine Industry,* 37–48. *Kings of Cocaine,* 28–41. **In April . . . were killed.** *Whitewash,* 40–42. The story about hiring the judge's brother is from Uribe. The killings of the *DAS* agents is from the *El Tiempo* retrospective on Pablo's life, 3B. **Pablo was . . . exceeded by profits.** *The Andean Cocaine Industry, plata o plomo,* 51, Pablo's business practices, 38–39. *Whitewash,* 34–65. **And what . . . Pablo's party.** *The Andean Cocaine Industry,* 39. *Death Beat,* 198. *Colombia: Democracy Under Assault,* 60.**With his multimillions . . . hardly noticed.** *Kings of Cocaine,* 75. My interviews with Centra Spike analysts. **After skating away . . . most popular citizen.** *Whitewash,* details of Nápoles and Pablo's partying lifestyle on 41, 51–52, 68; on Mario Henao, 41; and the church, 78–81. *Kings of Cocaine,* on Pablo's lifestyle at Nápoles, 11, on the church, 111–12. "On the Trail," Nápoles, 98. *The Andean Cocaine Industry,* on Pablo's civic outreach, 48–49. **In an interview . . . are disloyal."** *Whitewash,* interview with Auto y Pista, 53. **In private . . . unfortunate servant had.** Centra Spike analysts, Uribe, and Pablo's own writings. The story of drowning the servant is from Rubin. **Most of Medellín . . . to Colombia.** From fragments of Pablo's writings and Uribe. **Politics . . . president of Colombia.** *Death Beat,* 19–20. *The Andean Cocaine Industry,* 48, *Whitewash,* 66–75. **By then . . . north to south.** From my interview in Bogotá with Pardo. **The mistake . . . without a future."** *Medellín Cívica* interview quoted from *Kings of Cocaine,* which cites an undated edition of that publication from 1983, 96. **Pablo sponsored . . . the church.** *Kings of Cocaine,* 110–12. *Death Beat,* 25. **The only hint . . . political agenda.** *Whitewash,* 71–72. On the extradition treaty, 61. *The Andean Cocaine Industry,* 48, 99. **Pablo's election . . . his estate.** *Whitewash,* on Muerte a Secuestradores, 64. *The Andean Cocaine Industry,* 46. *Death Beat,* 4. The CIA attributed MAS to Fabio Ochoa in its June 28, 1983, National Intelligence Estimate "Implications for the U. S." The *Semana* article is quoted in *Whitewash,*

71. Also my interview with Uribe. I don't recall if the program *Miami Vice* ever specifically mentioned Pablo, but there was a steady theme of fashionably clad, violent, rich Colombians in the show presumed to inherit the top rung of the illicit cocaine ladder, any one of whom could have been modeled after him. There is a picture of the plane mounted over the front gate in *Kings of Cocaine,* on the eleventh page of the first photo insert. **He built . . . stop him.** *Mi Hermano Pablo,* 33–34.

3

Newly appointed . . . aspirations," he said. *Whitewash,* 90–94. *Death Beat,* 32. *Kings of Cocaine,* 105–10, 116–18. Renteria, *Semana,* April 6, 1993, "An Unforgettable Day." Annals of *El Congreso,* August 23, 1983, 1185–86. *El Espectador,* Wednesday, August 17, 1983, 1A-10A, Thursday, August 18, 1983, 1A-14A, *El Tiempo,* August 19, 1983, 4A *El Tiempo,* Thursday, August 25, 1983, 1A-8A. **Pablo complained . . . not have helped.** Uribe, Pablo's letters, *Whitewash,* 89–90. *Kings of Cocaine,* 138–43.

4

Pablo was right . . . the CIA report said. *Kings of Cocaine,* 69. "Implications for the U.S." 1–2. **The new U.S. . . . Lara was dead.** *Kings of Cocaine,* 103–104. On Tranquilandia, 133. *Whitewash,* 94–95. **His killing . . . hell to pay.** The quote from Caño is from *Death Beat,* 31, and reaction to Lara's death, 34. *The Andean Cocaine Industry,* 103. *Colombia: Democracy Under Assault,* 61–62. **Killing the justice minister . . . the United States.** *Kings of Cocaine,* 170–71. *Whitewash,* 100. *The Andean Cocaine Industry,* 50. **American involvement . . . our motherland."** From a copy of the letter to Tambs in Gaviria archives. **And, just like that . . . than he wanted.** Rubin, *The Andean Cocaine Industry,* 42. *Kings of Cocaine,* 172. *Panama,* 18. **Whatever the intentions . . . never forgive.** *The Andean Cocaine Industry,* 102–103. *Kings of Cocaine,* 174–77. *Death Beat,* 36. *Whitewash,* 100–103. Rubin. **Pablo didn't give up . . . hometown of Envigado.** Pablo's writings, seized in a Search Bloc raid circa 1990. **Pablo fled . . . hardship post.** Rubin. *Whitewash,* 104–105, 141. *Panama,* 59–60. *Kings of Cocaine,* 154–56, 160–69. A photo of Pablo helping load Seal's aircraft in Nicaragua appears on the sixth page of the second photo insert. **The near miss . . . letting him go.** *Kings of Cocaine,* 185. **After that . . . Colombia again.** *Whitewash,* 142.

5

For the rest . . . resigned the treaty. *Whitewash,* 138–60. *Kings of Cocaine,* 241–50, 300–308. **But victories . . . on a motorbike.** *Whitewash,* 152. *Kings of Cocaine,* 283–84. **Pablo's ugly struggle . . . Pablo's betrayal.** *Whitewash,* 154–55. *The Andean Cocaine Industry,* 50. **Still, the United States . . . in that country.** National Security Decision Directive 221, April 8, 1986, declassified 3/26/98. I obtained a copy from Michael Evans of the National Security Archive. For American troops joining in counterdrug operations see *Military Review,* March 1990. **Inside Colombia . . . genealogical tree."** Counternarcotics chief Jaime Ramirez was killed. *Whitewash,* 152. The Archive Chronology. The Colombian ambassador shot in Budapest was Enrique Parejo. An account of the kidnappings of Hoyos and current Colombian president Pastrana is from *Whitewash,* 170–71. The threatening letter is reproduced in *Colombia: Democracy Under Assault,* 61. **By the end of 1987 . . . martial law.** Gillespie's urgings and the NSC study are noted in "The Andean Strategy," 1. Martial law from the Archive Chronology. **Through it all . . . raging storm.** Uribe. **He was now . . . legitimate drugstores.** *The Andean Cocaine Industry,* 57. *Whitewash,* 168–69. **In March . . . out unhurt.** An account of the raid is in *Whitewash,* 175–76, and of the attack on Maza, 219. *Death Beat,* 131–33. **As these battles . . . efforts failed.** Uribe. *Whitewash,* 220–22. *The Andean Cocaine Industry,* 105–106. This passage records the attempt Escobar and other cartel leaders made to hire a firm that employed Jeb Bush and a firm owned by Henry Kissinger in an effort to gain ground with the Bush administration in their negotations. Accounts of the assassination attempt by former SAS soldiers led by Dave Tomkins and Peter MacAleese, 58. *Whitewash,* 180. **The future . . . had begun.** Gaviria, Pardo, Uribe, *Death Beat,* 152–54. *Whitewash,* 73, 84, 90, 118. **Pablo met . . . order the hit.** "This is How We Killed Galán." **On August 18 . . . the world.** Details of Galán's murder from *Whitewash,* 215. "This Is How We Killed Galán."

THE FIRST WAR: 1989–1991

1

In time . . . bought or bullied. Gen. Martinez, Delta Force soldiers. Franklin's death on August 18, 1989, is noted in "Escobar: 17 Anos," and *Whitewash,* 217–18. **He had steered . . . bottle of milk.** Uribe, *Whitewash,* 217. **Galán's killing . . . growing fight.** *Colombia: Democracy Under Assault,* 62. *Whitewash,* 220. The Archive Chronology. **The *narcos* could see . . . changed everything.** Delta Force soldiers, National Security Decision Directive 221, NSD 18, August 21, 1989. *The Philadelphia Inquirer,* June 10, 1989, "U.S. Weighs Assassination of Foreign Drug Traffickers," September 6, "Bush Outlines Drug Battle Plan/All U.S. Urged to Join the Fight," September 10, "Wider Role Is Seen for U.S. Troops/Military May Join Latin Drug Patrols." Archive Chronology. **In the four months . . . Colonel Martinez.** Gen. Martinez, Archive Chronology, Delta Force soldiers, *The Andean Cocaine Industry,* 99. **It was a position . . . new kind of help.** Gen. Martinez, Capt. Martinez, Gen. Trujillo, Gen. Serrano, Gen. Vargas.

2

This section is based on my interviews with six current and former members of Centra Spike, the DEA chronology, Murphy, and Busby. The British mercenary trainers are noted in *The Andean Cocaine Industry,* 53.

3

In the fall . . . on Galán. Centra Spike soldiers. Medellín's drug traffickers had first been listed in *Forbes* magazine's annual tally in the July 20, 1982, issue. Pablo was estimated to have $2 billion, while the three Ochoa brothers were thought to have an equal fortune. At that point the magazine had apparently not heard of Gacha, *The Philadelphia Inquirer,* December 17, 1989, "Killing of Drug Lord Wins Praise." **So the fat man . . . been prudent.** Centra Spike soldiers. **The hunt . . . target for assassination.** Alzate was interviewed at length by DEA agents Peña and Carlos Teixeira on April 4, 1994, and summarized in a four-page memo. Downing of the Avianca flight made international news. Details for this story are from *The Andean Cocaine Industry,* 52. *Whitewash,* 225–26. The quote from the Extraditables is from *Whitewash,* 222. **Ever since . . . community worldwide.** Pentagon sources, Centra Spike soldiers. The attempted Stinger purchase is noted in *The Andean Cocaine Industry,* 53. **Weeks after . . . so be it.** Pentagon sources, Centra Spike soldiers, Parks. Executive Order 12333. The Parks memorandum. The Justice Department decision was reported in *The Philadelphia Inquirer,* December 17, 1989, "Ruling Sees Wider Boundaries in Drug War." **The situation . . . unscathed.** DEA chronology. *The Andean Cocaine Industry,* 52. *El Tiempo,* "*Escobar: 17 Años.*" Maza's account of the blast is in *Death Beat,* 135–36. Duzan records the date of the blast as December 10, but both *El Tiempo* and the DEA chronology record the date as December 6. **The blasts . . . the United States.** Centra Spike soldiers, Delta Force soldiers, *Whitewash,* 227–28. *The Philadelphia Inquirer,* December 17, 1989, "Killing of Drug Lord Wins Praise." *The Washington Post,* December 18, "Body of Trafficker Dug Up in Colombia/Final Getaway for Cartel's Enforcer." *The New York Times,* December 17, 1989 "Drug Trafficker's Death Cheers Many Colombians." **A curious thing . . . Escobar was dead.** Centra Spike soldiers. Pablo's conversation with his brother and the Extraditables' communiqué are from *Whitewash,* 223–24.

4

Trouble at once . . . falling, too. DEA chronology. **Pablo concluded . . . radio or cell phone.** Centra Spike soldiers. The dialogue from the released tape is reprinted in Canon's *El Patrón.* Pablo had vehemently denied involvement in Jaramillo's murder, *Whitewash,* 236–37, arguing that the killing must have been done by right-wing paramilitaries, and stating, "I have never belonged to the right because it repulses me." The tape told a different story. **This made . . . colonel's men.** Centra Spike soldiers. DEA chronology. Interviews with Colombian members of the Search Bloc. Gen. Martinez denied threatening his men that he would shoot traitors in the head. The story was related to me by several of his men. He also denied the Centra Spike accounts of his men's reluctance to crawl in the dirt or fish information from latrines, or that two sources were beaten or thrown from helicopters. Martinez claimed that these accusations stemmed from statements made by Escobar during that time, and that he was vigilant in upholding the rights of prisoners. Escobar did accuse the then colonel of throwing men from helicopters, as reported in *Whitewash*, 263. The two men in question from this incident, Martinez told me, were turned over to the authorities and prosecuted for aiding a fugitive. The Centra Spike soldier I interviewed believed (perhaps wrongly) that the men had been killed, and reported this belief to Jacoby as I have recorded it here. **Two days . . . not to kill him.** Gaviria. *News of a Kidnapping*, 26. **Pablo shifted . . . August, 1989.** DEA chronology. *El Tiempo*, "*Escobar: 17 Años*." **But Gaviria . . . through carefully.** Gaviria. *News of a Kidnapping*, 70, 74–75. *Death Beat*, 252–56. **Pablo answered . . . know too much."** Gaviria. DEA chronology. *News of a Kidnapping*, 84–86, 90–93. *Whitewash*, 248. *The Andean Cocaine Industry*, 111–12. **But not . . . too much."** Gen. Martinez. *News of a Kidnapping*, 95. The dismembered body of Jaramillo, a sixty-six–year-old retired journalist, was not found until October 1997. **Pablo still had . . . biggest victory.** Gaviria. **So the dying . . . soul of stone."** Gaviria. *News of a Kidnapping*, 126, 144, 178. DEA chronology. **Monica de Greiff . . . to stop.** *Whitewash*, 224. Gaviria. **The drug boss's . . . from there?** Gaviria, Mendoza. **Just as Gaviria . . . say later.** Gaviria. *Whitewash*, 250. *News of a Kidnapping*, 186–87. **But his efforts . . . surrendered.** DEA chronology *El Tiempo*, "*Escobar: 17 Años*."

5

Pablo orchestrated . . . of honor." This account of the surrender is drawn from *News of a Kidnapping*, 280–87. *Whitewash*, 254–56. Newspaper accounts from June 20, 1991, in *El Tiempo, El Nuevo Siglo, El Espectador*, and *El Tiempo*, June 21. Visit to prison site earlier is reported in *Mi Hermano Pablo*, 39, 40. **It was over . . . very tall."** Gaviria, Mendoza, transcript of Pablo's confession hearing from *Semana*, February 11, 1992, translated by Ricky Ortiz. *The Andean Cocaine Industry*, 112. **So ended . . . public relations.** Gaviria Mendoza, Gen. Martinez. **He told . . . Colombia.** "I Won't Study Law," *El Colombiano*, translated by Ricky Ortiz. Murphy.

IMPRISONMENT AND ESCAPE: JUNE 1991–SEPTEMBER 1992

1

Pablo had fallen . . . back together. Uribe. **During the months . . . behind them.** DEA chronology. *The Andean Cocaine Industry*, 9 (chart), 99. Uribe. Description of the prison is from CIA videotape, DEA photographs, and Agent Peña's descriptions from his July 26, 1992, visit. *Mi Hermano Pablo*, 52–56. **It was not . . . and then.** Uribe. *The Andean Cocaine Industry*, 113. Pablo's attitude toward these excursions was expressed in a July 25 conversation with his attorneys recorded by Centra Spike. **To pass time . . . of ground.** Uribe, *Mi Hermano Pablo*, 52–58. **There were also . . . regular visits.** Uribe. DEA chronology. **President Gaviria . . . maneuver.** Mendoza, Gaviria, Estupinan.

2

Throughout the . . . to form suspicions. Gaviria, Busby, Mendoza, Estupinan, Gen. Martinez, de Greiff, Pardo. **Entrusted with . . . to act.** Gaviria, Mendoza, Uribe, DEA cables. *The Andean Cocaine Industry,* 48. *Whitewash,* 274.

3

Mendoza, Gaviria, Pardo. Dialogue is based on their memories. Also the minutes of the Colombian Security Council investigation of Pablo's escape (from Gaviria's archives).

4

Gaviria, Mendoza. Dialogue is based on their memories. Security Council minutes.

5

Morris D. Busby . . . Pablo Escobar. Busby, Christ, Gaviria, Toft, Wagner, Mendoza, Pardo, DEA cables.

6

On the day . . . the United States. Centra Spike soldiers. **Apart from . . . want a piece.** *Parameters,* summer 1997, Centra Spike soldiers, Pentagon sources. **Major Jacoby . . . the answer.** Busby, Centra Spike soldiers, Pentagon sources.

7

When Pablo . . . army patrols. Mendoza, Gaviria, Pardo, *Clear and Present,* 12. *Mi Hermano Pablo,* 64–69. **In a taped . . . comrades."** Pablo's statement is from Gaviria's archives, translated by Julie Lopez. **The day after . . . very much.** DEA cables, Gaviria, de Greiff, DEA cables from July 22–26. **Trying to cut through . . . good luck then."** Transcript of Pablo's conversation is from Gaviria's archives, translated by Julie Lopez.

8

Centra Spike soldiers, Delta Force soldiers, Pentagon sources, Busby, Toft, Wagner, Joulwon, Murphy, Gaviria, Burruss, Peña.

9

Busby, Centra Spike soldiers, Toft, Pardo, Gaviria, Wagner.

10

The colonel . . . is not clear. Gen. Martinez, Capt. Martinez, Murphy, Peña, DEA cables, Wagner, CIA videotape, CIA profile. **A week after . . . escape.** DEA cables, Centra Spike soldiers, Delta Force soldiers, Wagner, Reyes.

11

Transcript of September 8, 1992, RCN interview, translated by Maria Carrizosa.

LOS PEPES: OCTOBER 1992–OCTOBER 1993

This chapter is based on State Department and DEA cables, as indicated in the text, on the DEA chronology, the Archive chronology, and interviews with Busby, Wagner, Gen. Martinez, Capt. Martinez, Delta Force soldiers, Centra Spike soldiers, Toft, Murphy, Peña, Uribe, de Greiff, Londono, Pardo, and Sheridan. Pablo's note to Martinez was in Gaviria's archives, translated by Julie Lopez. Pablo's letter to Busby is from the former ambassador's files, translated by Eduardo Mendoza. The letter by Lehder and accounts of the debriefings of Ospina (SZE-92-0053) are from the DEA's Bogotá files. Twelve of Pablo's men were killed: Brance Muñoz and his brothers Paul and Jhon, Jhony River, Jhon Tobon, Wilmar Arroyava, William Trujillo, Juan Diaz, Jorge Zapata, William Echeverry, Juan Muñoz, and Carlos Arcila. Martinez said he turned over these men's names to de Greiff for prosecution, but that nothing was ever done, and he suggests that the former attorney general may have had some relationship with the death squad. De Greiff denies it.

THE KILL: OCTOBER 1993–DECEMBER 2, 1993

1

Colonel Martinez . . . his strength. Gen. Martinez, DEA cables, State Dept. cables, Peña, Delta Force soldiers, Busby, Capt. Martinez, members of the Search Bloc. The letters to Pablo from Maria Victoria and Juan Pablo were in the Bogotá embassy files and were translated by Julie Lopez.

2

Mendoza.

3

It was during ... operations worldwide. See *Black Hawk Down*. When I wrote the book about the October 3, 1993, battle, I had never heard of Centra Spike. Some of the same men who served with Delta in Colombia also fought in the Battle of Mogadishu, among them John Macejunas, Earl Fillmore, Joe Vega, and Dave McKnight. Fillmore was killed in Mogadishu. **It was in this climate ... their efforts."** "Exit El Patrón," 77–78. **Guillermoprieto's story ... in Colombia.** Sheehan, Powell, Sheridan, Slocombe, Pentagon sources.

4

Capt. Martinez, DEA cables, Gen. Martinez, Estupinan, Centra Spike soldiers, Delta Force soldiers.

5

Magee, Murphy, Peña, Busby, DEA cables, State Dept. cables, de Greiff, Rubin, and Gaviria.

6

Magee, videotape of the airport scene from Bogotá TV stations (collected by Mills and Doughenbaugh), DEA cables, State Dept. cables, Busby, Toft, Peña, Murphy, Gaviria, Pablo's letter to *Los Pepes* and accounts of his phone calls from Gaviria's archives, translated by Julie Lopez.

7

Capt. Martinez, Gen. Martinez, Centra Spike soldiers; description of the house is from DEA photos and videotape shot by camera crews working on the documentary *Killing Pablo*, and still photos shot by Akira Suwa of *The Philadelphia Inquirer*, DEA cables, Cepeda, Fernandez, details of Pablo's last day from *El Patrón*, chapter 19, translated by Ricky Ortiz. Pablo's last conversations from Gaviria's archives, translated by Julie Lopez.

AFTERMATH

Police on ... for so long. Capt. Martinez, Search Bloc members, Naranjo, autopsy photos and report for Pablo and Limón. Aguilar confirmed that he fired the fatal shot in an interview wth *El Tiempo*, November 17, 2000. Gen. Martinez asserted that the shot had to have been more than "one meter" away in the same *El Tiempo* article, and also to me. Murphy told me the story of the Search Bloc member selling his blood-splattered clothing. Capt. Martinez told me that it was Murphy who had shaved off one end of Pablo's mustache first, for a souvenir, and that the other end was then shaved off by Search Bloc members to complete the look. Murphy denies it. **The colonel . . . of victory.** Gen. Martinez, Capt. Martinez, Pardo. **Ambassador Morris . . . said Busby.** Busby, Canas. **Days before . . . successful mission.** Murphy, Peña, Delta Force soldiers, Toft, Gen. Martinez, Capt. Martinez. **Moments before . . . showstopper."** Toft, Vargas, Busby, Canas, Gaviria. I asked the former ambassador if his own cable didn't indicate that he believed there was a connection between *Los Pepes* and the Search Bloc, and he said that it did not. "I was never convinced of it," he said. **Colombian TV . . . and home."** Video of the death scene compiled by Mills and Doughenbaugh from Bogotá and Medellín TV files. Delta Force soldiers. **Analyzing the . . . all by himself.** Centra Spike soldiers, Murphy. Pictures of the party in Medellín from DEA files. **Hermilda . . . went through."** From a TV interview given by Hermilda. **After Pablo . . . all that."** Gen. Martinez, Capt. Martinez, DEA chronology. **In the days . . . or deportation.** Video compiled by Mills and Doughenbaugh. The account of Juan Pablo's visit to the embassy is from Busby and Toft. Uribe told me about the family's recent travails. **Centra Spike . . . much reduced.** Centra Spike soldiers, Pentagon sources. **The death . . . flowerpots.** Colombian news accounts, video compiled by Mills and Doughenbaugh, Busby, Murphy, photos of the grave by Akira Suwa. **Eduardo Mendoza . . . us all."** Gaviria, Mendoza. **Roberto . . . made it.** Uribe. **After his . . . the means"** Toft, DEA cables, Murphy, Peña, Magee, "Inside America's Troubled Wars."

ACKNOWLEDGMENTS

I'd like to thank all the people I can't name for their help on this book. The manhunt for Pablo Escobar is another of those complex missions in the modern history of the U.S. military, like the battle story told in *Black Hawk Down,* that otherwise would have remained largely unknown. The issue of whether the United States should target foreign citizens for assassination merits scrutiny and discussion, but I think this story makes it clear that on occasion it still does so.

Robert J. Rosenthal and David Zucchino at *The Philadelphia Inquirer* were enthusiastic about this story from the start, and supported me with it throughout. I'm grateful again to Morgan Entrekin for his careful editing and steady encouragement, to Brendan Cahill, for his always cheerful and efficient help, to Michael Hornburg, Beth Thomas, and Bonnie Thompson for their diligent copyediting, and Don Kennison, Chuck Thompson, and Diana Marcela Alvarez for their proofreading, and to all the warm, talented people at Grove/Atlantic. Thanks again to my agent, Rhoda Weyr, who never steers me wrong.

Major Fernando Buitrago of the *Policía Nacional de Colombia* was tremendously helpful to me on my first trip to Colombia, and Jay Brent and Gerardo Reyes were of invaluable assistance on my second. Maria Carrizosa was a very lucky find for me in Bogotá, and I'm grateful to Adriana Foglia for steering me to her. Eduardo Mendoza was extremely generous with his time, and his willingness to translate for me at a moment's notice enabled me to carry on extensive e-mail conversations with sources in Colombia. General Hugo Martinez was unfailingly polite and diligent in answering my questions, even about difficult matters. Organization of American States General Secretary César Gaviria was also a great help.

Thanks to Arthur Fergenson of Ballard, Spahr, Andrews & Ingersall, LLP, for the loan of office space in Baltimore, to Michael Evans of the National Security Archive for sharing his research, and to the U.S. Drug Enforcement Administration for allowing me to interview the agents who worked on this case. And, lastly, thanks again to Gail and my children for putting up with my long absences—even those that occur when I'm at home.

INDEX